G000256281

Transforming the Role of the SE

Transforming the Role of the SENCo

Achieving the National Award for SEN Coordination

Edited by Fiona Hallett and Graham Hallett

Open University Press

Open University Press
McGraw-Hill Education
McGraw-Hill House
Shoppenhangers Road
Maidenhead
Berkshire
England
SL6 2QL

email: enquiries@openup.co.uk
world wide web: www.openup.co.uk

and Two Penn Plaza, New York, NY 10121-2289, USA

First published 2010

Copyright © Fiona Hallett and Graham Hallett 2010

All rights reserved. Except for the quotation of short passages for the
purpose of criticism and review, no part of this publication may be
reproduced, stored in a retrieval system, or transmitted, in any form or
by any means, electronic, mechanical, photocopying, recording or
otherwise, without the prior written permission of the publisher or a licence
from the Copyright Licensing Agency Limited. Details of such licences (for
reprographic reproduction) may be obtained from the Copyright Licensing
Agency Ltd of Saffron House, 6–10 Kirby Street, London, EC1N 8TS.

A catalogue record of this book is available from the British Library

ISBN-13: 978-0-33-524241-2 (pb)
ISBN-10 0335242413 (pb)

Library of Congress Cataloging-in-Publication Data
CIP data has been applied for

Typeset by RefineCatch Limited, Bungay, Suffolk
Printed in the UK by Bell and Bain Ltd, Glasgow

Fictitious names of companies, products, people, characters and/or data that
may be used herein (in case studies or in examples) are not intended to
represent any real individual, company, product or event.

The **McGraw·Hill** Companies

Contents

Notes on contributors

Rachel Barrell is Course Leader for BA (Hons) Primary Initial Teacher Education at the University of Worcester. Prior to this, she has worked as a primary teacher and SENCO in both mainstream and special provision. Her current research focus is on attitudes towards special educational needs, looking at the development of inclusive practice in the United Arab Emirates.

Barbara Bradbury has taught in mainstream Primary schools in London and Sheffield in addition to SLD, MLD and ASD schools in Kirklees, Sheffield and Lancashire. She is currently Deputy Headteacher of The Loyne Specialist School in Lancashire and works closely with staff from the University of Cumbria on joint projects which benefit both educational settings.

Dr Angharad Beckett is Lecturer in Sociology and Social Policy and associate of the Centre for Disability Studies, University of Leeds. Her research focuses upon the nature of citizenship and she has interrelated interests in disability politics and education for equality and social justice

Lynne Cook is a Senior Lecturer in SEN/Inclusion at Oxford Brookes University. Previously she worked as a SENCo in mainstream schools, pupil referral units and as an advisory teacher for behaviour. Her current research interests focus on the changing role of the SENCo and behaviour management training in Initial Teacher Education.

Pam Davies has worked with children and young people from Reception to Sixth Form in a range of settings both urban and rural. She is currently Senior Adviser for SEN and Inclusion with Cheshire East Council. Her passion is for inclusion and the entitlement of all to experience a personal sense of achievement and satisfaction.

Dr Alison Ekins is a Senior Lecturer and Course Director at Canterbury Christ Church University, leading a range of Masters level courses on issues around SEN, Inclusion, Enabling Learning and School Development. Alison's research and publication interests are in inclusion, SEN and meeting the needs of all pupils through whole school approaches.

Niki Elliot leads the Professional Development Programme in Education at Sheffield Hallam University where she is principal lecturer in inclusion. Her research interests lie in the area of professionals' enquiries into and evaluations of their own practice. Niki has worked in both mainstream and special schools as SENCO, senior leader and as principal adviser for inclusion in a metropolitan borough.

Alison Feeney is a teacher educator (University of Cumbria), specialising in SEN and Inclusion. A passion for safe practice in schools, striving for the emotional well-being of vulnerable children and the imperative to hear their voices authentically grow from her work, and, both professionally and personally, from fostering and parenting her son.

Lani Florian is Professor of Social and Educational Inclusion at the University of Aberdeen where she is working with colleagues in the School of Education on the reform of initial teacher education programmes to ensure that all teachers are prepared to work in inclusive schools and classrooms. She has published widely in the areas of special and inclusive education. Current research projects focus on inclusive pedagogy and achievement and inclusion.

Bob Franks is currently a Principal Manager for SEND and Inclusion in a North-West LEA. His broad range of cross phase SEND experiences include working directly with SENCOs, Inclusion co-ordinators and headteachers in primary, secondary and special schools. His particular interest is related to developing the skills of SENCOs/Senior leaders, to use SEN data more effectively.

Anne Gager taught in a variety of schools over 17 years, before moving to the University of Cumbria in 2000. Anne has been a SENCo in both primary and secondary schools and has also taught in special schools. Anne's area of research interest is in the significance of special school placements for trainee teachers.

Philip Garner is currently Professor of Education at the University of Northampton, having previously taught in mainstream and special schools. He has published widely on issues relating to SEN and SEBD and is the Editor of *Support for Learning*.

Barry Groom is Senior Lecturer in the School of Education, University of Northampton. He has significant experience of working with both young people with SEBD and with SENCos. He has published in both these areas, and is currently researching SEBD issues in Estonia.

John Hattersley was at the 'chalk face' working with children with SEN for 25 years giving him the real practical experience to become a successful and highly experienced Senior Leader of Schools and Children's Services. He has a proven track record in improving outcomes for children through building partnerships, transforming attitudes and raising expectations.

Hazel Lawson is senior lecturer in special and inclusive education at the University of Exeter, having worked as a primary and special school teacher for 17 years. Her research interests are in the education of children and young people with severe, profound and multiple learning difficulties; conceptualizations of diversity; pupil participation and voice; and SEN in initial teacher education.

Linda Lyn-Cook taught in mainstream secondary schools and special schools, before taking on her current role as Consultant Teacher for Autism for Nottinghamshire County Council. She leads a specialist team of advisory teachers and teaching assistants in the area of autism, and is a visiting lecturer at Nottingham Trent University.

Bridget Middlemas has extensive experience in the education of SEN pupils, and has held teaching and management positions in both mainstream and segregated contexts. She is a Senior Lecturer in Special and Inclusive Education at Roehampton University, and has specific interests in the areas of autism, dyslexia, hospital education, and the use of ICT to aid learning and teaching.

Tricia Nash has over 28 years' experience as a researcher mainly in projects about children with SEN/disabilities or health needs, 21 at the University of Exeter. Her main research interests are families with children with these needs, the inclusion of such pupils, and research on hearing the voice of these children and young people.

Brahm Norwich is Professor of Educational Psychology and Special Educational Needs at the Graduate School of Education, University of Exeter. He has worked as a teacher, a professional educational psychologist, and university teacher and researcher. He has published widely in these fields; his books are on 'Moderate learning difficulties and the future of inclusion' (Routledge 2005); 'Special pedagogy for special children: pedagogies for inclusion' (with Ann Lewis – Open University Press, 2004); 'Dilemmas of difference, disability and inclusion: international perspectives' (Routledge, 2008) and 'Special Needs: a new look' (with Mary Warnock – Continuum Publishers, 2010).

Alison Patterson has taught in primary schools, where she was also a SENCO, and for two years within a special school. She currently works for Nottinghamshire County Council as a Specialist Teacher for the Early Years Inclusion Support Service and is also employed as a visiting lecturer at Nottingham Trent University.

Sue Pearson is Senior Lecturer in the School of Education, University of Leeds. She coordinates the MA(SEN) and the TDA funded Post Graduate Certificate in SEN Coordination. Her recently completed PhD was about the continuing professional development of SENCOs. She has undertaken a number of small-scale research projects for NASEN.

Lorraine Petersen is the Chief Executive Officer (CEO) of NASEN. Prior to her appointment, Lorraine held a number of teaching posts within mainstream schools in Sandwell, West Midlands, including serving as head teacher of two very diverse primary schools. Lorraine has many years' experience of working with pupils with special and additional needs within mainstream settings. In the last five years Lorraine has worked on numerous projects with the DCSF, the QCA and the TDA. In June 2009 Lorraine was awarded the OBE for services to education.

Gill Richards works at Nottingham Trent University in the School of Education as Director of Professional Development. Her teaching and research interests lie in inclusive education, involving national projects on inclusion and studies of practice in Canada, Japan, Italy and New Zealand. She currently tutors on the National Award for SEN Co-ordination.

Christopher Robertson is a lecturer in inclusive and special education at the University of Birmingham. He has co-authored books on special educational needs and inclusion, and written extensively on the role of the SENCO in England. He is particularly interested in education policy in the UK and international developments in inclusive education. Christopher is the editor of *SENCO Update*.

Dr Artemi Sakellariadis began her career as a special educator and taught in special schools for many years, before committing her energy to the development of inclusive provision for all in mainstream schools. Her writing and research interests include culture and pedagogy for inclusive education, identity formations of those at the margins and creative forms of academic writing. She is currently director of the Centre for Studies on Inclusive Education (CSIE), an independent organization promoting inclusive education as a basic human right of every child.

Cathy Svensson is principal lecturer and programme convener in Special and Inclusive Education in the School of Education, Roehampton University. Cathy has extensive experience in the field and a research interest in the discourses of Inclusion particularly related to communication difficulties.

Janice Wearmouth is currently Professor of Education at the University of Bedfordshire. She has a long history of teaching, research and publications in the area of special needs provision in mainstream schools, with particular foci on difficulties in literacy and behavioural concerns.

Note on the text

SENCo has become the accepted and common usage for the role of the Special Educational Needs Co-ordinator, with the variation Senco sometimes being seen. However, documentation surrounding the National Award for SEN Co-ordination uses the acronym SENCO. We have not tried to impose a standardized usage in this book; rather we have accepted the usage offered by each contributor. It will be interesting to see whether the new usage becomes accepted, or whether older practice is maintained.

PART I

Concepts and contexts of SEN

Introduction to Part I

There are just under 23,000 schools in England (DCSF, 2009a), and this means that there are at least that number of practitioners carrying out the role that is most commonly designated as Special Educational Needs Co-ordinator (SENCo). The ways in which this role has developed in schools since the publication of the first *SEN Code of Practice* (DfE, 1994) are as varied as the schools and settings in which the postholders are employed and the role is delivered.

It is clear that best practice has the role of the SENCo at the heart of the educational processes occurring within a setting, exerting an influence on teaching and learning for all. However, it is equally clear that the SENCo is not always placed at the centre of school development, in the way it seems to have been envisaged when the post was introduced. There will be many who are familiar, for example, with situations where the role is solely focused on administrative and bureaucratic procedures, in fulfilling the guidance laid down in the *SEN Code of Practice*, or in meeting the requirements of Local Education Authorities (LEAs) in ensuring the effective gatekeeping of funds delegated to SEN provision.

Perhaps the most common model sees the SENCo delivering interventions with those students characterized as having barriers to learning, offering SEN expertise in the setting, and discharging this through action. That this might be seen to de-skill other professionals in the setting might obscure the more important issue that the SENCo has little time to consider the potentially strategic nature of the role in supporting teaching and learning for all. A variation of this model, often found in larger primary and in secondary schools, sees the SENCo managing a learning support department, entrenching the view that meeting the needs of marginalized children is somehow separate from meeting the needs of those not in this category.

Postholders in such circumstances, while pivotal in ensuring appropriate practice for those with barriers to learning, are unable to influence how that practice is configured within the broader structures of school development and improvement. For example, in preparing for processes associated with monitoring, inspection and accountability, the prescribed focus for the SENCo is as likely to be in ensuring that existing practice is having an impact on outcomes, as it is on questioning or problematizing that practice.

These difficulties are exacerbated by inconsistencies in role expectation, for example, there are settings where procedures associated with the *SEN Code of Practice* (DfES, 2001) are carried out wholly by the SENCo, while elsewhere these functions are the remit of class teachers or the Headteacher. Further barriers can exist; it is not uncommon, for example, to find SENCos who have little knowledge of the SEN funding mechanisms that operate within their school; or who experience difficulties in ensuring liaison and shared planning between the SENCo and the Governor responsible for SEN provision; or for whom the development of multi-agency working and liaison lies outside of their responsibilities.

There would seem to be parallels here with other facets of school development. There is an extensive literature, for example, that addresses issues of school effectiveness. While this literature draws attention to the need to raise standards of achievement to support the needs of a knowledge economy in a changing world, it is not always the case that consideration is given to what constitutes effectiveness in schools, beyond a narrow agenda based on competency in attainment tests.

This has led to a concentration on school measures that promote raised standards measured summatively in national testing regimes. The headline results of this regime seem to deliver steadily increasing standards of attainment; unfortunately, this often seems to be at the expense of a group of students for whom the educational experience is marked by a seemingly intractable failure to provide successful outcomes.

Yet the Inclusion Statement, contained in the *National Curriculum* (DfEE/QCA, 1999), states that 'teachers should set high expectations and provide opportunities for all pupils to achieve'. In the documentation for the revised NC (DCSF, 2010b), this statement is expanded to include those with SEN and/or disability, pupils from all social and cultural backgrounds, and pupils from different ethnic groups, seemingly a recognition of the failure to meet the needs of these groups within previous structures.

In 2004, the *Building Schools for the Future* (BSF) initiative was launched. While this is a programme for the renewal of school buildings, the initiative has, as a key aim, the requirement 'for LEAs to develop a vision for education in their area that offers real innovation and enables teaching and learning to be transformed' (DfES, 2004a). It is undeniable that a major programme of renewing school buildings will have major benefits for many pupils; improved accessibility is a small, but significant gain from such a programme.

However, it is suggested that the transformation of teaching and learning, through a process of innovation, is much more in the hands of the practitioners who occupy those buildings, than it is in the buildings themselves. Indeed, it could be argued that the accomplishment of a more inclusive system requires current orthodoxy to be challenged by those involved with education. At the centre of such a debate lies an argument that is close to the heart of those involved with students who are marginalized by current educational policy and practice. This can be stated as a tussle between those who advocate measures designed to raise standards, often through a concentration on a narrowed curriculum of properly 'academic' subjects which seems to meet the needs of some pupils, and those who contend that current practice is driving out the broad, balanced, relevant and differentiated entitlement curriculum, that informed the premise on which the National Curriculum rests, one that seems to address the needs of all pupils. This might be configured as individualistic versus pluralistic, for example, or as academic (where this is measured through attainment) versus holistic (where this is measured through achievement).

That this is a current and relevant debate is suggested by several things. Recent evaluations of the National Curriculum such as the *Rose Report* (DCSF, 2009b) and the *Cambridge Review* (Alexander, 2009) have suggested the need to seek a better curriculum balance in terms of creativity, relevance and breadth. This has been mirrored by a change in perception of the role of the SENCo, both in practice, and in the central policy direction that frames the role.

It is clear in practice that the role of the SENCo is evolving. A broadening of the job description to that of Inclusion Manager is common, and this has been accompanied by an increased positioning of postholders within leadership and management teams. However, this shift in emphasis is perhaps of less significance than the structural changes to the role introduced in 2009. Regulations that came into force at that time (OPSI, 2009) require that anybody holding the post of SENCo must, by 2011, be a qualified teacher. The regulations also require that any newly appointed SENCo must obtain the newly instituted National Award for SEN Co-ordination (NASC); an extensive programme of training funded by the Teaching and Development Agency (TDA) has begun to make this possible.

It should be noted that the requirement to hold a statutory qualification in order to fill a position that exists in every school in England applies to only two positions: that of SENCo (NASC) and Headteacher (National Professional Qualification for Headship (NPQH)). This would seem to reflect a view that the SENCo is both an agent of change for individual pupils, and a change agent for schools; that is, it is both a process management role, and a strategic management role. This would seem to place the SENCo at the centre of the school development process, able to meet the needs of all pupils, while providing a specialist focus for those with additional needs.

That this amounts to 'transforming the role of the SENCo' gave us our title. The structure of this book seeks to draw together some of these disparate themes, to give a sense of how such a transformation may occur. Although divided into six parts, there is an intended difference between the first part and those that follow. The first part, which consists of Chapters 1–5, is intended to examine the contested and changing nature of the role of the SENCo; in this sense, it might echo the theme outlined above, of the SENCo as a change agent, placed at the heart of the school or setting, and driving an agenda that seeks to move practice in the direction of meeting the many, diverse, needs of the whole teaching and learning community of the setting.

The remaining chapters are divided into five parts that correspond to the divisions into which the Learning Outcomes of the National Award for SEN Co-ordination are split, namely the Professional Context; Strategic Development; Coordinating Provision; Leading, Developing and Supporting Colleagues, and Working in Partnership. In each of these parts, contributors drawn from education practitioners and providers of the National Award have written about practice that addresses the key Learning Outcomes of that division. An introduction has been included in each part, to prompt reflection on the links between the chapter and the Learning Outcomes of the award.

The remainder of this Introduction will give a summary of the main points made in the first five chapters, and how these relate to the National Award in general, but in particular to the potential for change that currently exists, both in transforming practice in schools and settings, and in transforming the role of the SENCo.

In Chapter 1, Lorraine Petersen, Chief Executive Officer of nasen, gives an overview of the genesis of the SENCo role and how it has developed since the first *SEN Code of Practice* (1994), and outlines the national context of training for SENCos. In tracking the processes that have been influential in the development of the role, Lorraine draws attention to two main points. First, she notes that responses in schools to the first *SEN Code of Practice* were varied because of the need to only 'have regard' to its recommendations. In some cases, the response was wholly congruent with the aspiration of the Code; in others, the response amounted to no more than 'a willing volunteer being sought', often without time or training being made available to fill the role.

Second, Lorraine draws attention to the increasing demand, from government agencies, committees and published sources, to enhance the scope and effectiveness of the role of the SENCo. These include the need to promote greater inclusion in schools and settings, to raise expectations for all young people in our schools, and to extend and develop best practice in teaching and learning, set against the introduction of an increasingly regulatory framework that will impose major changes on the scope of the work of the SENCo. This has led to the introduction, in September 2009, of regulations that impose a clear prescription of important elements of the role, including mandatory training for SENCos, a requirement that all SENCos must be qualified teachers, and requirements placing the management of SEN and/or disability in a much more strategic and central position within schools and settings.

This new emphasis, from a role bounded by a non-regulatory framework to one operating within statutory limits, requires a fundamental element of change in practice, as Lorraine notes that schools and governing bodies have the dual responsibility of ensuring that their school meets the standards laid down for them in the regulations, and of providing their SENCo with the 'training, time and resources to carry out their role effectively'.

Three further issues of importance to the role are then addressed. The issue of the changing nature of the school's workforce is considered, in the light of the expansion of the numbers of Teaching Assistants and Learning Support Assistants employed in schools, with the attendant development of the role and responsibilities of the SENCo in managing this workforce, and in ensuring that the SENCo is properly trained to fulfil the role demanded. The second issue follows from this, as Lorraine notes the further increased demands placed on the SENCo with the introduction of initiatives such as *Every Child Matters* (DfES 2004b), requiring a much greater level of inter-agency working and collaboration, which can often prove to be difficult to facilitate. Finally, training needs are considered, both within the role, and in developing the workforce within the school or setting. By drawing upon recent legislation and reports such as the *Lamb Inquiry* (DCSF, 2009d), Lorraine highlights a range of training and development requirements for twenty-first-century schools.

In concluding the chapter, attention is drawn to a demographic trend of significant proportion, concerning the need to recruit a substantial number of new SENCos in the next five years. While this might be seen as a major threat to the continuity of good practice, Lorraine prefers a much more positive analysis of the challenge, suggesting that this gives the opportunity to ensure that the SENCo will indeed become the leader for change in our schools.

Chapter 2 is by Artemi Sakellariadis, the Director of the Centre for Studies on Inclusive Education (CSIE), who gives an incisive overview of the challenges inherent in the work of supporters in inclusive schools.

Chapter 2 opens with an analysis of the current situation with regard to the development of inclusive schools. The argument for the inclusion of all pupils within the schools served by their local community is clearly stated; while it is recognized that this represents a moral position that is incontrovertible, the often cited pragmatic position that provision for those with some barriers to learning is not readily available within the mainstream is not seen to be necessarily contradictory to this position. What is clear, Artemi suggests, is that pragmatic solutions will become unnecessary with the development of more inclusive provision for all young people in the community in which they live.

The most recent contributions to this debate are then discussed, including an examination of the DCSF *White Paper* (2009c), the *Lamb Inquiry* (DCSF, 2009d), and the *Salt Review* (DCSF, 2010a). It is noted that these reports all call for substantial changes to the current situation regarding provision for pupils with special educational needs.

This section concludes, first, with an examination of the need for changes that encourage inclusive practice at the systemic level, rather than at the individual level. The case is then made for the building of social capital for all young people, where the most vulnerable members of society are enabled to benefit from extended contact with siblings, peers and potential friends in the local community, rather than being placed in settings that give the greatest benefit to those providing the education.

In a short section on terminology, a number of important issues are discussed. The use of terminology suggesting a 'within child' model of SEN and/or disability is challenged, and recognition is accorded to the growing use of concepts locating the barriers to learning as standing outside of the child, and resulting from 'society's failure to make adjustments and remove barriers'. The definition of a special educational need is also questioned, and is argued to be a tautology; the application of this term is strongly challenged, as tending towards promoting the stigma attached to labelling.

In an examination of recent research on the deployment of support staff, Artemi moves to the major theme of her argument. Her assessment of the research is based on the need to recognize an underlying assumption, which has been highlighted in this Introduction: that there is a need to exercise caution in assessing the effectiveness and usefulness of any practice in the complex social systems that characterize schooling, particularly where the measures of impact used focus on progress in a narrow range of 'core' subjects and give no indication of the benefits accrued beyond this focus.

This theme is developed in the rest of the chapter. It is suggested that the type and intensity of support provided should result from the expressed views of the pupil who is being supported, and ways in which these views might be elicited are explored. In particular, a cautious approach is advocated towards deciding what a pupil's needs might be, by drawing attention to processes by which disabled young people can state their priorities for support, and can identify practices they find unhelpful.

In Chapter 3, Brahm Norwich, who is Professor of Educational Psychology and Special Educational Needs, at the University of Exeter, identifies and discusses 'some of the key dimensions and tensions associated with the SENCo role'.

Chapter 3 begins with an overview of developments that have occurred since the introduction of the SENCo's role. Among the key themes outlined is the failure to properly address the needs of pupils with SEN and/or disabilities when the National Curriculum was introduced, the rise in exclusions that followed the introduction of a market-driven curriculum, and the increased demand for funded support for SEN that followed the introduction of school league tables.

The uncertainty surrounding the role of the SENCo and an increasing sense of the unmanageability of the demands of the role are then examined. In particular, a shift of focus resulting from the *SEN Code of Practice* (DfE, 1994) is noted, from meeting the needs of pupils with statements of SEN to meeting the needs of those with SEN but without statements. The extension of these responsibilities, first, to include a more strategic role in management and leadership, and latterly to a position of centrality in managing change, is then discussed. The section ends with an examination of the Learning Outcomes for NASC, which are summed up as showing a 'dual focus' on the operational and strategic aspects of the role.

In the main part of his chapter, Brahm identifies four inter-related aspects of the role, namely function versus role; justification and boundary of specialism; coverage of the function/role; and focus of co-ordination activities. In relation to the first aspect, it is noted that the set of functions of the role outlined in NASC 'might be better distributed across various staff roles'. The example illustrated is of the standards for middle managers in schools, which make only limited reference to functions associated with the needs of pupils with SEN, although in practice a greater alignment of function and role is likely to be required.

In considering the second aspect, that of 'justification and boundary of specialism', Brahm questions whether a distinct function for SEN co-ordination can be justified. It is suggested that this does not depend as much on the capability of the co-ordinator to fulfil the role, as on the willingness of others in the school to accept these responsibilities as integral to their already defined management roles. The argument is developed to consider whether this distribution of function could be extended to include all aspects of the role, rendering SEN co-ordination obsolete.

The third aspect identified is that of the coverage of the role/function. Building on the analysis explored in the previous section, Brahm suggests that, rather than creating a role with many functions that others might better discharge, a more inclusive role such as learning support/consultancy might be suggested. This would involve questioning whether the role should be broadened to include what is described as 'additional needs'. The section ends with a note of caution, to ensure both that pupils are not defined only by their additional need, and that expertise beyond the setting should not be overlooked.

The final aspect concerns the focus of the co-ordination activities. Here Brahm acknowledges the variety of ways in which the role of the SENCo has been configured, and suggests that the role, as currently defined, is beyond the effective capacity of a single person, unless the argument returns to the first issue, of function versus role.

In concluding, Professor Norwich makes the case for the distribution of most co-ordination functions to middle and senior management, leaving only specialist residual activities that reflect a concept of additional needs as a 'connective specialization'. The chapter ends with a challenge; a major re-examination of management roles will be needed in schools if an inclusive concept of co-ordination for those with additional needs is to be realized.

The editors of the book, Fiona and Graham Hallett have contributed the fourth chapter, which considers the role of the SENCo as a leader. An essential element of the current agenda to transform the role of the SENCo surrounds changes to the leadership and management functions of the role. This focuses on the SENCo as an agent of change in the learning and achievements of those with barriers to learning, and as a change agent promoting improvements to teaching and learning for all within schools, where 'all' is seen to include both pupils and adults within the setting.

The chapter develops three standpoints from which the role of the SENCo as an agent of change, and as a change agent, can be examined and evaluated. In the first of these, the current situation is examined. The leadership potential of the SENCo is seen to be shaped by the current policy agenda, and the practices that have developed in response, both in implementing that agenda, and in undermining its efficacy. Where the perceived policy message is ambiguous or contradictory, for example around inclusion, the response is likely to mirror this uncertainty, giving rise to role definitions that are entrenched in practice. This argument is exemplified through an examination of the *SEN Code of Practice*, and the *Every Child Matters* agenda, in relation to a research-generated typology that gives shape to extant practice. The outcome of personal responses to the demands of fulfilling the role of SENCo, and balancing the often contradictory expectations of policy-makers and senior managers, is examined through the concept of the street-level bureaucrat.

A second standpoint is then outlined; this is characterized as an interim position and is derived from the national policy aspiration that sees the role of SENCo as placed at the heart of school development, with the postholder being a member of the Senior Leadership or Management Team. This is seen as engendering two possible responses. In the first, the assimilation of the SENCo into the management hierarchy of the setting does not always lead to change, particularly in organizations where entrenched structures inhibit school development and promote subversive responses that work against collegiality. In an extended examination of social capital, it is suggested that the benefits of making connections between people with differing degrees of power and authority can be overstated unless linked to a willingness to embed autonomy in a core moral purpose that extends throughout the setting. It may also require a significant and disturbing reorganization of roles and responsibilities, which in the end serves only to preserve a narrow hierarchy that sustains bureaucratic process management.

In proposing an interim model, a more positive response can also be suggested. Here, the positioning of the SENCo role within the Senior Leadership team is seen as capable of unlocking the potential of a school to engage with raising the achievement and attainment of all pupils. While this will offer short-term benefits, the sustainability of such change is challenged, as it does not require the fundamental development of practice that moving to other models of leadership might bring to an organization.

This opens the possibility of a third standpoint. Drawing on work connected to distributive leadership, it is argued that a community of practice model would best serve the aim of moving the SENCo to a transformative position as a change agent. This embraces the concept of legitimate peripheral participation, where all members of the school community are 'leaders for learning and learning to lead' (MacBeath, 2009). The standpoint is developed through an examination of 'bridging' social capital, as a way in which community members, including pupils and parents, can express their agency, in the establishment of these communities of practice.

Three conditions are identified and developed as being prerequisites for the development of a distributive model of SEN Co-ordination: shared leadership; balanced accountability, both internal and external; and the removal of structures that atomize the role of the SENCo. With these in place, it is suggested that the opportunities offered by the National Award for SEN Co-ordination could find expression in a distributive model of leadership that promotes the role of the SENCo as serving the aims and aspirations of all learners, rather than only meeting the needs of those deemed to have special educational needs.

The fifth chapter develops the concept of inclusive pedagogy, and is contributed by Lani Florian, who is Professor of Social and Educational Inclusion at the University of Aberdeen. At the outset, the chapter identifies as problematic a policy agenda in England and Wales that rests on approaches that clearly identify those with barriers to learning while advocating for a more inclusive approach to meeting these needs, 'without specifying what these approaches might look like'.

In defining inclusive pedagogy as a response to individual difference, Lani focuses her argument on a 'socio-cultural perspective' of learning occurring in the 'community of the classroom'. In outlining the nature of this approach, it is made clear that inclusive pedagogy recognizes and responds to individual difference, but avoids approaches that target this difference, through differentiation, for example.

In developing this theme, Lani argues that a focus on meeting individual need as a way of promoting more inclusive practice can be challenged by examining five inter-related themes. The first suggests that such a focus serves to reinforce difference rather than lead to a resolution of it; it is suggested that this occurs because what is offered as 'inclusive education' does not rely on any significant change in practice, but simply replicates what was offered as 'special needs education'. This leads to a second theme which questions whether practice based on matching interventions to child characteristics is effective, drawing on research that suggests that 'different teaching strategies are not differentially effective with different types of learner'.

The third theme questions whether teaching strategies used are consistent with those suggested in literature on inclusion, and notes that teachers report that they differentiate as a response to a variety of individual differences, but that these were not 'dependent on, or specific to, the identification of special educational need'.

In the remaining themes, the complexity associated with meeting the learning needs of all children through the identification of difference is examined. The fourth theme notes the increasing use of categorizations in schools. It is suggested that the many sources of variation and difference within these groups make this requirement problematic and unhelpful. The fifth theme develops this point, by considering the degree to which membership of a group produces an intractable cycle which is difficult to escape. It is suggested that this often leads to the assumption that learners 'possess all of the characteristics of group membership to the same degree'.

In proposing a theoretical framework for inclusive pedagogy, Lani argues that the starting point, rather than being a model based on meeting needs that are 'different from' or 'additional to', should address a set of ideas about children, learning, teaching, curriculum, and the school and policy contexts in which these ideas are acted out, asserting that 'learning occurs in shared activity in shared contexts'.

This is characterized as taking place in the 'community of the classroom' to avoid connotations that inclusive pedagogy is simply whole class teaching. It is argued that the distinguishing characteristics of an inclusive pedagogy are marked by 'the ways in which teachers respond to individual difference, the choices they make about group work, and how they utilize specialist knowledge'. This difference is illustrated in an extended example from practice.

The chapter concludes by returning to the idea that marking some students as different leads to negative effects, including lowering expectations for those designated in this way, arguing that inclusive pedagogy can redress these limitations. The SENCo is seen to have an important role in shaping practice in this area, by considering the range and forms of provision available. Ultimately, it is argued, it is only through 'accepting the notion of individual differences among learners without relying on individualized approaches to responding to them' that the community of learners can be extended to include all pupils.

It is not the purpose of Part I of the book to suggest a 'manifesto' for transforming the role of the SENCo; rather, it is to be hoped that the chapters are seen as offering a varied but complementary view of some of the issues that need to be addressed if a change agenda is to become embedded in practice. However, in concluding this Introduction, some thought is given to generic themes that seem to emerge from the chapters.

It is clear that there is a changing landscape surrounding the role of the SENCo and the meeting of special or additional needs in schools. This is linked in the chapters to moves to make schools more inclusive; to the ambition to raise achievement and attainment, particularly for those pupils who are marginalized by current educational practice; and to make the best use of the resources, both physical and, most importantly, human, that are brought to bear on the school improvement agenda.

There is also a recurring focus on the need to examine the use of language, and the concepts that lie beneath this usage, in the debate surrounding special educational needs, disability, and inclusion, and the teaching and learning that occur in meeting these needs.

That the discharge of the role of SENCo is situated in the midst of a series of conflicting policy agendas is another important theme that emerges. It is hard to be clear about how the more creative approaches advocated in recent reports on, and reviews of, the National Curriculum are going to change practice in meeting the needs of all learners; whether this will encourage moves towards a more inclusive pedagogy, for example, or simply encourage the embedding of a slightly wider set of 'silo' subjects in the curriculum is yet to emerge.

The purpose of the SENCo role has also been placed under scrutiny. A conflict can be suggested, between the role as enhancing outcomes for individual pupils, and that as an agent of change for all, where existing management structures may inhibit the possibilities of the SENCo making a difference. A broader area of scrutiny concerns the need for the role of SENCo; on the one hand, there is a view that approaches that meet the needs of all pupils would render the role obsolete. On the other, the need to address the specific requirements of a broader group of pupils than currently reached by special educational needs procedures might transform the role to one of still greater specialization than current practice demands. Finally, this scrutiny should acknowledge and confront the debate that suggests that the existence of categories is the driver for identifying difference in pupils, and for sustaining bureaucratic structures and roles that best serve the interest of the system, rather than those of the pupils the system is devised to help.

The final theme identified acknowledges the current position of the SENCo as the lead practitioner for SEN in a school. Perhaps the way in which the role could be transformed to make the greatest contribution to the enhancement of achievement and attainment for all learners would be in the development of communities of practitioners, where management and leadership are vested in all, rather than in a hierarchy, in a whole school community of learners.

References

Alexander, R. (ed.) (2009) *The Cambridge Primary Review: Children, Their World, Their Education*. London: Routledge.

DCSF (2009a) *Statistical First Release: Schools, Pupils and Their Characteristics*. London: DCSF.

DCSF (2009b) *The Independent Review of the Primary Curriculum (The Rose Review)*. London: DCSF.

DCSF (2009c) *Your Child, Your Schools, Our Future: Building a 21st Century Schools System*. Norwich: TSO.

DCSF (2009d) *Lamb Inquiry: Special Educational Needs and Parental Confidence*. Nottingham: DCSF Publications.

DCSF (2010a) *Salt Review: Independent Review of Teacher Supply for Pupils with Severe, Profound and Multiple Learning Difficulties (SLD and PMLD)*. Nottingham: DCSF Publications.

DCSF (2010b) *The National Curriculum 2010*. London: DCSF.

DfE (1994) *Code of Practice on the Identification and Assessment of Special Educational Needs*. Nottingham: DfE.

DfEE/QCA (1999) *National Curriculum: Statutory Inclusion Statement*. London: DfES.

DfES (2001) *Special Educational Needs: Code of Practice*. Nottingham: DfES Publications.

DfES (2004a) *Building Schools for the Future*. London: DfES.

DfES (2004b) *Every Child Matters: Change for Children*. London: DfES.

MacBeath, J. (2009) A focus on learning. In J. MacBeath and N. Dempster (eds) *Connecting Leadership and Learning: Principles for Practice*. London: Routledge.

Office of Public Sector Information (OPSI) (2009) Education (Special Educational Needs Co-ordinators) (England) (Amendment) Regulations 2009. London: OPSI.

1

A NATIONAL PERSPECTIVE ON THE TRAINING OF SENCOs

Lorraine Petersen

Introduction

Up until the early 1990s the teaching of pupils with special educational needs (SEN) had been isolated from mainstream schooling, with the majority of children identified as having SEN being withdrawn from their classrooms by a SEN teacher. They would be taught basic, specific skills which had little connection to the curriculum that was being taught to the other children in their classroom and when returned to work alongside their peers were often given 'holding' work rather than being included in the wider classroom activities.

The 1993 Education Act promoted the requirement for all children to have the opportunity to access their education in a mainstream school and this was supported, in 1994, by the introduction of the *Code of Practice on the Identification and Assessment of Special Educational Needs* (DfE, 1994). This document gave schools guidance on how to make provision for children with SEN.

It was acknowledged that if a school was to be able to manage the process of integration in an effective way, there needed to be a managerial post in every school that would lead and support teachers in this process. The special educational needs co-ordinator (SENCO) was to be the key person given the responsibility for implementing the Code of Practice.

There was no recognition at this time that the role and responsibility of this post would be diverse and demanding and would need a teacher with a high level of training to ensure they had the skills, experience and knowledge to support the children effectively.

For many schools the appointment of the SENCO was made internally, a willing volunteer being sought from existing staff members. Many had full-time teaching commitments and were given very little time, resources or training to undertake the role effectively. Local Education Authorities would offer SENCO training sessions but these were often about raising awareness of local issues rather than professional development opportunities to meet the very individual needs in schools.

By the mid-1990s the inclusion agenda was well embedded in our schools, with the emphasis on the achievement of all children, including those identified with special educational needs. *The SENCO Guide* (DfEE, 1997) offered best practice examples on how the role was carried out in schools, how individual education plans (IEPs) were being used and how schools were developing and embedding their SEN policies.

The SENCO's role was becoming onerous and in many instances untenable with far too much time being spent on excessive paperwork (completion of IEPs) and taking sole responsibility for all aspects of SEN provision in a school.

The Government's Action Programme: Meeting Special Education Needs (DfEE, 1998) set out a broad agenda to ensure that the needs of all pupils with SEN were met through greater access to the curriculum and specific training for teachers.

The programme aimed to achieve successful inclusion of pupils with SEN by securing better training for teachers working with SEN pupils, and deploying teachers with specialist knowledge of SEN more effectively across schools, units and services, in order to do the following:

- raise expectations for pupils with SEN;
- promote their greater inclusion within mainstream schooling;
- encourage effective partnerships between special and mainstream schools in support of inclusion;
- develop the role of special schools to meet the continuing needs of some pupils with severe and/or complex difficulties; and
- promote stronger consortia arrangements in SEN provision.

The reality was that individual schools were trying to embed inclusive practice with very little training, support or advice.

The publication of *The National Standards for Special Educational Needs Co-ordinators* (TTA, 1998) offered structure and reinforced the key roles and responsibilities that this important post would have in the implementation of the action programme within schools.

These national standards set out:

- the main responsibilities of the SENCO role;
- the particular knowledge, understanding, skills, attributes and expertise needed by those co-ordinating SEN provision; and
- a definition of the context in which the co-ordination of SEN provision within a school is likely to be successful.

Their main aim was to do the following:

- set out clear expectations for teachers at key points in the profession;
- help teachers to plan and monitor their development, training and performance effectively and to set clear, relevant targets for improving their effectiveness;
- ensure that the focus at every point was on improving the achievement of pupils and the quality of their education;

- provide a basis for the professional recognition of teachers' expertise and achievements;
- help providers of professional development to plan and provide high quality, relevant training.

Using the National Standards for Special Educational Needs Co-ordinators (TTA, 1999b) offered help to professionals such as Headteachers and teachers on how to make more informed decisions about SEN in educational settings.

In theory, these standards should have offered a real opportunity for SENCOs and aspiring SENCOs to develop, through training, their skills, knowledge and understanding, enabling them to be more effective in their role. A lack of time, budget and training opportunities meant that many SENCOs meandered along with very little high quality professional development to support them in this ever demanding role.

The *National Special Educational Needs Specialist Standards* (TTA, 1999a) quickly followed the SENCO standards and offered an audit tool to help teachers and headteachers to identify specific training and development needs in relation to the effective teaching of pupils with severe and/or complex SEN.

Both the *National Standards for Special Educational Needs Co-ordinators* (TTA, 1998) and the *National Special Educational Needs Specialist Standards* (TTA, 1999a) have never been revised or superseded and much of their content is still applicable to the role of the SENCO today.

In 1998, the UK government, in their Action Programme, stated that they are 'committed to ensuring that all teachers have the training and support they need to do their job well and are confident to deal with a wide range of special educational needs'. By the end of the twentieth century there was still very little evidence that this training and support was available to SENCOs, let alone all teachers.

Twenty-first-century schools

The role of the SENCO has never been easy to define and has always been open to interpretation. It is a role that has had to move with the times and has evolved in schools, based on the needs of the individuals within each establishment.

The dawn of the new century brought with it a glimmer of hope in the form of the revised *Special Educational Needs Code of Practice* (DFES, 2001). This was to become (and still is) the SENCO's most thumbed document. Although not legislative, only guidance, a school should 'have due regard' to it for all their students with SEN.

Section 6.2 of the revised code states:

Provision for students with special educational needs is a matter for the school as a whole. In addition to the governing body, the school's headteacher, SENCO and learning support teams and all other members of staff have important operational responsibilities.

All teachers are teachers of pupils with special educational needs. Teaching such students is therefore, a whole school responsibility, requiring whole-school response. In practice the way in which this responsibility is exercised by individual staff is a matter for schools.

It is only now that we are beginning to finally see the role of the SENCO acknowledged as being one that should be closely involved in the strategic development of the SEN policy and provision, taking responsibility for the day-to-day operation of the school's SEN policy and for the co-ordination of the provision for students with SEN, particularly through School Action and School Action Plus.

Definitions of the role at each phase of education can be found in Sections 4.14, 5.30 and 6.32 of the *SEN Code of Practice* (DfES, 2001) where it clearly states that the SENCO should be taking the lead in providing professional guidance to colleagues to ensure high quality teaching for all children but especially for those with SEN. It was also assumed, but not made explicit, that the SENCO would be a qualified teacher, although with the increasing changes that were taking place within the school workforce it has to be acknowledged that some schools did not always appoint qualified teachers to this role.

The *SEN Code of Practice* (DfES, 2001) is also very clear in Sections 5.33 to 5.36 and 6.36 to 6.40 that the SENCO needed significant non-contact time to carry out their duties.

This was the ideal opportunity for schools to begin to raise the status of this key role within their school and offer training, pay and conditions that would support the SENCO in managing high quality educational opportunity for all children identified as having a special educational need. Unfortunately this happened in a very piecemeal fashion. Some schools took the guidance from the Code of Practice and implemented changes in their organizational practices with the SENCO being offered training, time and resources to manage the role effectively. Others saw it as only guidance and made very few changes at all. The financial constraints on schools meant that budgets did not take into account the need for a non-teaching SENCO to be able to meet the needs of the increasing number of vulnerable children within mainstream settings.

Changes to the school workforce including the appointment of a large number of teaching assistants had a significant impact on the role and responsibilities of the SENCO as it introduced a large number of non-teaching staff into classrooms to support children, many of these supporting pupils with SEN. The SENCO became the line manager of this ever increasing group and found themselves organizing timetables, planning work, holding meetings and often trying to broker collaboration between class teachers and support staff.

The *Every Child Matters* (HMSO, 2003) Green Paper and subsequent *Every Child Matters: Change for Children* (DfES, 2004a) introduced a much wider remit for schools in ensuring that opportunities and outcomes for all children were co-ordinated through a multi-professional approach with collaboration, information sharing and joined up service provision. For the SENCO, this meant not only additional responsibilities but an increased workload, often leaving them frustrated due to lack of co-operation from para-professionals from other agencies.

Removing Barriers to Achievement: The Government's Strategy for SEN (DfES, 2004b) outlined the current and future policies for SEN provision in England. This strategy clearly recognized that SENCOs should be a member of school leadership teams:

> SENCOs play a pivotal role, co-ordinating provision across the school and linking class and subject teachers with SEN specialists to improve the quality of teaching and learning. We want schools to see the SENCO as a key member of the senior leadership team, able to influence the development of policies for whole school improvement.
>
> (Section 3.14)

Despite the plethora of references to the roles and responsibilities of a SENCO being key to the raising of standards through supporting teachers in providing high quality teaching and learning experiences for their children, it was no surprise when the *House of Commons Education and Skills Select Committee Report on SEN* (HMSO, 2006a) was published, it offered a very adverse commentary on the role of the SENCO. This report, based on an overwhelming amount of written and oral evidence as well as research, highlighted that there was a very large gap between policy and practice in terms of the ever increasing role of the SENCO.

The Select Committee noted that the DfES had not ensured

> that SENCOs are always given the appropriate training – or the appropriate authority – to be able to undertake these significant responsibilities. Despite the recommendation in the Code of Practice that SENCOs should be part of the Senior Management this is not often the case.
>
> (para. 319)

The report recognized that many schools had in fact appointed teaching assistants to the role of SENCO, thus, not only were they not part of the leadership team, but in many cases they were carrying out administrative and peripheral duties and not the strategic role that had been envisaged.

It was also at this time that planning, preparation and assessment time (PPA) was introduced, and schools found themselves having to manage the need for all teaching staff to have their agreed time outside the classroom.

The introduction of Teaching and Learning Responsibilities (TLR) to replace responsibility points also gave rise to a great deal of anecdotal evidence that SENCOs had lost out both in terms of the time they had to carry out their SENCO duties and also on status and pay, due to loss of responsibility points without acknowledgement through the introduction of TLR.

There was a very clear view taken by the *House of Commons Education and Skills Select Committee Report on SEN* (HMSO, 2006a) in regard to the future role of the SENCO and what the government should do to address the disparity across England:

> Special Educational Needs Co-ordinators (SENCOs) should in all cases be qualified teachers and in a senior management position in the school as recommended in the SEN Code of Practice. Firmer guidelines are required rather than

Government asking schools to 'have regard' to the SEN Code of Practice. The role and position of a SENCO must reflect the central priority that SEN should hold within schools.

(Recommendation 84)

Special Educational Needs Co-ordinators (SENCOs) should be given ongoing training to enable them to keep their knowledge up to date as well as sufficient non-teaching time to reflect the number of children with SEN in their school. These baseline standards for SENCOs to be given training both on and off the job should apply to all schools, including academies and trust schools. Schools should set out in their SEN policy action to ensure that all SENCOs are adequately monitored and supported in their vital roles.

(Recommendation 85)

For the first time there was a very clear, prescriptive understanding of the role of the SENCO in a twenty-first-century school:

- They should in all cases be qualified teachers.
- They should be members of the senior leadership team.
- There should be stronger guidance from the government about the *SEN Code of Practice* to ensure that schools paid more than 'due regard' to its contents.
- The SENCO role should reflect the central priority that SEN should have within every school.
- SENCOs should be given on-going training to enable them to keep their knowledge up to date.
- SENCOs should have sufficient non-teaching time to reflect the number of children with SEN in school.
- Academies and Trust schools should embed the same standards for SENCOs in their schools.
- Schools should set out in their SEN policy action to ensure that all SENCOs are adequately monitored and supported in their vital role.

The government's response on this issue (HMSO, 2006b) was welcomed by many within the profession, since at last there was a very clear commitment to enhancing the role of the SENCO. It stated:

Special Educational Needs Co-ordinators (SENCOs) play a key role in building schools' capacity and skills in meeting children's SEN because of their crucial role in advising other members of staff on SEN matters and linking with parents. Each school is required, by regulations, to publish the name of the person with the role of co-ordinating the provision of education for children with SEN. In making the appointment, we would expect the head and governing body to take into account:

- the skills and experience required in connection with the role, and extent to which the candidate has demonstrated these or could acquire them;
- the range and complexity of SEN represented within the school; and
- practical issues such as authority (credibility) in relation to members of the teaching staff, parents and external parties.

The response continued by emphasizing three very specific aspects.

- We have reflected carefully on the Select Committee's comments on SENCOs. We share their view as to the importance and believe that the person taking on the lead responsibility should be a teacher and a member of the senior leadership team in a school (para. 21).
- We will be introducing an amendment to the Education and Inspections Bill to require governing bodies to make such an appointment for the purpose of co-ordinating the provision of education for children with SEN and to give the Secretary of State a power to make regulations relating to the role, responsibilities, experience and training required (para. 21).
- We have commissioned TDA to develop, in conjunction with interested parties, an accreditation system for SENCOs which will have at its heart an agreed training curriculum for co-ordinating staff covering both generic aspects such as implementing an SEN policy and securing help for pupils from external agencies, and knowledge of key areas such as autistic spectrum disorders. We will require all SENCOs to undertake nationally accredited training (para. 22).

In September 2008, the SENCO regulations came into force. All schools (community, foundation, voluntary schools and maintained nursery schools) in England had to comply with:

- Regulation 3 requiring the SENCO to be either a qualified teacher, the Headteacher or appointed acting Headteacher or a person carrying out the role for at least six months prior to the regulations coming into force, who has shown reasonable prospect for gaining Qualified Teacher Status (QTS) within a period of two years from the date the regulations come into force.
- Regulation 4 requiring SENCOs to be employed, i.e. not volunteers, and employed as teachers, not members of support staff.
- Regulation 5 requiring the governing body to define the role of the SENCO in relation to the leadership and management of the school.
- Regulation 6 requiring the governing body to monitor the actions of the SENCO in relation to key areas of the role.

The draft regulations had also required SENCOs to be a member of the Leadership Team but after consultation this was amended to recommend that, where the SENCO was not a member of the team, a member should be designated as champion of SEN and disability issues within the school.

Finally, to strengthen the role of the SENCO, the DCSF required all newly appointed SENCOs (September 2008) to undertake nationally accredited training, and commissioned the TDA to manage this process. The first cohort of these newly appointed SENCOs began their training in September 2009.

As we enter the second decade of the twenty-first century we finally have high quality, professional development opportunities for our next generation of SENCOs. The National Award for SEN Co-ordination has been a long time coming but very welcome and the first step in the raised status that SENCOs deserve. The basic principles of the SENCO as underpinned by the National Award are:

- senior leadership
- strategic
- relevant skills, knowledge, understanding and attributes
- raising standards
- school improvement
- lead teaching and learning.

Not a great deal different from those outlined in the SEN Code of Practice but they are now statutory and schools and governing bodies have to ensure that the SENCO in their school is meeting these exacting standards while providing them with the training, time and resources to carry out their role effectively.

It has to be acknowledged that supporting children and young people with special educational needs has never been more important and, as many of these learners are in our mainstream schools, the SENCO's role will be more challenging than ever. The numbers of new initiatives, guidance documents and legislation plus intervention programmes and training material that have bombarded our schools in recent years are testament to the increased impetus of government support for vulnerable children.

Removing Barriers to Achievement (DfES, 2004b) highlighted that all teachers were responsible for teaching children and young people with special educational needs and therefore there needed to be high quality professional development available to ensure that all staff had the necessary knowledge, skills and understanding to meet the individual needs of learners.

In 2007, the National Strategies launched the first phase of the *Inclusion Development Programme*, a professional development programme for all those working in schools.

The aim of the programme was to support schools and Early Years settings through the use of web-based materials, including teaching and learning resources, training materials, guidance on effective classroom strategies, models of good practice for multi-disciplinary teams, and information about sources of more specialist advice.

Covering the topics of dyslexia, speech, language and communication, the programme was intended to be disseminated through Local Education Authorities for individual schools to share with their staff. In many instances the SENCO became the key person in a school to disseminate this information, attempting to engage all teaching and non-teaching staff in the professional development activities within the programme.

This first programme was followed by two others: in 2008 for supporting the needs of children on the Autism Spectrum and in 2010 for supporting pupils with Behavioural, Social and Emotional Difficulties. The practicalities of trying to ensure that staff engage in all three programmes has been an immense challenge for many SENCOs and just one of the many new responsibilities they have had to take on.

In March 2008, Brian Lamb was asked by the Secretary of State to look at how parental confidence in the special educational needs system could be improved. The Lamb Inquiry was set up and emerging issues during the course of the inquiry expanded the remit by looking at SEN and disability information, the quality and clarity of statements, inspection and accountability, and what impact changes in the Tribunal system were having on parental confidence.

The final report, *The Lamb Inquiry: Special Educational Needs and Parental Confidence* (DCSF, 2009a) made 51 recommendations. All of these were agreed by the Secretary of State and reinforced in the implementation plan published by the DCSF, *Improving Parental Confidence in the Special Educational Needs System* (DCSF, 2010).

Many of the 51 recommendations will have an impact on schools and many will add a further range of challenges for the SENCO as schools respond and begin to implement them. The following examples reflect just six of these:

- The principles of Achievement for All are to be embedded within school leadership, continuing professional development and initial teacher training to ensure that as wide a range of children, parents and schools as possible benefit from the effective practices developed. SENCOs will need to be aware of the good practice examples from the ten local authority pilot projects and begin to embed them within their school practice.
- SENCOs will be able to access specialist support and advice from the additional 4000 specialist dyslexia teachers being trained to support schools.
- New specialist SEN and disability resources are to be introduced to support initial teacher training. This will result in student and newly qualified teachers requiring additional support and guidance during their early teaching careers. The SENCO will need to be able to guide, direct and support new teachers in their schools.
- SENCOs will be required to play a crucial role in leading teaching and learning of pupils with SEN, and advising other staff within the school on effective approaches and interventions.
- New guidance will be issued on the effective deployment of teaching assistants. As the majority of SENCOs line manage TAs, this will directly impact on the work and support that they give.
- New governor training will give a high profile to governors' responsibility for SEN and disability, with a particular focus on progress and outcomes. It is vital

that SENCOs are involved in the training of their governing body and develop a strong relationship with the governors responsible for SEN.

The White Paper *Your Child, Your Schools, Our Future: Building a 21st Century Schools System* (DCSF, 2009b) outlines the key challenges that face us in the future:

- Families are becoming more diverse and some families are under more pressure, so we need to ensure our response is tailored to their needs.
- The need to keep the most vulnerable children and young people safe, especially in the face of greater-than-ever pressure on children's social care, helping young people to develop resilience and knowledge to avoid risky behaviours.
- Increasing demand for higher skills with very few jobs available for people with low or no skills.
- Increasing numbers of children and young people using our services while resources are tighter.

These challenges will demand an increase in the voice of both parents and pupils, a stronger link between all the professionals working with families, schools ensuring good behaviour, strong discipline and safety and an effective personalization of teaching that will meet the needs of all pupils.

There will need to be increased collaboration between schools taking expertise, experience and models of good practice and sharing this with local schools to ensure the best outcomes for all children. Special schools will become centres of excellence offering support, guidance and specialist training to mainstream schools.

There will also be increased pressure to reduce the number of young people who are Not in Education, Employment or Training (NEETS) by ensuring that those individuals who are disaffected and/or at risk of exclusion are able to access an education that is appropriate and accessible to meet their individual needs.

SENCOs will play a pivotal role in all of these challenges, engaging with parents, pupils, external agencies, colleagues from other schools and both Early Years and Further Education practitioners to ensure smooth transition through the educational journey of an individual.

At a time when we are facing proposed changes to the distribution of funding to schools through the Dedicated Schools Grant, financial constraints and reduction in school budgets, it is more important than ever that SENCOs have a full understanding of the delegated school budget and the specific amounts available to support children and young people with special educational needs. The formula for this delegation will differ from one local authority to another but additional funding will be allocated to support early identification and intervention and for those children in School Action and School Action Plus. It is widely acknowledged that this funding is not ring-fenced and can be used for other purposes. The SENCO must take responsibility for this funding and work with the leadership team and governing body to ensure that the most vulnerable children in their school receive not only the resources allocated to them but additional provision if necessary.

The SENCO must also ensure that children and young people with a Statement receive the full provision highlighted within their statement. There is a legal responsibility to ensure that the individual has adequate support to meet the needs of the Statement, this is another challenge for the SENCO if the funding that supports this is hidden within the school budget.

The SEN Value for Money Toolkit produced by the Audit Commission (2007) will support the SENCO in ensuring that the appropriate resources are available to meet the needs of all children and young people

During the past 20 years we have seen a significant increase in the number of children with special educational needs in our mainstream schools. The inclusion agenda has ensured an equality of opportunity for all, supporting an individual's needs through a personalized approach to ensure each child reaches their full potential. Children with more complex needs are entering our schools daily and we need to ensure that we have well-trained and experienced teachers to be able to identify, assess and develop the pedagogy to enable all of these children to be able to access an educational experience that will meet their diverse and complex needs.

The SENCO will be pivotal to meeting this challenge. A large percentage of our current SENCOs will be retiring in the next five years and we need to ensure that we have teachers who begin to aspire to the role of the SENCO as part of their career pathway. We need well-trained, flexible and experienced leaders who are able to challenge, support and collaborate to ensure that the teaching and learning in every school are meeting the needs of all children.

Twenty-first century SENCOs need to have the time, status and support to enable them to be able to react and meet the demanding and challenging responsibilities that are now central to the role. No longer can we have a willing volunteer or a caring friend to carry out this extensive and diverse role. The professional SENCO has to be at the centre of change if a school wants to raise standards and improve its overall performance.

References

Audit Commission (2007) available at: www.sen-aen.audit-commission.gov.uk

DCSF (2009a) *Lamb Inquiry: Special Educational Needs and Parental Confidence*. London: DCSF Publications.

DCSF (2009b) *Your Child, Your Schools, Our Future: Building a 21st Century Schools System*. London: DCSF Publications.

DCSF (2010) *Improving Parental Confidence in the Special Educational Needs System: An Implementation Plan*. London: DCSF Publications.

DfE (1994) *Code of Practice on the Identification and Assessment of Special Educational Needs*. Nottingham: DfE.

DfEE (1997) *The SENCO Guide*. London: DfEE.

DfEE (1998) *The Government's Action Programme: Meeting Special Educational Needs*. Nottingham: DfEE.

DfES (2001) *Special Educational Needs Code of Practice*. London: DfES Publications.

DfES (2004a) *Every Child Matters: Change for Children*. London: DfES.

DfES (2004b) *Removing Barriers to Achievement: The Government's Strategy for SEN*. London: DfES Publications.

HMSO (2003) *Every Child Matters: Green Paper*. Norwich: The Stationery Office.

HMSO (2006a) *House of Commons Education and Skills Select Committee Report on Special Educational Needs*. London: TSO.

HMSO (2006b) *Government Response to the Select Committee Report on Special Educational Needs*. London: TSO.

TTA (1998) *National Standards for Special Educational Needs Co-ordinators*. London: TTA.

TTA (1999a) *National Special Educational Needs Specialist Standards*. London: TTA.

TTA (1999b) *Using the National Standards for Special Educational Needs Co-ordinators*. London: TTA.

2

THE CHALLENGE OF SUPPORTING THE SUPPORTERS IN THE INCLUSIVE SCHOOL

Artemi Sakellariadis

As I said, Tanya[1] is leaving this year. Yeah. 12½ hours gone that is, out of my time. And although Hassib is in Year One, it won't be enough hours for me, so I've just started looking around for another job. But that's why I've been to three different schools in five years. Because last in, first out. So, because I've had to keep moving, I'm always the last in! [laughs loudly]

Introduction

This quotation an extract from an unpublished interview with a learning supporter,[2] conducted in 2005 as part of my doctoral research. Although the role of learning supporters and the contexts in which they work has been continuously evolving in recent years, a number of issues remain challenging. This chapter considers the presence and role of learning supporters in the context of the whole school community, then explores challenges for the SENCO or Inclusion Manager in organizing support for pupils and for adults in the school.

Facilitating the learning and development of all children and young people in ordinary local schools

Embracing the changing landscape

An increasing number of disabled children and young people or those said to have special educational needs are nowadays educated in their local school. While many see this as a sign of progress on a matter of social justice, the issue of inclusion for all remains controversial. Some schools do not see why they should develop provision for all learners when separate special schools, thought to offer tailor-made provision, still exist. The imperative for mainstream provision for all is not yet widely understood. It involves a re-examination of conventional ways of seeing disability and a reconceptualization of how educational provision is organized and delivered. Children who spend their school years separated from their brothers, sisters, friends and potential friends from their local community, often end up living their adult life at the margins of society. Disabled adults remind us that if we are all to live in a society together, we all need to go to school together. There is, therefore, a strong argument for developing provision for everyone in ordinary local schools. At the same time, there is still strong support for the continuation of separate special schools, on the grounds that they offer provision not readily available in mainstream schools. I would argue that the former represents a moral position and the latter a partial reflection on existing practice. In this sense the two statements are not mutually exclusive and, therefore, should not be perceived to represent conflict. A detailed exploration of these issues is beyond the remit of this chapter.

What is of relevance here is the fact that ordinary local schools are increasingly being called upon to develop more inclusive provision for all learners. From national[3] and international[4] legislation, government guidance[5] and strategy[6] for special educational needs, to Audit Commission[7] and Ofsted[8] reports, the case has consistently been made for developing more inclusive provision for all young people in the communities in which they live. The simple truth is that UK law stipulates every child's right to a mainstream school place and inclusive education for all has been officially promoted since the early 1980s. However, as I have argued elsewhere (Sakellariadis, 2007), granting children the right to mainstream education without developing mainstream schools to provide for disabled children, is like issuing a ticket and keeping the door locked.

Recent developments lend further weight to the call for more inclusive provision for all children and young people to be developed in ordinary local schools. In June 2009, the UK government published the White Paper *Your Child, Your Schools, Our Future: Building a 21st Century Schools System* (DCSF, 2009b) which made a clear commitment to 'greater inclusion and participation for pupils with special educational needs and disabilities'. The Lamb Inquiry into parental confidence in the SEN framework produced its final report in December 2009; this calls for a major reform of the current system and contains 51 recommendations (DCSF, 2009a). In response to this inquiry the government has set up the *Achievement for All* project, aiming to improve outcomes for all children and young people said to have special educational needs and disabilities. The *Salt Review*, published in March 2010, looked at the teaching profession's capacity to provide for children and young people with labels of 'severe' and 'profound and multiple' learning difficulties; it identified a range of examples of good practice but suggested that initial teacher education does not leave newly qualified teachers feeling adequately prepared to teach young people identified as having severe or profound and multiple learning difficulties. In its Introduction, the report states that there are 38,000 school-aged children in England identified as having severe learning difficulties (SLD) or profound and multiple learning difficulties (PMLD), around 9,500 of whom are being educated in mainstream schools (DCSF, 2010).

It is important to remember that promoting disability equality is a whole school approach and not a matter for a particular class or teacher. Developing provision for a wider range of young people than the school has previously catered for is more likely to be successful if fully supported by the senior leadership team and embraced by the whole school community. The question, if one needs to be asked, should not be 'can we?' but 'how can we?'

A number of resources are available to help schools on this journey. In 2006, the (then) Department for Education and Skills (DfES), together with the (then) Disability Rights Commission, produced and made available to schools free of charge, a detailed resource to help schools meet the disability equality duty. *Implementing the Disability Discrimination Act in Schools and Early Years Settings: A Training Resource for Schools and Local Authorities* (DfES and Disability Rights Commission, 2006) provides information on how schools' commitments under the Disability Discrimination Act fit in with the framework for special educational needs and includes a DVD with inspirational examples of reasonable adjustments made by ordinary local schools to provide for a wide range of disabled children and young people. The CSIE publication *Index for Inclusion: Developing Learning and Participation in Schools* (Booth and Ainscow, 2002) is a set of materials to support inclusive school development through a self-review of the school's cultures, policies and practices. Although not specifically designed to have a focus on the inclusion of disabled pupils or those said to have special educational needs, the indicators and questions listed in the *Index* can be of considerable help to schools wanting to develop more inclusive provision for all learners.

Before closing this section I want to briefly expand on the simple statement that *all means all*. A number of children and young people considered to have the most complex needs are frequently excluded from their local neighbourhood schools. This is widely considered unproblematic, even though such practice often commits them to a lifetime on the margins and, therefore, hinders their life chances; it is also inconsistent with current moral values, policy and legislation. As I have written elsewhere (CSIE staff and associates, 2010), current ideas about schooling were established over 100 years ago, when many children with unusual bodies or minds were not expected to ever have a place in mainstream society. Although cultural norms have significantly shifted in recent years and disabled people are being increasingly valued as members of mainstream society, current educational practice has yet to embrace these changing attitudes. In assessing children's 'needs', many professionals continue to focus on physical, sensory or mental impairments and place children in educational institutions alongside others with similar impairments. No adult would choose their workplace by these criteria. At a time when all schools are increasingly expected to provide personalized learning, there is no reason why tailor-made provision has to take place in separate schools. There is nothing that happens in special schools that cannot take place in mainstream ones. A perceived need for daily contact with adult specialists should not be allowed to trump young people's need for daily contact with their brothers, sisters, friends and potential friends from the local community (not to mention the sense of belonging to one's local community, which most of us take for granted). To do so is to deprive some of the most vulnerable young people of the opportunity to build social capital: to establish friendships and helpful networks of support that can last a lifetime.

In a beautiful and often-quoted short piece entitled *Welcome to Holland*, Emily Kingsley reflects on the experience of parents having a child that seems to be different from the one they were expecting. She draws an analogy of setting off for a holiday in the sun but unexpectedly finding yourself in Holland, where you have to stay. You begin to address all the practical implications such as clothing and phrasebooks, while at the same time dealing with a sense of resentment at the irreversible change of plan. You gradually get to realize that you haven't arrived at a terrible, ugly place, only a different place to the one you were expecting. In fact, in time, you get to like it. After a while, you may even stop minding about everyone else around you bragging about their wonderful holiday in Italy (Kingsley, 1987). Many parents of disabled children or those said to have special needs will resonate with this story and the emotional journey it represents. Ruth MacConville reminds us that 'Just as parents do the important work of preparing themselves, their family and friends to welcome their baby, so schools also need to prepare themselves to welcome the pupil' (MacConville, 2007).

Thinking about the words that we use

The language we use shapes our thinking, and vice versa, so a word about terminology is called for. As I have written elsewhere (CSIE staff and associates, 2010), a major shift in how people understand disability has gathered momentum in recent years. Disabled adults have called for an examination of common assumptions and a clarification of what is meant by 'impairment' and what by 'disability'. The conventional way of thinking (the view that people are disabled by physical or mental impairments and, consequently, need management or treatment) has become known as the medical model of disability. An alternative, known as the social model of disability, is increasingly being understood and becoming more widely accepted. According to this, a person who has an impairment (a long-term loss of physical or mental function) may become disabled if reasonable adjustments are not provided in relation to that impairment. In other words, people are not disabled by the impairment itself but by society's failure to make adjustments or remove barriers. 'Disability', in this sense, is understood as an experience. For this reason, in the UK, the term *disabled people* is preferred to the term *people with disabilities*. The two models are clearly described by Richard Rieser in 'Disability discrimination, the final frontier' (Rieser, 2000).

A word about the term 'special educational needs' is also called for. The *Special Educational Needs Code of Practice* (DfES, 2001b) offers this definition: 'Children have special educational needs if they have a *learning difficulty* which calls for *special educational provision* to be made for them.' Baroness Warnock, who chaired the committee which first introduced the term in this country's education system (though not responsible for actually coining the term) had this to say:

> The definition, as you probably know, which comes in the 1981 Education Act is the purest vicious circle you will ever know. A special need is defined as 'any need that the school needs to take special measures to meet'. Well, that is not much of a definition but it is the only definition there is.
>
> (Warnock, 2005)

A major challenge of applying this generic term is clearly articulated by David Galloway and his colleagues:

Despite the humanitarianism apparently contained in the notion of 'catering for special needs' or 'acting in the child's best interests', children receiving the label become marginalized members of the society. The stigmatic social identity becomes a means by which children can be segregated from their peer group, friends, home and local community, denied access to the educational experiences offered to 'normal' children and offered a curriculum which may subsequently deny them access to further education, training or most types of employment.

(Galloway et al., 1994)

An interesting perspective, and one that is consistent with the social model of disability, has been put forward by Alan Dyson:

'Special educational needs are needs that arise within the educational system rather than the individual, and indicate a need for the system to change further in order to accommodate individual differences'.

(Dyson, 1990)

As I have argued elsewhere (CSIE staff and associates, 2009), the difference between whether a child 'has' or 'experiences' difficulties is similar to whether a child 'brings' or 'finds' difficulties at school. To many this might seem like a futile word game; to others such differences are of paramount importance, not least because they can have a strong impact on children's sense of identity. It is for this reason that throughout this chapter I have adopted the potentially cumbersome alternative of 'disabled young people or those said to have special educational needs'.

Finally, I would like to briefly address what is meant by 'the inclusive school' in the title of this chapter. It seems inappropriate to assume that there is a stage of development that a school can reach, which would render it to be an 'inclusive school'. 'I see inclusion as a never-ending process, rather than a simple change of state, and as dependent on continuous pedagogical and organizational development within the mainstream' (Ainscow, 1999). As the CSIE publication *Index for Inclusion* suggests:

Inclusion involves change. It is an unending process of increasing learning and participation for all students. It is an ideal to which schools can aspire but which is never fully reached. But inclusion happens as soon as the process of increasing participation is started. An inclusive school is one that is on the move.

(Booth and Ainscow, 2002)

Equipping young people for adult life

Research undertaken at the University of London's Institute of Education hit the media headlines in September 2009, following the publication of the final report on the deployment and impact of support staff in schools (DISS) project. This was a large-scale five-year study covering England and Wales, which reported that learning supporters boost teachers' productivity but not pupils' progress in English, Maths and Science. When a government-funded report claims that learning supporters impair young people's progress, perhaps the time has come to sit up and reconsider what is unproblematically accepted as common practice.

It is true that among the most significant ways in which schools help prepare the vast majority of children and young people for adult life is progress in core curriculum subjects and, later, other curriculum subjects of their own choice. Although it seems self-evident that this is not relevant to a small minority, for example, some young people with high level support needs, undue weight on academic achievement continues to skew educators' perceptions and give rise to a rather narrow view of progress. It is important to remember that the best preparation for adult life that school can offer some young people is to provide the opportunity and develop the capacity to establish social relationships, some of which may last a lifetime. Learning supporters have a key role to play in this and, therefore, often make a positive qualitative impact on young people's lives which is all but impossible to measure. It remains true that every single learning supporter stands to have a hugely significant impact on the experience children have in mainstream schools and on everyone's sense of belonging in the school community.

Children and young people also learn about values and develop a personal sense of identity during their time at school. Here, too, the contribution of learning supporters can be enormous, particularly if the temptation to concentrate time and effort on academic achievement can be sufficiently resisted. All schools now have a duty to promote disability equality, yet prejudice and stereotypes often continue to go unchallenged. As Mike Oliver reminds us:

> [Disabled children] also see themselves as pitiful because they are socialised into accepting disability as a tragedy personal to them. This occurs because teachers, like other professionals, also hold to this view of disability, curriculum materials portray disabled people (if they appear at all) as pathetic victims or arch villains, and their education takes place in a context in which any understanding of the history and politics of disability is absent.
>
> (Oliver, 1993)

Finally, it is important to remember that learning does not only take place in classrooms. Lunch and other break times make up a significant part of children's and young people's school day and afford them considerable opportunities to make or lose friends, develop social skills and learn or unlearn behaviours. These moments are every bit as important in preparing young people for adult life as the learning that goes on in the classroom, if not more. It is important to plan for learning supporters to be available during these unstructured times of the school day, while all the time being mindful not to compromise young people's need for independence. Learning supporters can model and facilitate interactions, then step back and let play activities and friendships flourish.

Co-ordinating support in ordinary local schools

Support for children and young people

When it comes to co-ordinating learning support, many SENCOs or Inclusion Managers may justifiably feel that they can write an Individual Education Plan (IEP) standing on their head. The key challenge here would be to consult with all stakeholders as appropriate. The ease with which a key function can be executed, after all, should not be confused with the benefit it stands to bring to the person concerned. No matter how able and experienced a SENCO or Inclusion Manager might be, IEPs need to be negotiated with the young person whom they are written for, as well as their parents and teacher. Any other member(s) of staff called upon to implement the IEP should also have agency in its content.

The Code of Practice specifies:

> Children and young people with special educational needs have a unique knowledge of their own needs and circumstances and their own views about what sort of help they would like to help them make the most of their education. They should, where possible, participate in all the decision-making processes that occur in education including the setting of learning targets and contributing to IEPs, discussions about choice of schools, contributing to the assessment of their needs and to the annual review and transition processes. They should feel confident that they will be listened to and that their views are valued.
>
> (DfES, 2001b)

It might be easy to assume that this is not always possible, but with sufficient will and creative thinking, it is hard to imagine when it would not be. Julia Hayes, an educational psychologist in Nottingham, has developed visual annual reviews as a creative way to increase the meaningful participation of young people in this process. Visual annual reviews are based on MAPs (Making Action Plans), a person-centred approach to planning using graphics, developed in Canada by Marsha Forest, Jack Pearpoint and John O'Brien (Forest et al., 1996). This approach places at the centre of the process the young person, who becomes directly involved in reviewing their strengths and goals as well as planning for the future (Hayes, 2004).

One of the greatest challenges in co-ordinating support for learning is to arrive at a joint understanding, shared by all concerned, of what a young person's 'needs' are. 'Putting the needs of the child first' can be seen as a cliché to which most, if not all, practitioners would aspire. Any reference to 'the child's needs', however, can harbour a number of assumptions, for example, what these 'needs' are and their relative significance, how they have arisen, what constitutes an appropriate response to them, or who has the authority to determine an answer to any of these questions. John Swain and his co-authors remind us that interventions thought to be helpful may easily be experienced as intrusive and/or unwelcome. 'Many other practices, which are undertaken in the name of "care", have been identified as abusive by disabled people. These include medical practices (such as excessive physiotherapy)' (Swain et al., 2003).

The Alliance for Inclusive Education's publication *The Inclusion Assistant: Helping Young People with High Level Support Needs in Mainstream Education* (Alliance for Inclusive Education, 2001) includes a 'Charter for Learning Support Assistants' drawn up by disabled young people who reflected on their experiences and considered what they had found helpful, including qualities they appreciated and practices or attitudes they had found difficult to deal with. Their resulting charter is reproduced here with the Alliance's permission.

Charter for Learning Support Assistants

1 LSAs must know about inclusion.
2 LSAs must be committed to learning everything they can about the needs of the young person they work with, including knowing when to interfere and when not to.
3 LSAs must be able to speak up for young people even when they are talking to a boss.
4 LSAs must be educated enough to understand what the young person is learning and help them understand it.
5 LSAs must be attached to one disabled young person and build a relationship with that person.
6 LSAs must be willing to learn new things and be trained by the young person.
7 LSAs must understand that they are not experts. They are there to assist, not [as] a carer.
8 LSAs must understand how to actively support young people's relationships with other people.
9 LSAs must negotiate proper professional boundaries with young people.
10 LSAs must know when to act as a responsible adult in the interests of the young person.
11 Communicators must be willing to learn from the young deaf person.

Support for adults

As the CSIE's publication *Learning Supporters and Inclusion* (Shaw, 2001) flagged up nearly a decade ago, learning supporters are often being asked to take on considerable extra responsibility at low pay, minimum job security and often with insufficient training. In a system that seems to be held together largely by the goodwill and commitment of the individuals sustaining it, the time for change is long overdue. The challenge to ensure that learning supporters feel valued members of the school community could be significant.

The role of learning supporters has been continuously evolving and many are now regularly taking on significantly greater responsibility for children's learning and development than was previously common. It is important to have a clear and shared understanding of how responsibility for the learning and development of young people said to have special needs is shared between class teachers and learning supporters. It is also important to articulate these understandings and to ensure that what happens in practice is in line with them. All too often I have visited schools and heard that the class teacher has overall responsibility for children's learning and development, only to find that a teacher had to consult with a learning supporter in order to answer questions about the progress of a particular child. The development of inclusive school communities is, in part, dependent upon an equitable and collaborative relationship between teaching and learning support staff.

One of the most significant challenges in co-ordinating support for adults is to strike a good balance between accessing the expertise of others outside the school and empowering staff to value and draw on resources available within the school. Ensuring that all teaching and non-teaching staff have sufficient access to continued professional development should go without saying. A range of impairment-specific training is widely available, and should be made accessible to those who would find it helpful. Knowledge about particular impairments, however, is only a small part of relevant training available. The Alliance for Inclusive Education regularly offers training for professionals involved in training or supporting learning supporters. A one-day course enables participants to deliver *The Inclusion Assistant* training pack. This is a unique resource drawing on the perspective of young disabled people and disabled adults within the Independent Living Movement, which helps create a pathway from school to a supported adult life in the community, for people who will continue to need one-to-one assistance throughout their lives.

In addition, professionals outside the school who have knowledge and experience that can be helpful to school staff can be expected to make a valuable contribution. A danger to be alert to is the possibility that, by engaging in unnecessary comparisons and identifying themselves as someone who does not have expert knowledge or experience, staff may feel disempowered from taking initiatives or implementing actions themselves. Potentially widespread, this is not helpful. After all, if only those claiming to have expert knowledge and experience were expected to implement any intervention, no new parent would ever begin to look after their own child. Without wishing to detract from the importance of consulting with those who claim expertise, I suggest that considerable expertise is already available within most schools. In some schools, staff may shy away from seeking the advice or support of their colleagues, for fear that this may be misconstrued as a sign of weakness or inadequacy. However, every incident is unique and sometimes collaborative thinking can generate more answers to a question than one individual can, no matter how experienced they are. Collaborative thinking (which carries more positive connotations than collabora-tive problem-solving) can be a standing item on the agenda of every staff meeting. Let us not forget that, in schools that are striving to develop more inclusive practices, staff would aim to treat each other with respect and feel comfortable about discussing work challenges with one another, in the spirit of collaboration.

Notes

1   Not her real name. Names and/or other identifying details of staff or pupils mentioned in this chapter have been changed, to protect the privacy of the people concerned.

2   In this chapter I have adopted the term established and explained in the earlier CSIE publication *Learning Supporters and Inclusion* (Shaw, 2001). Learning supporters are taken to be adults other than teachers who support children's and young people's

learning in schools. The term seems preferable over numerous alternatives currently in use, primarily because it defines people by what they do and, therefore, acknowledges their contribution to young people's development.

3   Current UK law stipulates that children said to have special educational needs should be educated in mainstream schools, provided that this does not conflict with parental wishes or affect the efficient education of other children (Section 316 of the Education Act 1996, as amended by the Special Educational Needs and Disability Act 2001).

The Disability Discrimination Act 1995, as amended by the Special Educational Needs and Disability Act 2001, renders it unlawful for schools to treat a disabled pupil, actual or potential, less favourably than another for a reason related to their disability, without attempting to make 'reasonable adjustments' to avoid placing disabled pupils at a disadvantage.

The Disability Discrimination Act 2005 established in the field of education the 'disability equality duty'. Schools must have regard to the need to: promote equality of opportunity between disabled and other people; eliminate discrimination and harassment, promote positive attitudes to disabled people; encourage participation by disabled people in public life; and take steps to take account of disabled people's impairments, even if this requires more favourable treatment.

Disability discrimination legislation defines a disabled person as one who 'has a physical or mental impairment which has a substantial and long-term adverse effect on his ability to carry out normal day-to-day activities' and provides clarifications and exclusions to this definition.

4   Every child's right to education without discrimination is also enshrined in international human rights law. The UK has ratified a number of international human rights treaties which place the government under an obligation to provide an education free from discrimination for all children and young people. Two human rights instruments are particularly relevant to the education of children said to have special educational needs:

(a)   The United Nations Convention on the Rights of the Child (1989, ratified by the UK government in 1991) is the main international instrument covering children's rights. The Committee on the Rights of the Child, which monitors the implementation of the Convention, has adopted a number of general comments – documents clarifying its interpretation of the Convention – relevant to inclusive education. General Comment No. 9 on the rights of children with disabilities (2006) was adopted in recognition of the poor situation of many disabled children. It states: 'Children with disabilities are still experiencing serious difficulties and facing barriers to the full enjoyment of the rights enshrined in the Convention. The Committee emphasizes that the barrier is not the disability itself but rather a combination of social, cultural, attitudinal and physical obstacles which children with disabilities encounter in their daily lives.'

The Committee on the Rights of the Child last examined the UK's implementation of this Convention in 2008. With regard to inclusive education for all children and young people, the Committee noted the lack of a comprehensive national strategy for the inclusion of disabled children into society and recommended legislative and other measures to address this.

(b)   The United Nations Convention on the Rights of Persons with Disabilities (2006, ratified by the UK government in 2009) covers the rights of disabled people. Article 24 (Education) asserts the right of all disabled young people to an 'inclusive education system at all levels' and suggests that they should be able to access an inclusive, quality and free primary and secondary education on an equal basis with others in the communities in which they live. The UK government has ratified this Convention, but placed a reservation and an interpretive declaration on Article 24 (Education), expressing its intention to continue placing some disabled children and young people in segregated provision a long way from home; it also confirmed its commitment to developing more inclusive provision for all children and young people in ordinary local schools.

5   When the Special Educational Needs and Disability Act (SENDA 2001) was introduced, the Department for Education and Skills (DfES) published guidance for schools on the new framework for inclusion of children with special educational needs into mainstream schools. The guidance confirmed that the general duty is to educate all children in mainstream schools and clearly explained: 'The starting point is always that children who have statements will receive mainstream education' (DfES, 2001a).

6   Following the proposals for the reform of children's services in *Every Child Matters*, the DfES published a key document setting out the government's vision for offering children said to have special educational needs and disabilities the opportunity to succeed: *Removing Barriers to Achievement: The Government's Strategy for SEN* (DfES, 2004). A commitment to inclusive education for all children and young people in mainstream schools was clearly articulated: 'All teachers should expect to teach children with special educational needs (SEN) and all schools should play their part in educating children from their local community, whatever their background or ability.'

7   In 2002, the Audit Commission for Local Authorities and the National Health Service in England and Wales undertook extensive research into provision for children with special educational needs, describing SEN as 'a very broad term, covering the full range of children's needs – from mild dyslexia to behavioural problems to complex medical conditions' (Audit Commission, 2002a: 4) and published two reports: (1) *Statutory Assessment and Statements of SEN: In Need of Review?* This raised concerns about the existing framework and suggested it leads to inequitable provision of SEN resources and is at odds with inclusion (Audit Commission, 2002a); (2) *Special Educational Needs: A Mainstream Issue.* This suggested that even though one in five children are thought to have special educational needs, they have remained a low priority and schools may be reluctant to admit them.

> The existence of separate structures and processes for children with SEN may have allowed their needs to be seen as somehow different – even peripheral – to the core concerns of our education system. This needs to change . . . 'SEN' must truly become a mainstream issue.
>
> (Audit Commission, 2002b)

8   In October 2004, Ofsted published a report on the quality of provision of mainstream schools for pupils said to have special educational needs. The report praised a minority of schools but noted that

> a high proportion of the schools visited in this survey have still a long way to go to match the provision and the outcomes of the best. They are generally not reaching out to take pupils with more complex needs, especially if their behaviour is hard to manage.
>
> (Ofsted, 2004)

In July 2006, Ofsted published a report on the quality of provision for 'pupils with learning difficulties and disabilities' in a range of settings. The report found that best outcomes are determined not from type but from quality of provision. 'Effective provision was distributed equally in the mainstream and special schools visited, but there was more good and outstanding provision in resourced mainstream schools than elsewhere.' The report also identified a number of weaknesses in provision, including the impact of learning supporters as key providers (Ofsted, 2006).

References

Ainscow, M. (1999) *Understanding the Development of Inclusive Schools.* London: Falmer.

Alliance for Inclusive Education (2001) *The Inclusion Assistant: Helping Young People with High Level Support Needs in Mainstream Education.* London: Alliance for Inclusive Education.

Audit Commission (2002a) *Statutory Assessment and Statements of SEN: In Need of Review?* London: Audit Commission.

Audit Commission (2002b) *Special Educational Needs: A Mainstream Issue.* London: Audit Commission.

Booth, T. and Ainscow, M. (2002) *Index for Inclusion: Developing Learning and Participation in Schools.* Rev. edn. Bristol: Centre for Studies on Inclusive Education.

CSIE staff and associates (2009) *The Welcome Workbook: A Self-review Framework for Expanding Inclusive Provision in Your Local Authority.* Bristol: Centre for Studies on Inclusive Education.

CSIE staff and associates (2010) *Developing a Single Equality Policy for Your School: A CSIE Guide.* Bristol: Centre for Studies on Inclusive Education.

DCSF (2009a) *Lamb Inquiry: Special Educational Needs and Parental Confidence.* Nottingham: DCSF Publications.

DCSF (2009b) *Your Child, Your Schools, Our Future: Building a 21st Century Schools System.* Norwich: TSO.

DCSF (2010) *Salt Review: Independent Review of Teacher Supply for Pupils with Severe, Profound and Multiple Learning Difficulties (SLD and PMLD).* Nottingham: DCSF Publications.

DfES (2001a) *Inclusive Schooling: Children with Special Educational Needs.* Nottingham: DfES Publications.

DfES (2001b) *Special Educational Needs: Code of Practice.* Nottingham: DfES Publications.

DfES (2004) *Removing Barriers to Achievement: The Government's Strategy for SEN.* Nottingham: DfES Publications.

DfES and Disability Rights Commission (2006) *Implementing the Disability Discrimination Act in Schools and Early Years Settings: A Training Resource for Schools and Local Authorities.* Nottingham: DfES Publications.

Dyson, A. (1990) Special educational needs and the concept of change. *Oxford Review of Education,* 16(1): 55–66.

Forest, M., Pearpoint, J. and O'Brien, J. (1996) 'MAPS' – Educators, parents, young people and their friends planning together. *Educational Psychology in Practice,* 11(4): 35–40.

Galloway, D., Armstrong, D. and Tomlinson, S. (1994) *The Assessment of Special Educational Needs: Whose Problem?* London: Longman.

Hayes, J. (2004) Visual annual reviews: how to include pupils with learning difficulties in their educational reviews. *Support for Learning,* 19(4): 175–80.

Kingsley, E. P. (1987) Welcome to Holland. Retrieved March 2010 from http://www.ndsccenter.org/resources/package1.php.

MacConville, R. (2007) *Looking at Inclusion: Listening to the Voices of Young People*. London: Paul Chapman.

Ofsted (2004) *Special Educational Needs and Disability: Towards Inclusive Schools*. London: Ofsted Publications Centre.

Ofsted (2006) *Inclusion: Does It Matter Where Pupils Are Taught?* London: Office for Standards in Education.

Oliver, M. (1993) Disability and dependency: a creation of industrial societies?, in J. Swain, V. Finkelstein, S. French and M. Oliver (eds) *Disabling Barriers: Enabling Environments*. London: Sage.

Rieser, R. (2000) Disability discrimination, the final frontier: disablement, history and liberation, in M. Cole (ed.) *Education, Equality and Human Rights: Issues of Gender, 'Race', Sexuality, Special Needs and Social Class*. London: RoutledgeFalmer.

Sakellariadis, A. (2007) Voices of inclusion: perspectives of mainstream primary staff on working with disabled children. Unpublished PhD thesis, University of Bristol.

Shaw, L. (2001) *Learning Supporters and Inclusion: Roles, Rewards, Concerns, Challenges*. Bristol: Centre for Studies on Inclusive Education.

Swain, J., French, S. and Cameron, C. (2003) *Controversial Issues in a Disabling Society*. Buckingham: Open University Press.

Warnock, M. (2005) Select Committee on Education and Skills: Minutes of oral evidence taken on 31 October 2005. Retrieved March 2010 from http://www.publications.parliament.uk/pa/cm200506/cmselect/cmeduski/478/5103103.htm.

3

WHAT IMPLICATIONS DO CHANGING PRACTICES AND CONCEPTS HAVE FOR THE ROLE OF SEN COORDINATOR?

Brahm Norwich

Introduction

This chapter takes an overview of the historical origin and position of the SEN coordinator role and uses this to identify some of the key dimensions and tensions associated with this role. There have been many studies on and discussions of the role of the coordinator since its formal inception in the 1990s. Some of these will be drawn on to illustrate the dimensions under discussion. This leads onto a brief examination of current debates and of recent developments in the field and what these might mean for the SEN coordinator role. The role of the SEN coordinator has been described as 'pivotal' for policy and practice in the government's recent Inclusion Strategy *Removing Barriers to Achievement* (DfES, 2004: 116). This is not surprising as there is such high, if not unrealistic, policy expectations about what teachers in this role can do for the education of pupils with special educational needs and disabilities. From another perspective, it could be argued that this role was likely to be constructed following the landmark *Education Act* (1981) with its increased commitment to educating pupils with special educational needs in ordinary schools. However, the uncertain position of the role is evident from the fact that one commentator was wrong, if not premature, in predicting some years ago that SEN coordinators were a 'dying breed' (Dyson, 1990: 116), while another more recent author considers that the role is still 'under construction' (Cole, 2005: 303).

The origins of the role arise from practical moves to enable the development of whole school provision for pupils identified as having SEN. These moves reflect the commitment of specialist teachers in the 1970s to widen their remit to supporting pupils with SEN beyond the confines of special classes. The key point in the official development of the role can be seen as the interaction of two key school policy developments, the *Education Act* (1981) and the *Education Reform Act* (1988). As mentioned above, the 1981 Act introduced the first explicit commitment to what we would nowadays call inclusive education. The onus was to educate as many pupils in ordinary schools as possible, subject to various conditions. This implied that ordinary schools had to consider how to develop and support whole school policies for special educational needs (Thomas and Feiler, 1988). However, seven years later, the

Conservative Government introduced radical changes to the school system with the *Education Reform Act* (1988), which introduced the National Curriculum and national testing system alongside the introduction of a quasi-market system of funding schools and more local management of schools. These measures were designed to raise standards through increasing competition between schools.

At the introduction of the 1988 legislation there were mixed feelings among those interested in special educational needs about these significant and complex changes to the school system. On one hand, the principle of a common curriculum for all including pupils with SEN was welcomed, but on the other, the central direction of the curriculum design for national assessment purposes, was seen to have none of the flexibilities required for those with SEN/disabilities. It is notable that the introduction of the National Curriculum adaptations for pupils with learning difficulties and the P levels came a decade later (QCA, 2001). This assessment-driven curriculum was part of the central establishment of more competition between schools for pupils as a way of driving up academic standards. School performance was to be judged by parents as users of schools in terms of average school attainment levels. With school funding becoming linked to pupil numbers, the introduction of a quasi-market system became a dominant feature of the school system. It was anticipated at the end of the 1980s that schools would became less tolerant of those presenting behaviour difficulties. This was what happened, as shown by the growth in permanent exclusions into the 1990s. Schools also tended to focus more on increasing attainment levels in the school league tables and sought further funding to support pupils with SEN. This was indicated by the increase in the level of Statements of SEN through the 1990s, which only flattened out at about 3 per cent in the early 2000s.

The tension between the push for externally visible standards and providing inclusively and flexibly for pupils with SEN had been recognized since the implementation of the 1988 Act (Weddell, 1988). The concerns aroused by the 1988 legislative changes and the resulting turbulence led to moves to focus more on the needs of those pupils with SEN without Statements. The 1981 legislation had focused predominantly on those with more significant SENs (2–3 per cent with more significant SENs) and not the larger group in ordinary schools (12–13 per cent). The introduction of the Code of Practice in 1994 (DfE, 1994) was the government's response to these problems. Among other guidance, a graduated model of identification and individual planning for pupils with SEN was to be introduced and all schools were required to have a SEN Coordinator. Seven areas of responsibility were set out for this role in the 1994 Code:

1   Daily operation of SEN policy.

2   Liaising with and advising fellow teachers.

3   Coordinating provision for pupils with SEN.

4   Maintaining school's register of SEN; overseeing records on pupils with SEN.

5   Liaising with parents.

6   Contributing to in-service training.

7   Liaising with external agencies.

There have been a series of research reports and publications about the SENCo role since 1994, by the government, teacher unions and researchers. It is not the aim of this chapter to review these findings and conclusions (for this, see McKenzie, 2007). However, it is relevant to this chapter to note the recurrent concerns about the role from surveys, for example, about time available for the role, unmanageability of role, support of the Headteacher/senior management, issues about understanding SEN funding in their schools, whether teaching assistants act as SENCos and training opportunities. McKenzie concludes her review in terms of the difficulty of generalizing about the SENCo's work which varies according to local circumstances, e.g. phase, membership of senior management team, extent of direct class teaching responsibilities and the same person having the SENCo and other responsibilities.

Another point relevant to this chapter is the consensus that the SENCo's role has widened since the 1994 Code of Practice (Cheminais, 2005; McKenzie, 2007). This widening involved the SENCo in more strategic work in schools concerned with management and leadership. This conception of the SENCo role was first formally set out in the Teacher Training Agency's attempt to capture the core purpose of the role in its SENCo National Standards (TTA, 1998). Not only was the SENCo to be responsible for the day-to-day provision for pupils with SEN but also for the guidance and leadership of other staff. The four areas identified were:

1   strategic direction and development of SEN provision;
2   teaching and learning;
3   leading and managing staff;
4   efficient and effective deployment of staff and resources.

Though the revised Code of Practice (DfES, 2001) did not change the main conception of the role set out originally in the 1994 Code, the widening of the role was also underlined by the government's inclusion strategy *Removing Barriers to Achievement* (DfES, 2004). Not only were SENCos expected to be members of senior management teams, but they were supposed to be central to managing change without any clear specification of what this involved. The most recent learning outcomes for the National Award for SEN Coordination (TDA, 2009) specifies these outcomes in terms of five areas which clearly show the dual focus on the operational and strategic aspects of the role:

1   *Professional context*: national/local frameworks, SEN/disability knowledge, evidence-based practice.
2   *Strategic development*: SEN policy and procedures: work with senior colleagues, finance, budget resource use, improve learning outcomes.
3   *Coordinating provision*: using data systems, deploying staff, managing resources.
4   *Leading, developing and supporting colleagues*: staff development, professional direction of others.
5   *Partnership working with pupils, families and professionals*: using external support/ expertise, consulting, engaging others.

Important dimensions of the SENCo role

The main aim of this chapter is to identify and discuss some of the key dimensions and tensions associated with the SENCo role which have arisen since the 1990s.

The following four inter-related aspects will be discussed:

1   Function versus roles.
2   Justification and boundary of specialism.
3   Coverage of the coordination function/role.
4   Focus of the coordination activities.

In analysing these aspects, I assume that central government guidance and strategies are applied to the school system with the aim of promoting particular practices in the name of special educational provision. I will also assume that some of the basic issues confronted in carrying out the SENCo role arise from differences in how special educational provision are understood, while other issues arise from the way that a general model of the coordination role does not exactly fit the par-ticularities of schools. This lack of fit can be understood in terms of differences associated with:

1   School phase (primary–secondary).
2   School size (number of staff, distribution of roles).
3   School priorities (inclusive and learner-centred commitment-in-action).
4   Local Authority setting (special needs/inclusion policies and practices).

These four dimensions and others will emerge as having a bearing on the discussion of the above four aspects of the SENCo role under consideration in what follows.

1 Function versus role

Not only have there been practical questions about time availability to undertake the SEN coordinator role, but, as shown above, the role has operational and strategic functions. The role of the SENCo as set out in the Code of Practice since 1994 has been focused around a cycle of individualization of teaching; that is, the assessment of pupils with SEN, the development of individual educational plans (IEPs), the implementation of teaching to these plans, their review and further adaptive planning. Much of the criticism of the overload of the role has been attributed to the bureaucratic nature of the IEP process, especially in larger schools with more pupils identified as having SEN. It is notable that the 2001 Code reduced the workload for SENCos by reducing the need to have IEPs through introducing group educational plans (GEP) where pupils had similar needs. Frankl (2005) showed that using GEPs reduced the number of IEPs in some primary schools and released SENCos from paperwork, enabling them to work with teachers and supported class teachers in taking more responsibility for pupils with SEN.

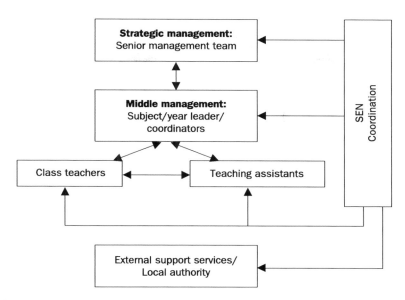

Figure 3.1 Levels of activity relevant to SEN coordination

That GEPs can reduce the workload of the SENCo and at the same time enable class teachers to be more responsible for planning for pupils with SEN raises questions about how the SENCo role and its associated responsibilities relate to other roles and responsibilities in schools. The range of responsibilities set out in the 2009 outcomes for SENCo training (see above) involves strategic development (policy, procedures, budgets), coordinating provision (data systems, deploying staff, managing resources), leading, developing and supporting, colleagues and partnership working with pupils, families and professionals (see Figure 3.1). Is this range of responsibilities best located in a single role? SEN coordination as a set of functions might be better distributed across various school staff roles. In Figure 3.1 the arrows going from SEN coordination to various functions represent how SEN coordination contributes to these generic functions, which do not officially take on and inter-relate with these specialist functions. This lack of shared responsibility in the official government position was pointed out by Garner (2001), when he identified that though the first SENCo standards (TTA, 1998) were meant to be allied to subject coordinator standards, these middle management standards made no reference to their role in relation to pupils with SEN. As Garner argues, the implication is that it is for SENCos 'to develop and sustain collaborative practice' (2001: 123) and that middle management responsibility for pupils with SEN is not formally and specifically recognized. The same point can also be made with respect to senior management standards. In only two of the six areas set out in the TDA (2004) standards for headteachers is there reference to inclusion and diversity, with no references specifically to disability/SEN. Under the 'Shaping the Future' area, heads are expected to be committed to 'Inclusion and the ability and right of all to be the best they can be' and under the 'Leading Learning & Teaching' area, they are expected to have knowledge of 'the development of a personalised learning culture within the school' and 'strategies for ensuring inclusion, diversity and access'.

This analysis indicates a significant imbalance in the official guidance about the inter-connections between and respective responsibilities of senior/middle management and SEN coordination. It is evident that this imbalance might not be reflected in the particular practices in schools, where there might be a sharing of responsibilities and collaborative approach to providing for pupils with SEN. However, it is reasonable to assume that the official imbalance does reflect a dominant trend in school practices, where school priorities and practices are not as inclusive and whole learner-centred as they could be (see the conclusion of the *Lamb Inquiry Report* (DCSF, 2009)).

Some of this trend may reflect internal school factors, but schools also operate within a national policy context with strong pressures to meet national priorities, such as raising attainments in a way that is in tension with and undermines inclusive priorities (MacBeath et al., 2006). This discussion leads on to the second key aspect of the SENCo role to be addressed in this chapter.

2 Justification and boundary of specialism

In this section I discuss whether there can be a justification for distinct SEN co-ordination as a function. There are two parts to this question: one about whether there is a need for specialist coordination, whatever it is called, apart from middle and senior management general coordination of school provision; the other, whether this kind of coordination should be labelled as and confined to SEN? These issues parallel the on-going debates about whether the term 'special educational needs' continues to be useful and justified.

One way to consider the question about specialist coordination as apart from middle and senior management coordination is to weigh up the arguments against and in favour of a specialist function. A specialist function can be justified if there is something distinctive and useful about the knowledge and skills that others cannot easily acquire or do not have the time to acquire. But, it is not just a matter of capability, but also whether others have an interest and willingness to acquire the knowledge/skills and use it. For example, a curriculum subject coordinator could be trained to lead, develop and support colleagues, one of the SENCo's functions, in her/his subject area as regards pupils with SEN. In practice, many do this to some extent, but perhaps without identifying this as an important part of their role. And, in this case the curriculum coordinator might not be particularly interested in this aspect of the role and come to depend on the SEN coordinator to do this function. However, in a more inclusive and collaborative school context, the subject coordinator might collaborate with the SEN coordinator, and so take on some of the coordination functions. From the SEN coordinator's perspective, this may be seen as distributing the coordination function.

This kind of middle management collaboration could be seen as good practice in terms of promoting shared responsibility for inclusive provision. But, how far could this handing over go? Could it go so far that specialist coordination 'does away with itself'? Would middle and senior management be willing to take over what is to be

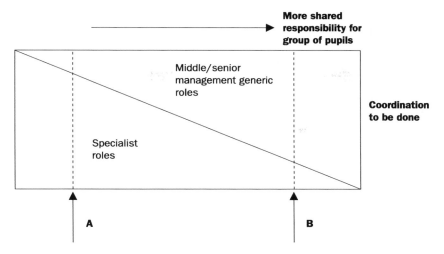

Figure 3.2 The balance between specialist and generic roles as responsibility for group of pupils is increasingly shared

done for a specific group of pupils, however defined, so that there would be no further requirement to have specialist coordination and a role to cover this function?

Figure 3.2 schematically shows one way of understanding the balance between specialist and generic coordination in an area such as SEN. The vertical axis in the rectangle represents the amount of coordination to be done. How this is shared between specialist and generic roles depends on the extent to which responsibility for this group is shared across roles. At position A on the left of Figure 3.2, where there is less shared responsibility, the balance is towards much more specialist coordination in a specialist role and rather little in a generic role. However, at point B, which is in the direction of more shared responsibility, there is more coordination in generic rather than specialist roles, but with some specialist role retained.

It seems that, even if much of the specialist capability/expertise can become generic, it is likely that there will be some residual specialist functions. This could be because of the specific knowledge that may be required in the field, but more important is the degree of commitment and interest in the particular field. If this kind of coordination is seen to require something additional to generic coordination and those doing generic roles feel low levels of responsibility for this additional aspect, then their interest will be in separating the functions and finding others to undertake it. However, not only is there a tendency in these circumstances to externalize the coordination outside generic responsibilities, but there are those within schools who identify with and are committed to particular groups, e.g. SEN and disabilities, and wish to champion their interests and advocate for them. In this way there can be a settlement between those willing to take on responsibilities for specific aspects of coordination and those with generic coordination responsibilities wishing to externalize them. It may be that the interest of the champions for this group of pupils arises in response to the externalizing of responsibility by those in generic roles, but it is also possible that those who come to champion this group of pupils developed these interests from experiences outside schools, for instance, in their families.

3 Coverage of coordination function

The third of the four aspects under discussion relates to the question raised in the previous section: whether the specific coordination should be labelled as and confined to SEN? In this section I discuss and analyse some of the issues about whether it is justified that coordination in schools is identified with a group, such as those with SEN.

Figure 3.3 represents some of the different areas where there can be specialist coordination and their relationships to each other. At the top of Figure 3.3 is the overarching learning support consultancy function. Dyson (1990) argued 20 years ago that the SEN coordinator role would be better framed as learning support consultancy. The reasons for this are to do with having a broader role that is not confined to pupils with SEN, that focuses on teaching and teachers and avoids the negative labelling of support functions. Though learning support has a more generic connotation as all pupils, not just a minority, might require such support at some time, this label has not become as established as Dyson anticipated. There are two main reasons for this: first, the coordination functions become labelled in accordance with government policy initiative and guidance, and, second, the potential breadth of the function cannot be managed by a single role.

There are two interpretations of 'learning support' as a specialist function, one that recognizes additional needs and another associated with a radical inclusion

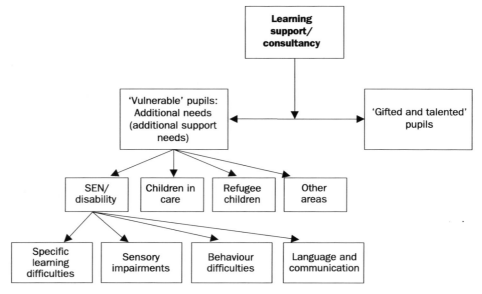

Figure 3.3 Levels and areas for specialist coordination
Note: Not all sub-areas are represented.

commitment that rejects any concept associated with 'needs'. By opting for a broader concept of 'additional needs' coordination, we do not avoid issues about the nature, scope and origins of these needs. 'Additional needs' might appear to offer a way of adopting an approach to inclusive schooling, which is presented and justified in terms of removing barriers to participation and learning, support for learning and the social model (Booth et al., 2000). However, I will argue that this is not a justifiable position. Many current advocates of the social model criticize and reject the concept of 'needs', whether it is 'special' or 'additional needs' (Runswick-Cole and Hodge, 2009). This is because of the assumed negativity of 'needs' and its association with the medical model rather than a social model of disability and educational rights. So, it follows that there is no place within an Inclusion Index model and other allied models for specialist coordination whether under the title of SEN and additional needs coordination.

There is a tension over the labelling of specialist coordination for a subgroup, whether a smaller one, such as SEN/disability, or a larger one, such as additional educational needs. The labelling restricts the coordination to a 'vulnerable' minority, with stigmatizing and devaluing risks; but on the other hand, to leave learning support coordination open to all learners, risks not focusing the coordination on those who require it. This tension is an example of the dilemmas of difference found in other aspects of specialist provision (Norwich, 2008b). There are different ways of resolving this dilemma over coordination which involve weighing up the respective risks and opting for the option with the lesser risks. I favour a resolution which recognizes that SEN as about learning difficulties and disabilities has outlived its usefulness (Norwich, 2008a), but that retains a concept of need (taken as implying a requirement that takes account of individual strengths and difficulties) as useful and necessary (Warnock and Norwich, 2010). Rights are critically important and, in practice, rights and needs are compatible and complementary. But what rights have traditionally not done is take account of individual functioning, as rights have been predicated on group membership (as in the phrase 'the rights of the disabled'). A commitment to what is required for an individual pupil means that we use a concept beyond rights that protects the additional resourcing for that pupil. Perhaps the term 'needs' should be replaced by another, perhaps it could be 'capabilities' (Terzi, 2007) or 'needs' could be used with a more positive meaning. This can be achieved through recognizing and using a more elaborate model of needs in which all pupils have common needs and through using it for pupils who are not identified as 'vulnerable', such as those identified as gifted and talented.

In arguing for learning support coordination based on additional needs, it is still important to note that the SENCo function is probably the best and longest estab-lished of the coordination functions established for 'vulnerable children'. It is notable that when other coordination functions were subsequently established, e.g. the 'desig-nated teacher' for children in care (Children and Young Persons Act, 2008) and for 'coordinators' for gifted and talented pupils, these have not been formally linked to the SENCo functions and role. These functions share common pedagogic and administrative aspects concerned with promoting appropriate provision relevant to minority groups of 'exceptional' pupils. They can be integrated into an overarching function in which there are still specialisms, as set out in Figure 3.3. That coordination for pupils identified as 'gifted and talented' and 'vulnerable' has not been integrated in national guidance might be to do with historic separation of these kinds of provision, though some schools have additional needs departments that integrate functions as regards 'vulnerable' and gifted/talented pupils.

That there has not been national guidance about the integration of the 'vulnerable' pupil area at school level, given the Every Child Matters integration at Local Authority level, reflects a significant and regrettable aspect of current English policy. Though some schools have established 'Inclusion managers' and 'Inclusion coordinators', despite the Common Assessment Framework (CAF) for assessing and planning for the needs of 'vulnerable' children, including those with SEN/disabilities, the new SENCo standards have not been formulated to include the wider group of those with 'additional needs' as defined in the CAF (TDA, 2009). This can be attributed to the influence and interests of the SEN lobby groups in the national policy arena, where the specific areas of SEN have become more vocal and powerful in promoting their specific interests, such as autism, dyslexia and hearing impairment. The reluctance of the Lamb Inquiry to recommend the broadening of the scope of SEN and link it up, as in Scotland and Wales, with a wider additional needs remit (Lamb Inquiry Report, 2009), is also regrettable.

Though there are benefits to the integration of the coordination of provision for pupils with exceptional needs, there are also risks involved. One of the benefits is that pupils do not always fall into neat categories, so the integration of coordination can bring together different forms of knowledge and skills. For example, a pupil may have a SEN and be a child in care or have a specific learning difficulty and be gifted at mathematics. One kind of risk is that pupils come to be defined predominantly in terms of their area of additional need and their other needs that are common to all pupils and their needs that are unique to them as individuals can be overlooked. To meet these common and individual needs requires the sharing of responsibility of all staff in schools. Another risk in integrating the coordination across the range of additional needs is that some specific kinds of additional needs may be overlooked or not given enough attention. This is where outside support services working at Local Authority or cross-school level might be better able to provide the specific knowledge, skills and consultancy required, but unavailable from school staff, for example, complex SEN including autistic and severe behaviour difficulties. Being aware of the range of additional needs and identifying where the appropriate knowledge and skills reside and drawing on them depends on economies of scale. The scarcer the knowledge and skills, the fewer people will have them and so the more likely that they may reside outside ordinary schools. This may be why coordination for additional needs may require sharing staff across ordinary schools, for example, jointly employed additional needs coordinators, and why special schools or units may be a useful source of support and consultancy knowledge and skills.

4 Focus of the coordination activities

The last aspect to be analysed and discussed is about the focus of coordination activities. As discussed above, the areas of activities for coordination have grown since the 1994 SEN Code of Practice. The scope of coordination activities relates to

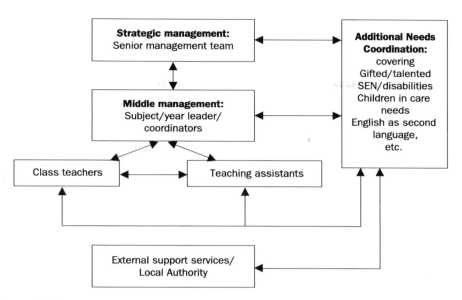

Figure 3.4 Levels of activity relevant to additional need coordination in organization with shared responsibility for pupils with such needs

strategic and middle management as well as coordination with respect to class teachers and teaching assistants, as well as liaising with external services, as shown in Figures 3.1 above and 3.4. One of the main themes of this chapter is the gap between official models of the SENCo role and responsibilities and what happens in the variety of particular schools. The scope of SEN coordination makes it possible for different interpretations of the role, as shown in a study by Kearns (2005) that identified and typified a range of different roles. Some SENCos operated as 'arbiters' in which they oversaw the rationalizing and monitoring of special educational resources, while helping teachers and parents clarify their concerns and supporting them to be positive about inclusion and provision. Others were portrayed as 'rescuers', who focused on pupils and undertook close work with specific class teachers. Kearns suggested that these SENCos created demand for their support and this resulted in time management problems. The 'rescuers' tended not to focus on or influence management, leading to less influence on the staff overall. Another approach, 'auditers', were focused more on procedures such as managing IEPs, organizing meetings, record keeping, analysing data, etc. 'Collaborators' focused on sharing practices within and across schools, engaged teachers in curriculum development and tended not to see boundaries between managers and teachers. Interestingly, only a minority of the study sample saw themselves as 'experts'; those who did, tended to have relevant qualifications or were in charge of specialist units. That there are such different interpretations of the SENCo role shows how broad is the scope of the role and how general is the official formulation of its functions.

Clearly the focus of coordination activities depends on many contextual factors, such as those identified above, school phase, school size, etc. It is also evident that the official model of SEN coordination is not one that can be effectively fulfilled by a single person, even if this teacher has specialist qualifications, e.g. has the National Award for SEN Coordination. In this respect the recent government requirement that SEN coordinators were not to be Higher Level Teaching Assistants (HTLAs) is an important recognition of the declining importance accorded to this role in some schools and the need for appropriately qualified teachers to become involved. It is evident that the focus of the SEN coordination cannot be separated from the function versus role discussion above. SEN coordination with its multiple foci cannot all be located in a single role. This becomes all the more necessary if the SEN coordination functions are integrated into other specialist coordination functions for other groups of exceptional pupils. So, the discussion shows how the different aspects are inter-connected, and this brings us back to the point where the overall argument of the chapter will be summarized and conclusions drawn.

Conclusion

The main aim of this chapter has been to highlight some of the key tensions and opportunities associated with SENCo roles and responsibilities. The discussion has shown how inter-connected are the aspects under analysis: function versus roles, the justification and boundary of a coordination specialism, the coverage of the functions and roles, and the focus of the coordination activities.

In Figure 3.4, I have represented the range of activities that can be associated with what I call additional needs coordination in an organization where there are shared responsibilities for these needs. Figure 3.4 has similarities with Figure 3.1 in terms of setting out the kinds and levels of activities and relationships, but it has two major differences from the earlier figure. The first difference is that the arrows show two-way interactions. This is used to represent that the coordination activities with the different levels of school provision (strategic and middle management and class teaching) are shared between the generic and specialist roles. This is one of the main implications arising from this analysis. I am aware that questions of ownership and responsibility reflect issues of the balance of power and priorities about schooling, but if inclusive education means anything, it is that there is some distribution of specialist coordination roles beyond those in labelled specialist roles. It is clear also that the recommendations of the *Lamb Inquiry Report* (2009), the most recent expression of government policy, imply the need for whole school practical commitments to quality provision for those with SEN. Finding ways to integrate specialist coordination functions in senior and middle management will be one way forward, so making the residual specialist functions attributed to the coordinator role more manageable and effective. This conclusion is one that reflects a concept of special educational or additional needs as a 'connective specialisation' (Norwich, 1996). Connective implies that special/additional is not separated from generic responsibilities in schools, but is integral to generic coordination.

The second difference between Figures 3.4 and 3.1 is to do with the integration of the various areas of specialist coordination into an additional needs coordination function. This integrates SEN coordination into related areas where the same pupil might come under different systems and titles as well as link coordination for 'vulnerable' pupils with those identified as gifted and talented. Such links might also promote the ownership of responsibilities for 'vulnerable' children and counteract the resistance of some teachers to take on shared responsibilities for them. One can expect pressures to separate out these aspects of coordination, but again a commitment to adequate provision for all pupils implies this kind of integration.

I conclude this chapter with a summary of the implications of the above analysis of the SENCo role and responsibilities. If inclusive provision for pupils with disabilities and difficulties in learning is to be a whole school matter, then the co-ordination for these pupils, usually identified in terms of SEN/disabilities, is best integrated under a broader additional needs title. It has been argued that this broader category needs to specify the range of overlapping areas of additional need and to cover not only pupils identified as 'vulnerable' in various ways. The inclusion of those with very high abilities and attainments, currently identified as gifted and talented, makes administrative sense and will also contribute to the positive connotation of the 'needs' term in additional needs. It has also been argued that additional needs might also be associated with a learning support function, but not learning support without a specific focus. The specific focus on additional needs, despite its risks, preserves the principle of protected coordination for a minority, whether the term 'need' is used or replaced by another term. Inclusive provision, it has also been argued, requires shared responsibility and collaboration between generic and specialist roles. This implies that generic senior and middle management roles take on explicit aspects of coordination for pupils with additional needs. Were this to happen, the additional needs coordination role will become more manageable than it has been since its inception. However, as argued above, central government models need to be flexible enough to take account of school particularities. The challenge of defining an inclusive concept of coordination for pupils with additional needs requires an examination and redefinition of middle and senior school management.

References

Booth, T., Ainscow, M., Black-Hawkins, K., Vaughn, M. and Shaw, L. (2000) *Index for Inclusion: Developing Learning and Participation in Schools*. Bristol: CSIE.

Cheminais, R. (2005) *Every Child Matters: A New Role for SENCOs*. London: David Fulton.

Cole, B.A. (2005) Mission impossible? Special educational needs, inclusion and the reconceptualization of the role of the SENCO in England and Wales, *European Journal of Special Needs Education*, 20(3): 287–307.

DCSF (2009) *Lamb Inquiry: Special Educational Needs and Parental Confidence*. London: DCSF.

DfE (1994) *Code of Practice on the Identification and Assessment of Special Educational Needs*. London: DfE.

DfES (2001) *SEN Code of Practice*. Nottingham: DfES.

DfES (2004) *Removing Barriers to Achievement: The Government's Strategy for Inclusion*. Nottingham: DfES Publications.

Dyson, A. (1990) Effective learning consultancy: a future role for special needs coordinators? *Support for Learning*, 5(3): 16–27.

Frankl, C. (2005) Managing individual educational plans: reducing the workload of the SEN coordinator. *Support for Learning*, 20(2): 77–82.

Garner, P. (2001) What is the weight of a badger?, in J. Wearmouth (ed.) *Special Educational Needs in the Context of Inclusion*. London: David Fulton.

Kearns, H. (2005) Exploring the experiential learning of special educational needs co-ordinators, *Journal of In-Service Education*, 31(1): 131–50.

MacBeath, J., Galton, M., Steward, S., MacBeath, A. and Page, C. (2006) *The Cost of Inclusion*. Cambridge: Victoire Press.

McKenzie, S. (2007) A review of recent developments in the role of the SENCo in the UK, *Support for Learning*, 34(4): 212–18.

Norwich, B. (1996) Special needs education or education for all? Connective specialization and ideological impurity, *British Journal of Special Education*, 23(2): 100–4.

Norwich, B. (2008a) Has SEN outlined it usefulness?, in Special Educational Needs Policy Options Group (2009) *Has SEN Outlived its Usefulness: A Debate*, available at: nasen website (accessed 5 March 2010).

Norwich, B. (2008b) *Dilemmas of Difference: Inclusion and Disability*. London: Routledge.

QCA (2001) *Planning, Teaching and Assessing the Curriculum for Pupils with Learning Difficulties*. London: QCA/DfES.

Runswick-Cole, K. and Hodge, N. (2009) Needs or rights? A challenge to the discourse of special education, *British Journal of Special Education*, 36(4): 189–203.

TDA (2004) *National Standards for Headteachers*. London: TDA.

TDA (2009) *Standards for National Award for SEN Coordination*. London: TDA.

Terzi, L (2007) Beyond the dilemma of difference: the capability approach to disability and special educational needs, in L. Florian and M. McClaughlin (eds) *Categories in Special Education*. London: Sage.

Thomas, G. and Feiler, A. (1988) *Planning for Special Need: A Whole School Approach*. Oxford: Blackwell.

TTA (1998) *National Standards for SEN Coordinators*. London: TTA.

Warnock, M. and Norwich, B. (2010) *Special Educational Needs: A New Look*. London: Continuum Publishers.

Weddell, K. (1988) Special educational needs and the Educational Reform Act, *Forum*, 31(1): 19–21.

4

LEADING LEARNING
THE ROLE OF THE SENCo
Fiona Hallett and Graham Hallett

Introduction

The creation of the SENCo role was undoubtedly viewed by many as an imaginative and progressive move. To nominate an agent who would coordinate provision for learners with all forms of special educational need and/or disability was clearly envisaged as a means by which schools, parents and successive governments could ensure that all children would be given equal opportunities for educational success. The original SEN Code of Practice (DfE, 1994) and subsequent revision (DfES, 2001) set out the areas of responsibility for the SENCo which were predominantly phrased in terms of 'maintaining' records, 'liaising' with stakeholders and 'contributing' to staff development rather than in terms of strategic leadership even though it was suggested that the SENCo should be a member of the Senior Leadership Team (SLT).

Reviews of practice conducted in the past five years have, somewhat unsurprisingly, reported that the reality of the role is clearly varied (Kearns, 2005; Layton, 2005; McKenzie, 2007) and very much dependent upon context and interpretation of sometimes contradictory legislation. In particular, the emergence of Teaching Assistants (TAs) as SENCOs in some settings gave cause for reconsideration of the ways in which the SENCo role had been envisaged with the *House of Commons Education and Skills Select Committee Report on SEN* (2006) urging the government to address this unanticipated development.

The government response to this report included the introduction of the National Award for SEN Coordination (TDA, 2009) which has a clear focus on strategic leadership. This chapter aims to explore what this might, and should, mean in terms of 'leadership for learning' which is described by John MacBeath as 'the capacity for leadership to arise out of powerful learning experiences and opportunities to exercise leadership to enhance learning' (MacBeath, 2009: 83). While we acknowledge that this may be the very model that currently informs the practice of some SENCos and their schools, we would suggest that this only occurs when the existing school culture (and core beliefs of the SENCo) align to this vision; that is, it happens despite current legislation and initiatives rather than as a result of them. Our concern is that current practice is so embedded in the culture and ethos of school settings that to require SENCos to adopt a leadership role may do little to enable them to exercise leadership to enhance learning.

Kearns' study, while limited to interviews with just 18 SENCos, offers us five useful metaphors for the way in which the SENCo role is currently practised that resonate with similar studies (Layton, 2005; McKenzie, 2007). These metaphors allow us an instantly recognizable typology of the SENCo role as: 'auditor', 'rescue', 'expert', 'collaborator' and 'arbiter', any of which can dominate, overlap and co-exist. In fact, when we consider the guidance offered by the Codes of Practice (DfE, 1994; DfES, 2001), it is no surprise that such variation exists. At present, the Code of Practice acts as non-statutory guidance in that a school must pay regard to the Code without necessarily adopting all of the processes that it advocates. Nonetheless, the 'auditor' role, identified by Kearns, indicates that accountability and procedural management dominate the lives of many SENCos, often leading to role anxiety and overload (McKenzie, 2007). Those who adopted this role focused on legalities and administration, asserting that a critical phase of their personal growth was 'the introduction in the school of the official Code of Practice for Special Educational Needs' (Kearns, 2005: 141).

The leadership implications for 'auditor' SENCos could result in what Argyris and Schön (1978) described as 'single loop learning' which characterizes much of the managerial and audit agenda, caught up in the self-perpetuating loop of targets, strategies, implementation and evaluation, in effect, a means by which to 'tame the wild' (Perkins, 2003) and reduce individual autonomy. Therefore, while the Code of Practice purports to offer guidance, rather than a legally binding rubric, it is, perhaps, unsurprising that SENCos view it as a 'rule book' and quickly become overwhelmed by what they see as their procedural duty or by what their colleagues encourage them to see as their role. Fullan (2003: 51) notes that 'relational trust atrophies when individuals perceive that others are not acting in ways that are consistent with their understanding of the others' role obligation'; it is all too easy for the newly appointed SENCo to adopt the behaviours expected by their colleagues and by doing so create a situation where some can be absolved of their responsibility for all learners.

Another of the metaphors highlighted by Kearns was that of SENCo as 'rescue'. While the *Every Child Matters* (DfES, 2004) agenda is not specific to learners with SEN and/or disability, it looms large on the political landscape and lends itself to this role construct. The five outcomes of the Every Child Matters agenda, that all children should: be healthy, stay safe, enjoy and achieve, make a positive contribution and achieve economic well-being, while vague and somewhat benevolent in articulation, demonstrate an expectation that certain children will be identified as being at risk of not achieving these outcomes as a result of their home circumstance or social background. The fact that these outcomes are phrased in relation to children experiencing social deprivation lends them a deterministic slant predicated on a notion of 'surrogate need', by virtue of their social circumstance, rather than the 'perceived need' based upon the range of evaluative judgements required by the *SEN Code of Practice* (DfES, 2001). As such, predictive categorization of learners by social background is, perhaps, an inevitable response to Every Child Matters. The leadership potential of the well-intentioned 'rescue' SENCos who are influenced by such agendas could lead to a situation where staff align themselves to factions which may be seen as oppositional with, on the one hand, educators determined to anticipate potential risk, and on the other, educators determined to achieve predetermined academic standards. Such demarcation lines have been termed 'Balkanisation' (Hargreaves, 1994) and serve to obscure the moral purpose of education which is grounded in equity, justice and the desire to enable all individuals to achieve their full potential. While both the *SEN Code of Practice* (DfES, 2001) and *Every Child Matters* (DfES, 2004) are framed within similar precepts, and almost all educators would espouse views of this nature, the enactment of these principles can seem impossible to achieve in the current climate.

If SENCos, in response to beneficent, but vaguely articulated, guidance, develop localized practice determined by particular policy initiatives, of which there are many, the result can often be described as what Michael Lipsky (1980) termed 'street-level bureaucracy'. The notion of 'street-level bureaucracy' reflects a belief that policy implementation in the end comes down to the people who implement it, limited resources, the need to negotiate targets and relations with 'clients'. In terms of the SENCo role it is clear to see how such pressures, and scope for individual inter-pretation of policy, can produce an instrumental approach predicated on one, or more, policy initiatives. Reports on the current role of the SENCo mirror Lipsky's notion of street-level bureaucracy in that it is often described in terms of powerless-ness and a need to develop practice from conflicting, or unclear, policy guidance (Layton, 2005).

As argued earlier, the policy agenda has now shifted more explicitly towards advocacy of the SENCo as a member of the Senior Leadership Team in school settings. This representation of the SENCo role has been idealized since the first *SEN Code of Practice* (DfE, 1994) and is clearly shaping the National Award for SEN Coordination. While we recognize the value of this model and would promote this as a 'stepping stone' that could move current practice forward, we are also arguing that this could result in surface-level change where 'what is being proposed sounds good and contains all the right concepts, where leaders can talk a good game and even mean it, but where the ideas never get implemented with consistency or integrity' (Fullan, 2003: 31).

The next section of this chapter explores the potential limitations of responding to concerns about current practice by simply moving the SENCo to the Senior Leadership Team. The purpose of this is to argue for an alternative model which we have termed a 'distributive model for SEN coordination'. This nomenclature reflects a reconceptualization of SEN coordination that harnesses the moral imperative of leadership for learning in order to mobilize the commitment of all members of the school to improve the experiences of all students, including closing the achievement gap.

The SENCo as a member of the Senior Leadership Team: an interim model?

By describing the SENCo as a member of the Senior Leadership Team as an 'interim model', we would suggest that this is a necessary response to a flawed system. We argue this despite the fact that the desire to raise the status of the SENCo, to one in which they become a leader of SEN Coordination across the school, would appear to enable macro-analysis of SEN Coordination; potentially widening the narrow focus on resource limitation and targets described above to a more expansive view of teaching and learning across the setting. Indeed, we recognize that appointing the SENCo to the leadership team could, in theory, reduce both the temptation to micro-manage the administration of SEN coordination and reduce the perceived need to 'rescue' certain learners. However, we also caution that if schools are to avoid the limited role constructs highlighted in the first section of this chapter, the purpose of the SENCo role, whether central to the SLT or not, requires some thought.

First, as Gunter (2007), Stevenson (2007) and MacBeath (2010) have argued, new divisions of labour have served to create a divorce between those who plan and those who execute; between teaching and pastoral care. Some consideration of why the SENCo should be a member of the Senior Leadership Team is necessary if we are to address this concern. If a SENCo becomes a member of the Senior Leadership Team merely to plan a school response to policy initiatives and legislation, the response from teachers and teaching assistants may mirror the aforementioned street-level bureaucracy as they attempt to navigate targets, negotiate the demands of 'clients' and compete for funding; shifting the street-level bureaucracy to class teams rather than developing cohesive and collaborative approaches to teaching and learning for all pupils. Without a reconceptualization of the interplay between leader-ship and learning, and how this might lead to 'leadership for learning' (MacBeath, 2006, 2009) promoting the SENCo to the leadership team might do little to address the concern that 'most systems have enacted accountability policies in the absence of conceptualising and investing in policies that will increase the capacity of educators to perform in new ways' (Fullan, 2003: 25).

Alternatively, if the SENCo is appointed to the Senior Leadership Team in order to influence teaching and learning across a school, the role of the Deputy Head-teacher in many primary schools, or Curriculum Leaders in Secondary Schools, may need to be reviewed. This raises fundamental questions about responsibility for the planning and execution of strategies to meet the needs of all learners, including those with SEN and/or disabilities. If the SENCo, as senior leader, moves away from planning interventions and executing individualized learning programmes for learners with SEN and moves towards planning and executing strategies that enable class communities to assume ownership of teaching and learning, it could be argued that the role of the Deputy Headteacher, or Curriculum Leader will require re-thinking.

Each of these alternatives highlights the importance, and potential impact, of role definition upon 'social capital' (the connections within and between social networks). Putnam (1999), Szreter (2000) and MacBeath (2009) discuss the difference between three forms of social capital: bonding social capital, bridging social capital and linking social capital. 'Bonding' social capital relates to relatively few strong connections between people creating a small number of strong groupings which can lead to insularity. In terms of educational settings, these groups might be the SLT, teaching staff or support staff. Bonding social capital of this nature would be evident in schools adopting hierarchical approaches to leadership where, for example, the SLT meet to decide policy, the teachers meet to discuss the curriculum and the support staff meet to discuss individual learners. If bonding social capital dominates an educational setting, the opportunities for the SENCo to implement leadership for learning may not be enabled by simply relocating them to the Senior Leadership Team.

If we take the example of provision mapping, a SENCo, appointed to the SLT, could retain ownership of provision mapping across the setting in order to lead the creation of something akin to Group Education Plans (Frankl, 2005) for an identified body of learners. While Frankl has described Group Education Plans as having the potential to reduce administration for SENCos and devolve planning responsibility to class teams, this is, once again, little more than a much needed response to a flawed system. If Individual Education Plans (IEPs) can be little more than a document produced to achieve the procedural expectations set out in the *SEN Code of Practice* (DfES, 2001), the Group Education Plan could go some way to creating a less bureaucratic and more inclusive system. However, it must also be recognized that such systems in themselves can often become a new form of bureaucracy and are only the driver for collaboration in a culture that embodies collective responsibility. As such, the narrowness of the SENCo role, as is reported by those not appointed to senior leadership teams (Layton, 2005), could be reproduced from within the leadership team, strengthening 'bonding' social capital rather than enabling more collegial forms of leadership for learning to develop.

In contrast to 'bonding' social capital, 'linking' social capital operates vertically, making connections between people with differing degrees of power and authority. Such social links are evident in educational settings that seek to create connections between groups that possess bonding social capital, for example, between teachers and the Senior Management Team or between subject coordinators and teaching assistants rather than to redistribute autonomy across a setting. While a SENCo may be able to enact a desire to effect 'linking' social capital by becoming a member of the Senior Leadership Team, one must question the moral purpose of such a move.

It is therefore of some interest to this discussion that Layton (2005: 59) reported that 'most especially, however, the greatest barrier to achieving their moral purpose as SENCos was identified as not being a member of the senior leadership team'. While it is clear, from Layton's study, that SENCos believed membership of the Senior Leadership Team to be an essential precursor to improved status for themselves and for all learners within their setting, we would caution against viewing such membership as a panacea. In fact, we would question any differentiation between the moral purpose of SENCos, which was articulated by the SENCos in Layton's study as a 'deeply held commitment to serve the best interests of all their pupils' (2005: 58), and that of any member of the teaching profession.

Five major virtues central to the moral character of teaching professionalism were defined by Sockett (1993, 2006) as: honesty, courage, care, fairness, and practical wisdom. As these virtues are arguably no more, or less, central to the role of the SENCo than to any other teacher, to argue for membership of the Senior Leadership Team for one member of staff on the basis of enabling them to achieve their moral purpose ignores both the collective moral purpose of the school and the moral responsibility of all staff for all learners.

Indeed, simply promoting the SENCo to the Senior Leadership Team may do little more than redistribute accountability without embedding a philosophy that encourages what Eisner (1991) termed 'connoisseurship' which MacBeath (2009: 74) describes as knowing 'how to suspend preconception and judgement; to know what they see rather than seeing what they already know'. While connoisseurship may lend itself to the development of a collective moral purpose, the ability to suspend preconception requires a culture that moves beyond performativity in order to develop genuine dialogue around the intention, purpose and impact of education for all of our learners; in essence, a culture that embraces distributive and reciprocal practices that are driven by a core moral purpose.

A distributive model of SEN coordination: leadership for learning?

The third type of social capital cited by Putnam (1999), Szreter (2000) and MacBeath (2009) is described as 'bridging' social capital which occurs when social links are relatively weak but more numerous and are 'outward looking connecting people with others beyond their immediate reference group, opening up new ways of seeing, relating and learning' (Swaffield and MacBeath, 2009: 45).

Crucially, settings that enable 'bridging' social capital reconceptualize leadership away from a process-led accountability view towards 'leadership for learning' which is concerned, above all, with keeping alive bridging social capital in the belief that 'it is the many and weak links that provide the scope and space for the exercise of agency in respect of both leadership and learning' (Swaffield and MacBeath, 2009: 46). The notion of agency (people being able to make choices and make a difference) is central to this approach. The degree to which learners, parents and educators can each express their agency will clearly inform the moral purpose of the school and the extent to which accountability for learning is shared and valued.

By advocating a distributive model of SEN coordination, we are arguing that we should view educational settings as 'communities of practice' (Lave and Wenger, 1991) focused upon the process and activity of learning rather than as a series of hierarchical structures focused upon the product of learning and the attendant processes of SEN coordination. Central to the 'communities of practice' approach is an acceptance of what has been termed 'legitimate peripheral participation', where novices become experienced members of a community of practice or collaborative project (Lave and Wenger, 1991). In this way, novices are valued for their contribution, rather than viewed as individuals whose practice requires correction, recognizing that participation is an 'encompassing process of being active participants in the *practices* of social communities and constructing *identities* in relation to these communities' (Wenger, 1999: 4). This notion operates on two levels. Firstly, in terms of staff participation, this approach does not seek to permit harmful or neglectful practice; rather, the need to embrace legitimate peripheral participation recognizes that practice varies in levels of expertise but that expertise is not the only measure of value. In particular, this philosophy recognizes the moral imperative of all practitioners above the particular expertise of some. Secondly, this perspective persuades us to view learning as participation both for students and staff, enabling us to move beyond the 'competency traps' (Cousins, 1996: 79) of a standards-driven philiosophy that necessarily marginalizes and labels those deemed to be failing. By reconceptualizing learning in terms of participation, rather than simply as achievement, the ethos shifts to one which encompasses a belief that 'teaching a child to read is an important contribution, but inspiring him or her to be an enthusiastic, life-long reader is another matter' (Fullan, 2003: 29). Similarly, it could be argued that inspiring all members of a school community to be enthusiastic and life long agents of change offers more than creating inflexible hierarchies of management or attainment. This encourages learning communities to unleash their moral imperative and increase autonomy and agency in order to enable 'double loop learning' (Argyris and Schön, 1978). In contrast to 'single-loop learning' which adopts a 'plan, act, evaluate' approach where plans are created in response to targets that are rarely questioned, 'double-loop learning' requires a much deeper critique of the purpose of targets and the underlying assumptions of action. 'Double-loop learning' is intolerant of routine and simplistic answers to complex issues in the belief that 'the valuing of consistency leads to competency; the valuing of inconsistency leads to learning' (Argyris and Schön, 1996).

We recognize that for many SENCos, this will be a challenging approach to take, in that they may believe that the actions of some members of the school community require correction and redirection reaffirming the 'SENCo as rescue' and 'SENCo as auditor' roles identified by Kearns (2005). Nevertheless, until we recognize, and give permission for, legitimate peripheral participation the two, very limited and limiting, SENCo roles described above may prevail.

As mentioned earlier in this chapter, Kearns (2005) reported a further three roles identified by the SENCos in his study: 'SENCO as arbiter' (negotiating, rationalizing and monitoring the use of SEN resources in their schools), 'SENCo as expert' and 'SENCo as collaborator'. In order to avoid SENCos identifying solely, or predominantly, with only one of these roles the whole school community must recognize and develop the forms of teaching and learning practice on offer for all learners, including those with special educational needs. This recognition can move schools away from process management aimed at certain groups of learners towards leadership for learning and learning for leadership where any member of a school society can learn to effect change and the 'headteacher becomes the head learner' (MacGilchrist et al., 1997). Aside from the fact that the National College for School Leadership recognizes that the potential 'influence from distributive leadership is up to three times higher than that reported for an individual leader' (NCSL, 2006: 12), this change in focus enables anyone to 'take on leadership as a right and responsibility rather than it being bestowed as a gift or burden' (Swaffield and MacBeath, 2009: 44). In this way conceptualizing learning as 'participation in social practice' can serve to challenge the prevailing staff and learner hierarchies and encourages all members of a school community to explore the relationship between learning and the social situations in which it occurs (Lave and Wenger, 1991).

This ideal has real implications for transforming the role of the SENCo beyond that of a powerless negotiator of policy and practice: the street-level bureaucrat (Lipsky, 1980), as evidenced in reports of current practice. It also demands some recognition of the fact that membership of the Senior Leadership Team, in itself, might do little to empower all staff to take responsibility for diverse groups of learners. A distributive model of SEN coordination requires a radical re-think of practice.

Fullan (2003) discusses 'complexity theory' in this regard, arguing that transformation cannot be effected in a top-down or linear fashion. In developing this argument he makes reference to the many disruptions that can occur within the most meticulously planned strategies when individuals within the system choose to exert their autonomy. This raises a crucial point; in a hierarchical system individual autonomy, or agency, whether in the form of street-level bureaucracy or in the individual expression of one's moral purpose, can be viewed as dissent or unprofessional practice. This can even be the case when the expression of individual autonomy, when viewed beyond the hierarchical system, exhibits those dispositions described by Sockett (2006), earlier in this chapter, as representative of teacher professionalism.

As such, a distributive model of SEN coordination requires three conditions. First, it requires a commitment to ensure that every member of the educational community is given the space to learn to lead and to lead to learn. This is not to argue that a school does not need a Headteacher but it does require some consideration of the additional statutory roles in schools such as a Deputy Headteacher, SENCo and the myriad leadership roles that exist in many settings. Indeed, the desire to become an 'intelligent school' where 'change comes from within, from the staff and pupils, rather than imposed from above' (MacGilchrist et al., 1997: 108) requires school leaders to analyse whether they create hierarchical layers of narrowly defined positions merely to sustain bureaucracy or whether these serve a legitimate purpose.

The second condition for a distributive model of SEN coordination relates to the balance between internal and external accountability (MacBeath, 2010) a review of which is necessary before an educational environment can begin to develop communities of mutually accountable practitioners. This is not to extol a naïve ignorance of external accountability; rather, we would suggest that a much needed reconsideration of the forms of accountability that drive practice is called for, recognizing that 'what is worth fighting for is more of an internal battle than an external one' (Fullan, 2003: 19) and that moral accountability to all members of the school community may serve a higher purpose than presumed bureaucratic accountability to national directives.

The final condition that we feel to be central to a distributive model of SEN coordination is some recognition of the de-professionalization that occurs, as evidenced in Kearns' (2005) study, when we create structures that serve to atomize the SENCo role. These structures can occur whether or not the SENCo is appointed to the Senior Leadership Team. In fact, if we return to the dispositions that Sockett (2006) describes as the moral purpose of teaching, a distributive model of SEN coordination would need to be designed so that all educators can develop such dispositions, not by decree or correction, but by negotiation, collaboration and a commitment to shared accountability.

The demands and implications of the three conditions described here explain the need, in some settings, for the 'interim model' described above. However, for those settings with the drive and vision to review the purpose of leadership structures, the role of the SENCo could be situated within an ethos where 'learning and leadership are conceived of as "activities" linked by the centrality of human agency within a framework of moral purpose' (Swaffield and MacBeath, 2009: 42). In this way, the National Award for SEN Coordination could empower SENCos to become the catalyst for a reinvigoration of the moral purpose of education and a review of the potential for leadership for learning across educational settings. The resulting climate could be one which extols 'deliberately shared leadership of vision building, people development, organisational structuring and teaching and learning management' (Dempster, 2009: 29). The evolving nature of the SENCo role envisaged by the National Award for SEN Coordination could very well be the vehicle for such change for those schools and SENCos with the imagination and foresight to maximize this unique opportunity.

References

Argyris, C. and Schön, D. (1978) *Organizational Learning: A Theory of Action Perspective*, Reading, MA: Addison-Wesley.

Argyris, C. and Schön, D. (1996) *Organizational Learning II: Theory, Method and Practice*, Reading, MA: Addison-Wesley.

Cousins, B. (1996) Understanding organised learning for leadership and school improvement, in K. Leithwood, J. Chapman, D. Corson, P. Hallinger and A. Hart (eds) *International Handbook of Educational Leadership and Administration*. Dordrecht: Methuen.

Dempster, N. (2009) What do we know about leadership?, in J. MacBeath and N. Dempster (eds) *Connecting Leadership and Learning: Principles for Practice*. London: Routledge.

DfE (1994) *Code of Practice on the Identification and Assessment of Special Educational Needs*. London: DfE.

DfES (2001) *SEN Code of Practice*. Nottingham: DfES.

DfES (2004) *Every Child Matters: Change for Children*. London: DfES.

Eisner, E. (1991) *The Enlightened Eye*. New York: Macmillan.

Frankl, C. (2005) Managing individual educational plans: reducing the workload of the SEN coordinator, *Support for Learning*, 20(2): 77–82.

Fullan, M. (2003) *The Moral Imperative of School Leadership*. London: Sage.

Gunter, H. (2007) Remodelling the school workforce in England: a study in tyranny, *Journal for Critical Education Policy Studies*, 5(1): 1–11.

Hargreaves, A. (1994) *Changing Teachers, Changing Times: Teachers' Work and Culture in the Postmodern Age*. London: Continuum.

HMSO (2006) *House of Commons Education and Skills Select Committee Report on SEN* (2006). London: HMSO.

Kearns, H. (2005) Exploring the experiential learning of special educational needs coordinators, *Journal of In-Service Education*, 31(1): 131–50.

Lave, J. and Wenger, E. (1991) *Situated Learning: Legitimate Peripheral Participation*. Cambridge: Cambridge University Press.

Layton, L. (2005) Special educational needs coordinators and leadership: a role too far? *Support for Learning*, 20(2): 53–60.

Lipsky, M.(1980) *Street-level Bureaucracy: Dilemmas of the Individual in Public Services*. New York: Russell Sage Foundation.

MacBeath, J. (2006) *Leadership as a Subversive Activity*, Monograph, University of Melbourne, ACEL/ASPA.

MacBeath, J. (2009) A focus on learning, in J. MacBeath and N. Dempster (eds) *Connecting Leadership and Learning: Principles for Practice*. London: Routledge.

MacBeath, J. (2010) Stories of compliance and subversion in a prescriptive policy environment, *Educational Management Administration and Leadership*, 36(1): 123–48.

MacGilchrist, B., Myers, K. and Reed, J. (1997) *The Intelligent School*. London: Paul Chapman.

McKenzie, S. (2007) A review of recent developments in the role of the SENCo in the UK, *Support for Learning*, 34(4): 212–18.

NCSL (2006) *Impact and Evaluation Report 2004/05*. Nottingham: NCSL.

Perkins, D. (2003) *King Arthur's Round Table: How Collaboration Creates Smart Organisations*. Hoboken, NJ: John Wiley and Sons, Ltd.

Putnam, R. (1999) *Bowling Alone: The Collapse and Revival of American Community*. New York: Touchstone.

Sockett, H. (1993) *The Moral Base for Teacher Professionalism*. New York: Teachers College Press.

Sockett, H. (ed.) (2006) *Teacher Dispositions: Building a Teacher Education Framework of Moral Standards*. Washington, DC: American Association of Colleges for Teacher Education.

Stevenson, H. (2007) Restructuring teachers; work and trades union responses in England: bargaining for change?, *American Educational Research Journal*, 44(2): 224–51.

Swaffield, S. and MacBeath, J. (2009) Leadership for learning, in J. MacBeath and N. Dempster (eds) *Connecting Leadership and Learning: Principles for Practice*. London: Routledge.

Szreter, S. (2000) Social capital, the economy and education in historical perspective, in S. Baron, J. Field and T. Schuller (eds) *Social Capital: Critical Perspectives*. Oxford: Oxford University Press.

TDA (2009) *Standards for National Award for SEN Coordination*. London: TDA.

Wenger, E. (1999) *Communities of Practice. Learning, Meaning and Identity*. Cambridge: Cambridge University Press.

5

THE CONCEPT OF INCLUSIVE PEDAGOGY
Lani Florian

Introduction

Beginning with the 1997 Green Paper, *Excellence for All Children*, and continuing in more recent policy documents, the UK government has acknowledged that there is no single best route to inclusion for students identified as having special educational needs (SEN) in England and Wales. National policies have consistently proposed retaining traditional approaches (i.e. identification and assessment of individual need, individualized education plans (IEPs), and specialist facilities for those who choose them), while at the same time advocating for more inclusive approaches without specifying what such approaches might look like or how they might be achieved. Consequently, there are numerous interpretations of inclusion, and a great deal of variability in practice, not all of which is positive. As the recent Lamb Inquiry on Special Educational Needs and Parental Confidence noted:

> In talking with parents of disabled children and children with special educational needs (SEN), we met some of the happiest parents in the country and some of the angriest. Many had children who are well-supported and making good progress. But we also met parents for whom the education system represents a battle to get the needs of their child identified and for these to be met. The crucial issue is that both experiences happen within the same system. While the aims of the SEN framework remain relevant, implementation has too often failed to live up to them.
>
> (DCSF, 2009: 2)

Clearly, this variability raises important questions about the nature and quality of provision in schools. As Lamb has shown, how schools as organizations, and individual teachers within those organizations, respond to students identified as having special educational needs is of paramount importance. This will be reflected in the culture of the school, including its admission, behaviour and exclusion policies and practices. It is also reflected in the approaches that teachers take and the responses that they make when students encounter difficulties in learning. Ensuring that the aims of the SEN framework are implemented in ways that support the social and academic well-being and progress of all students is a key responsibility of the SENCO.

The aim of this chapter is to introduce the concept of inclusive pedagogy as an important response to individual differences between learners. As will be shown, inclusive pedagogy is based upon a socio-cultural perspective on learning that focuses on how learning occurs in the community of the classroom (Florian and Kershner, 2009). It is different from notions of special and inclusive education that assume that students identified as having special educational needs are those who need something 'additional to' or 'different from' the educational provision generally made to children of a similar age. It challenges the idea of inclusion as differentiation according to individual need, in favour of an alternative approach that responds to individual differences but avoids the stigma that can occur when individual differences are isolated and targeted for intervention. In so doing, the inclusive pedagogical approach aims to avoid the negative effects (such as labelling, stigma and separation) that can occur when teachers provide for 'all' by differentiating for 'some'.

Background to the approach

For many years, researchers interested in special and inclusive education have focused on the influence of school factors in learning and in student outcomes. Research in the 1980s explored how school structures could create special educational needs (Tomlinson, 1982). Moses et al. (1987) described how special needs teams in mainstream schools might develop a whole school approach to intervention. Ainscow (1991) argued that school factors were likely to be more powerful in their effects than individual differences between learners. The special needs task, as he put it, needed to be reconceptualized to focus on school development. As researchers began to study how schools were implementing the ideal of inclusion, a series of case studies, and action research projects, many of book length, documented the efforts that schools were making to become more inclusive (i.e. Thomas et al., 1998; Allan, 1999; Dyson and Milward, 2000; Benjamin, 2002; O'Hanlon, 2003, to name a few). This work showed that inclusive education was a complex endeavour, characterized by dilemmas (Norwich, 1993, 2008) that could be mediated (Rouse and Florian, 1997) as part of a process of increasing participation and reducing exclusion (Booth and Ainscow, 2002). Such work was theoretically principled (Slee, 1993; Thomas and Loxley, 2001) and required imagination (Hart, 1996, 2000). Subsequent efforts have involved development tools based on individualized approaches such as the *SEN Toolkit* (DfES, 2001), and whole school approaches such as *Leading on Inclusion* (DfES, 2005), and the *Index for Inclusion* (Booth and Ainscow, 2002).

While certain structural features of schools can help to create special educational needs, it is important to point out that this is the case only 'when the forms of provision and approaches to teaching that are generally available and effective for most students do not appear to work in particular cases' (Florian and Kershner, 2009: 173). In other words, by extending the quality of what is generally available to an increasing range of students, schools can become more inclusive. This is an important but subtle change in focus that is the basis upon which the inclusive pedagogical approach (inclusive pedagogy) is based.

Why a change in focus?

There are five interrelated reasons why a change in focus is needed, and all of them can be linked to the intractable problems of individualization. First, a focus on individual difference has been shown to be more likely to reinforce than solve what has been called the dilemma of difference. That is, as Minow (1990) has shown, when remedies that are put in place to protect vulnerable groups depend on the identification of difference, they are likely to reinforce the very difference that the remedy is intended to redress. Such has been the case with special needs education where policies intended to ensure access to education have paradoxically created problems of equity within it (for example, students from particular minority groups are more likely to be identified as having special educational needs). Although notions of inclusive education have challenged the concept of special educational needs as 'different' or 'additional' to that which is provided to the majority of children, much of the provision associated with inclusive education reproduces the problems of marginalization which occur when students who experience difficulties in learning are identified as needing something different. This is because many conceptualizations of inclusion have done little more in practical terms than replace the phrase 'special needs education' with 'inclusive education'.

This is problematic because of the historical presumption that the identification of individual students who need something different has direct implications for educational interventions. The idea of matching child characteristics with interventions remains popular despite the knowledge that different teaching strategies are not differentially effective with different types of learners (Ysseldyke, 2001). This is the second reason a change in focus is needed. To date, efforts to define what is special about special needs education have concluded that the teaching strategies used in mainstream education can be adapted to assist students identified as having additional needs in learning (Vaughn and Linan-Thompson, 2003; Davis and Florian, 2004; Lewis and Norwich, 2005; Kavale, 2007). The process of making an accommodation is an important element of any pedagogical approach but does not constitute pedagogy in itself. As will be argued, knowledge about human differences is important (a student who is an English language learner is different from a student who has been diagnosed as having autism; a 6-year-old is different from a 10-year-old, and so on), but the relationship between cognitive processing and learning is still too crude to be directly helpful in educational assessment or intervention (Howard-Jones, 2007). In practice, teachers use strategies that are matched to the purpose of the learning, and they adapt these strategies in response to differences between learners.

Moreover, and this is the third reason a change in focus is needed, teachers themselves have reported that they do not differentiate among types of students when planning lessons. For example, Florian and Rouse (2001) studied the extent to which classroom practice in the various subjects of the National Curriculum was consistent with that which is promoted as effective by the literature on inclusion. A questionnaire designed to examine possible relationships between subject taught and teaching strategy used included an open-ended comments section to aid the interpretation of the data. Teachers commented that the use of some strategies was resource dependent (e.g. use of computer-assisted instruction), while others depend on administrative arrangements and support (e.g. 'team teaching and co-teaching are difficult to organise but they work'). Some teachers went out of their way to comment that they made no distinction between pupils with SEN and others when it comes to teaching strategy although others made very specific comments about how they included pupils with SEN in terms of behavioural strategies (i.e. 'give the pupil a responsibility vital to the lesson'). These findings suggested that the ways in which the teachers were responding to individual differences was not dependent on, or specific to, the identification special educational need.

Fourth, while inclusive education is based on the principle that local schools should provide for *all* children, some way of determining 'all' has to be established. In England, the Ofsted (2000) guidance for school inspectors specifies that in order 'to identify what it means to be an inclusive school' inspectors must attend 'to the provision made for and the achievement of different groups of pupils within a school'. The Ofsted (2000: 4) groups are:

- girls and boys;
- minority ethnic and faith groups, Travellers, asylum seekers and refugees;
- pupils who need support to learn English as an additional language (EAL);
- pupils with special educational needs (SEN);
- gifted and talented pupils;
- children 'looked after' by the local authority;
- other children, such as sick children; young carers; those children from families under stress; pregnant school girls and teenage mothers; and
- any pupils who are at risk of disaffection and exclusion.

A focus on groups of learners as a way of determining 'all' is problematic because of the many sources of variation within and between any identified groups of learners. Yet provision is often organized in this way (for example, according to year groups, students with SEN, EAL, and so forth), despite the fact that individual learners usually fit into more than one category. Even seemingly discrete categories like year groups are not straightforward because each one will contain learners of different ages who will vary considerably. Whatever can be known about a particular category of learners will be limited in the educational purposes it can serve because the variations between members of a group make it difficult to predict or evaluate provision for each of the individuals within it.

Nevertheless schools are organized by grouping pupils according to commonly agreed categories, and the utilitarian principle of the greatest good for the greatest number (e.g. statistical norms of ability distributed according to a bell-shaped curve). In this way, what is ordinarily provided will meet the needs of most learners, while a few at the tail ends of the distribution may require something 'additional' to or 'different' from that which is ordinarily available. Indeed, this is the definition of special needs education and additional support in many countries, and this is the fifth problem: when students who encounter difficulties in learning are identified as having 'special educational needs', an intractable cycle is formed – students are assigned membership of the group because they are judged to possess the attributes of group membership, and they are believed to have the attributes of the group because they are members of it. The problem is that identification of 'special educational needs' can also lower a teacher's expectations about what it is possible for a student to achieve.

One example is that of autism spectrum disorder (ASD). For this rapidly growing group, identification depends on a clinical assessment of a 'triad of impairments' associated with difficulties in social communication, social understanding, and flexibility of thought and imagination (Wing and Gould, 1979). The National Autistic Society (NAS) in the UK defines ASD as:

> A complex lifelong developmental disability that affects the way a person communicates and relates to people around them. The autism spectrum includes the syndromes described by Kanner and by Asperger but is wider than these two subgroups (Wing and Gould, 1979).
>
> Many people have a mixture of features from these two syndromes but do not fit neatly into either. The whole spectrum is defined by the presence of impairments affecting social interaction, social communication and social imagination, known as the triad of impairments. This is always accompanied by a narrow, repetitive range of activities.
>
> A range of other problems is also commonly found in association with the triad but the three basic impairments are the defining criteria.
>
> Individuals who are considered to be on the autism spectrum are all very different. The range of intellectual ability extends from severely learning disabled right up to normal or even above average levels of intellect. Similarly, linguistic skills range from those who are mute to those who display complex, grammatically correct speech.
>
> (NAS, http://www.nas.org.uk/nas/jsp/polopoly.jsp?d=1048&a=2224)

Clearly this definition describes a condition that contains many sources of variation. As the definition itself specifies, 'many people have a mixture of features . . . but do not fit neatly into either'. Here, variation between the individuals within the ASD group suggests that there will be degrees of difference between members with regard to the many characteristics thought to affect learning. And yet, tacit judgements are often made about learners based on assumptions that they possess all the characteristics of group membership to the same degree. Moreover, the identification of the difficulties in learning associated with ASD is often assumed to require specialist teaching. Questions about the nature of such teaching are often answered with information about ASD itself, including what learners on the ASD spectrum can *not* do by virtue of their impairments, rather than focusing on the learning that might be possible. In this way, the categorization of ASD, and the assumed cognitive impairments that are associated with it, arguably put a ceiling on learning and achievement.

As this example shows, a focus on learner types is problematic because of the many sources of variation within and between identified groups of learners that make educationally relevant distinctions between them difficult to observe and judge. Thus, whatever can be known about a particular category of learners will be limited in the educational purposes it can serve because the variations between members of a group make it difficult to predict or evaluate provision for individuals in it. Clearly the limitations and problems of focusing on individual difficulties suggest that alternative approaches for responding to them are needed.

Theoretical framework for inclusive pedagogy

The inclusive pedagogical approach described below has emerged from a synthesis of research projects and the literature on inclusive education and specialist pedagogy. It was developed in response to the problems identified above. It sets out to replace traditional approaches to teaching children, identified as having special educational needs, that are based upon the argument that such children necessarily require something 'different from' or 'additional to' that which is ordinarily available, and that what is needed can be matched to learner characteristics. To this end, the approach is located within a socio-cultural framework on pedagogy (Alexander, 2004) where the complexities inherent in providing for differences among students are subsumed within a set of interrelated ideas about children, learning, teaching and curriculum, as well as the school and policy contexts by which they are legitimized (for a discussion, see Florian and Kershner, 2009).

A socio-cultural perspective is important because it permits a consideration of individual differences as something to be expected and understood in terms of the interactions between many different variables rather than fixed states within individuals. Difference is not the problem; rather, understanding that learners differ and how the different aspects of human development interact with experience to produce individual differences become the theoretical starting point for inclusive pedagogy. A sociocultural perspective assumes that 'all children have much in common, including the fact that their individual characteristics and preferences uniquely interrelated rather than neatly categorisable' (Florian and Kershner, 2009: 174). As such, it offers a productive way of thinking about how to understand and respond to the complexities inherent in educating diverse groups of learners and encourages open-ended views of all children's potential for learning. This is consistent with what Susan Hart and her colleagues (Hart et al., 2004) have called the core idea of *transformability* to assert the principled belief that 'children's capacity to learn can change and be changed for the better as a result of what happens and what people do in the present' (2004: 166). Their argument is that how teachers respond in the present can affect any child's capacity to learn and in part determines what will be achieved.

Finally, a socio-cultural perspective on learning steers the teacher to focus on how to access and use knowledge about how people learn when helping children who are experiencing difficulties. Here it is productive to think about learning in terms of the development of expertise, and how novices differ from experts (Bransford et al., 2000), rather than to differentiate groups of learners on the basis of perceived limitations. While socio-cultural factors produce individual differences, learning occurs through shared activity in social contexts. Thus, the teacher must think about everybody in the class and how they will work together, as opposed to differentiating for some on the basis of judgements about what they cannot do compared to others of similar age.

This is not to suggest that individual differences are unimportant. As Ravet (in press) has noted, a teacher may have two students, both of whom are experiencing similar difficulties in learning (her example is with understanding common idioms), but differences between the students (a learner with English as a second language and a learner on the autism spectrum) means that the nature of the misunderstanding is different in each case necessitating different responses to the difficulty in learning. She worries that an inclusive pedagogical approach might lead to 'an over-reliance on generalist teacher practices' at the expense of attention to individual differences. As will be shown below, the inclusive pedagogical approach does not ignore individual differences between students. Rather it encourages the teacher to extend the range of options that are available to *everyone in the community of the classroom*. This is a subtle but important shift in thinking about individual differences between learners that focuses on learning as a shared activity and thereby avoids the potentially negative effects of treating some students as different.

The inclusive pedagogical approach

Extending what is generally available

The approach to inclusive pedagogy detailed below has emerged from a series of research projects and the literature on inclusive education. It sets out to replace traditional approaches to teaching children identified as having special educational needs that are based upon the argument that such children necessarily require something 'different from' or 'additional to' that which is ordinarily available because of the unintended negative effects of such approaches. The research builds on previous work (Black-Hawkins et al., 2007), which examined how some schools have developed strategies to raise the achievement of all their children, while safeguarding the inclusion of those who are more vulnerable to exclusion and other forms of marginalization. While the earlier study explored schools as institutions and considered how values and beliefs within a school's culture shape the teaching and learning that takes place, the second stage of the research focused on teacher 'craft knowledge' about how they extend what is 'generally available' to all (Florian and Black-Hawkins, 2010). This was supplemented by the findings from a further study of how teachers can be prepared to use inclusive pedagogy (Florian and Linklater, in press).

The studies were informed by the view that learners vary across many dimensions and teachers are constantly making multiple decisions about how to respond to all kinds of differences. Differences themselves are a matter of degree rather than categorical distinctions. It is only when the magnitude of difficulty experienced by a learner exceeds the teacher's capacity to know how to respond that the learner is considered to have special or additional needs. Findings from these projects suggest that teachers engaged in inclusive pedagogical practice work out what they can do to support the learner while maintaining a commitment to everybody (Hart et al., 2004), and avoiding situations that mark some students as different. This does not rule out the use of specialists or specialist knowledge but it does not require the identification of special educational need *within* individual learners. While this may happen as a result of seeking support, it is often because administrative rules require such identification rather than because of a teacher attribution of a 'problem' within the learner. Where specialists are consulted, it is in support of the teacher's effort to ensure that the learner is meaningfully engaged in the community of the classroom. The phrase 'community of the classroom' is used purposefully to avoid the idea that our approach is merely advocating whole class teaching. It is in the *ways* that teachers respond to individual differences, the *choices* they make about group work and *how* they utilize specialist knowledge that differentiates inclusive practice from other pedagogical approaches.

Focusing on how teachers extend what is generally available in a classroom lesson or activity offers an alternative perspective from which to consider inclusive educational practice to those of traditional approaches to teaching children, identified as having special educational needs, that are based upon the argument that such children necessarily require something 'different from' or 'additional to' that which is ordinarily available. Cooper and McIntyre (1996) suggested that there was much to be learned from studying how teachers develop their professional craft knowledge as they go about doing their jobs. By studying the craft knowledge of teachers' practice, an understanding of how teachers committed to the principles and ideals of inclusion by attending to individual differences while avoiding the stigma of marking some students as different is beginning to emerge. This is illustrated in Table 5.1 where the inclusive pedagogical approach is contrasted with a special additional needs approach to inclusive practice. While this approach (also referred to as the 'additional needs' approach to inclusion) focuses only on the student who has been identified as in need of additional support, the inclusive pedagogical approach focuses on everybody in the community of the classroom.

As is shown, inclusive pedagogy is defined not in the *choice* of strategy but in its *use*. This required the provision of rich learning opportunities that were sufficiently made available for everyone, so that all learners are able to participate in the community of the classroom (Florian and Linklater, 2009). For additional examples of this approach, see Florian and Black-Hawkins, 2010.

Conclusion

Inclusive pedagogy rejects the idea that it is educationally helpful to base teaching approaches on categories of learners, particularly when the categories are described in terms of attributes about people. The approach has been developed in part as a response to the concern that an emphasis on studying human differences perpetuates the belief that they are predictive of difficulties in learning and potential achievement. This is highly problematic because of the well-documented negative effects of marking some students as in need of something 'different', particularly with regard to the lowering of expectations for achievement.

Instead, the concept of inclusive pedagogy that is emerging from studies of

Table 5.1 Contrast of 'additional needs' and inclusive pedagogical approaches

| Additional needs approach to inclusion | Most and some | | Everybody |
	Manifest in terms of inclusion	Manifest in terms of exclusion	Inclusive pedagogical approach
A student with autism uses Voice4Me on an iPod Touch to communicate with his teacher and peers during a field trip to an historic airfield. The tool is selected specifically because a visual approach will reduce the 'processing burden' for the student and enhance both his learning and enjoyment of the trip. He selects a sequence of symbols/icons/pictures, which represent words and/or phrases to tell stories about the trip. The student uses an iPhone to collect photos and videos of the site, assign meta-tags, and upload the content to a website of the group's field trip.	Student participates in the trip. Student works alongside peers. Student participates in learning activities by contributing photographs to a webpage, which is created by all the class illustrating selected idioms.	Peers of the student complain it is unfair that they are not allowed to use their digital phones. Student with autism is marked as different because he is getting special treatment.	Focus is on everybody in planning for the school trip, and the building of a webpage to document the trip. While a visual approach is likely to be supportive for some students, immersion in the social context of the site will be more relevant for others. All students are involved in planning how to document the trip – types of information (such as narrative accounts, photographs, audio recordings, maps to illustrate where they went, statistical information such as distance travelled). Students then plan how this data could be collected and negotiate who would be responsible for the different tasks. Returning from the trip, the class collate their different forms of data to generate stories about the event and develop the website page.

teacher craft knowledge located in a socio-cultural perspective on learning can be seen as a strategy to address adverse school influences in the production of special educational needs. Specifically, inclusive pedagogy is concerned with redressing the limitations on learning that are often inadvertently placed on children when they are judged 'less able'. This occurs when judgements are made about what is possible for a learner to achieve based on particular teacher understandings of the factors that are considered to interfere with learning. It does not deny differences between learners but moves to accommodate them by extending what is ordinarily available to all rather than by differentiating for some. Here there is a shift in focus away from the idea of inclusion as a specialized response to some learners that enables them to have access to or participate in that which is available to most students. Extending what is ordinarily available to all learners, taking account of the fact that there will be individual differences between them is a subtle but profound difference in approaching teaching and learning for all that is the hallmark of inclusive pedagogy.

The SENCO's work must begin with an understanding of the variability in identification and type of special educational need and an acknowledgement that the range and forms of provision available can lead to important new insights about how teachers are able to be both effective and inclusive in their practice. For example, while some schools exclude, or refuse to include, certain students on the grounds that teachers do not have the requisite knowledge and skills to teach them, teachers in other schools have been able to include students with many different types of special educational needs. This raises questions about what constitutes the necessary knowledge and skills teachers need to learn in order to work with *all* of the members of a classroom community *together*. In answering these questions, the study of individual teachers' successful practice is providing an articulation of inclusive pedagogy as a way of working with all of the members of a classroom community together (*everybody*), as opposed to individualizing for each student. By accepting the notion of individual differences among learners without relying predominately on individualized approaches to responding to them, teachers, with the support of SENCOs, can help to ensure that the promise of inclusive education to provide good quality educational opportunities and experiences for *all* is less variable and less difficult to secure for those students who experience difficulties in learning and have not had positive experiences of mainstream education.

Acknowledgements

The research projects that have informed the view of inclusive pedagogy reported represent the work of many colleagues over the years at the universities of Aberdeen and Cambridge. Nigel Beacham, Kristine Black-Hawkins, Ruth Kershner, Holly Linklater, Jackie Ravet, Martyn Rouse, Jenny Spratt and Kathryn Young have all contributed in various ways to the development of the ideas expressed in this chapter.

References

Ainscow, M. (1991) *Effective Schools for All*. London: David Fulton.
Alexander, R. (2004) Still no pedagogy? Principle, pragmatism and compliance in primary education, *Cambridge Journal of Education*, 34(1): 7–33.
Allan, P. (1999) *Actively Seeking Inclusion: Pupils with Special Needs in Mainstream Schools*. London: Falmer Press.
Benjamin, S. (2002) *The Micropolitics of Special Educational Needs: An Ethnography*. Buckingham: Open University Press.
Black-Hawkins, K., Florian, L. and Rouse, M. (2007) *Achievement and Inclusion in Schools*. London: Routledge Falmer.

Booth, T. and Ainscow, M. (2002) *The Index for Inclusion: Developing Learning and Participation in Schools*, revised edition. Bristol: CSIE.

Bransford, J.D., Brown, A.L. and Cocking, R. (2000) *How People Learn: Brain, Mind, Experience and School*. Washington, DC: National Academy Press.

Cooper, P. and McIntyre, D. (1996) *Effective Teaching and Learning: Teachers' and Students' Perspectives*. Buckingham: Open University Press.

Davis, P. and Florian, L. (2004) *Teaching Strategies and Approaches for Pupils with Special Educational Needs: A Scoping Study* (Research Report 516). London: DfES.

DCSF (2009) *Lamb Inquiry Report: Special Educational Needs and Parental Confidence*. London: DCFS. Retrieved 15 February 2010 from: http://www.dcsf.gov.uk/lambinquiry/related.shtml.

DfES (1997) *Excellence for All Children*. London: HMSO.

DfES (2001) *SEN Toolkit*, DfES 0558–2001. Available at: http://publications.teachernet.gov.uk/default.aspx?PageFunction=productdetails&PageMode=publications&ProductId=DfES+0558+2001 (accessed 15 February 2010).

DfES (2005) *Leading on Inclusion*, DfES 1183–2005 G. London: HMSO.

Dyson, A. and Milward, A. (2000) *Schools and Special Needs: Issues of Innovation and Inclusion*. London: Paul Chapman.

Florian, L. and Black-Hawkins, K. (2010) Exploring inclusive pedagogy. *British Educational Research Journal*, First published on: 20th July 2010 (iFirst)

Florian, L. and Kershner, R. (2009) Inclusive pedagogy, in H. Daniels, H. Lauder and J. Porter (eds) *Knowledge, Values and Educational Policy: A Critical Perspective*, London: Routledge, pp. 173–83.

Florian, L. and Linklater, H. (in press) Enhancing teaching and learning: using 'Learning without Limits' to prepare teachers for inclusive education. *Cambridge Journal of Education*.

Florian, L. and Rouse, M. (2001) Inclusive practice in English secondary schools: lessons learned. *Cambridge Journal of Education*, 31(3): 399–412.

Hart, S. (1996) *Beyond Special Needs: Enhancing Children's Learning through Innovative Thinking*. London: Paul Chapman.

Hart, S. (2000) *Thinking Through Teaching: A Framework for Enhancing Participation and Learning*. London: David Fulton.

Hart, S., Dixon, A., Drummond, M.J. and McIntyre, D. (2004) *Learning Without Limits*. Maidenhead: Open University Press.

Howard-Jones, P. (2007) *Neuroscience and Education: Issues and Opportunities, A Commentary by the Teaching and Learning Research Programme*. London: Economic and Social Research Council. Retrieved 22 September 2008 from: http://www.tlrp.org/pub/commentaries.html

Kavale, K. (2007) Quantitative research synthesis: meta-analysis of research on meeting special educational needs, in L. Florian (ed.) *The Sage Handbook of Special Education*. London: Sage.

Lewis, A. and Norwich, B. (eds)(2005) *Special Teaching for Special Children? Pedagogies for Inclusion*. Maidenhead: Open University Press.

Minow, M. (1990) *Making All the Difference: Inclusion, Exclusion and American Law*. Ithaca, NY: Cornell University Press.

Moses, D., Hegarty, S. and Jowett, S. (1987) *Supporting Ordinary Schools*. Windsor: NfER/Nelson.

National Autism Society, website: http://www.nas.org.uk/nas/jsp/polopoly.jsp?d=1048&a=2224 (retrieved 9 March 2009).

Norwich, B. (1993) Ideological dilemmas in special needs education: practitioners' views. *Oxford Review of Education*, 19(4): 527–45.

Norwich, B. (2008) *Dilemmas of Difference: International Perspectives and Future Directions.* London: Routledge.

Ofsted (2000) *Evaluating Educational Inclusion Guidance for Inspectors and Schools.* London: Ofsted.

O'Hanlon, C. (2003) *Educational Inclusion as Action Research: An Interpretive Discourse.* Buckingham: Open University Press.

Ravet, J. (in press) Inclusive/exclusive? Contradictory perspectives on autism and inclusion: the case for an integrative position, *International Journal of Inclusive Education.*

Rouse, M. and Florian, L. (1997) Inclusive education in the marketplace. *International Journal of Inclusive Education,* 1(4): 323–36.

Slee, R. (1993) *Is There a Desk with My Name on it? The Politics of Integration.* London: Routledge.

Thomas, G. and Loxley, A. (2001) *Deconstructing Special Education and Constructing Inclusion.* Buckingham: Open University Press.

Thomas, G., Walker, D. and Webb, J. (1998) *The Making of the Inclusive School.* London: Routledge.

Tomlinson, S. (1982) *A Sociology of Special Education.* London: Routledge & Kegan Paul.

Vaughn, S. and Linan-Thompson, S. (2003). What is special about special education for students with learning disabilities? *The Journal of Special Education,* 37(3): 140–7.

Wing, L. and Gould, J. (1979) Severe impairments of social interaction and associated abnormalities in children: epidemiology and classification, *Journal of Autism and Childhood Schizophrenia,* 9: 11–29.

Ysseldyke, J. E. (2001) Reflections on a research career: generalizations from 25 years of research on assessment and instructional decision making, *Exceptional Children,* 67(3): 295–309.

PART II

The professional context

Introduction to Part II

It is tempting to think that the way to demonstrate compliance with the 55 Learning Outcomes for the National Award for SEN Coordination (NASC) is to take each outcome in turn, assemble evidence that shows that the outcome has been met, and place these in a sequentially organized folder. To demonstrate accountability, it might be that several pieces of evidence should be provided for each outcome. There would need to be an examination of what constitutes evidence, how recent the evidence should be, and some consideration of whether the evidence should simply be descriptive, or whether it should contain a reflective element to demonstrate understanding as well as knowledge and skills.

In asking contributors to write a chapter on a specific element of the Learning Outcomes, we hoped to demonstrate that there might be a different way of completing this task, that had the further advantage of tackling the subtlety and nuance required in work at Master's level and beyond. The resulting 15 chapters are all successful in meeting that challenge, in outlining an evidential base that clearly demonstrates the Learning Outcomes. Furthermore, each contributor has taken a personalized approach in meeting the requirement; these approaches range from surveys of the field in the area selected, written within an analytical framework, to first person evaluative and reflective case studies.

In addition, because each author is writing from extensive experience in working with young people with SEN and/or disability, their work cannot help but give evidence of the complexity of the role of the SENCo, and in so doing, overlap into areas covered by Learning Outcomes outside the particular section under study.

It follows from this, in our opinion, that there might be a more creative and cohesive way of demonstrating that standards have been met. In writing about their work, in all of its variety, intensity and range, SENCos can evidence a wealth of knowledge, experience and skill; this will occur whether the starting point is the child, the class or the school or setting. By reflecting on this writing, whether developed as an assignment at Master's level, as a reflective portfolio, or in a seminar or VLE discussion, the SENCo can produce evidence that meets Learning Outcomes in imaginative and thoughtful ways. If this writing is illustrative of the work done in a specific situation relating to a child experiencing significant barriers to learning, it is likely that many Learning Outcomes will be addressed, at least in part. A series of reflections of this nature will be likely to extend this coverage, both in breadth and depth, without the need to produce disconnected and unrelated 'evidence' that does little to develop understanding, enhance practice, or initiate change, in the role of the SENCo.

The three chapters in Part III have been designed to explore aspects of the Professional Context of the SENCo role. In Chapter 6, Janice Wearmouth tackles the four areas of need identified within the *SEN Code of Practice* (DfES, 2001) and examines *Every Child Matters* (DfES, 2004). This chapter serves a number of purposes. Primarily, it offers a nucleus of information about the legislative position in schools, the pedagogical implications of the four areas of need and the inherent complexities of the Every Child Matters agenda. As such, this chapter focuses on a number of Professional Context Learning Outcomes, which include:

- laws and associated guidance on SEN, including the policies and procedures set out in the SEN Code of Practice; their implications for the school, the SENCo and others; and how to put them into practice;
- the principles and outcomes of *Every Child Matters* and how the school can help pupils with SEN and/or disabilities to achieve those outcomes;
- causes of underachievement, including those related to SEN and/or disabilities;
- the four areas of need set out in the SEN Code of Practice and the educational implications of these.

Thus, at a superficial level, it would be easy for the reader to conclude that this is all that Chapter 6 achieves. Nevertheless, on closer examination, far more can be discerned about this chapter. For example, Janice raises important points about the need to look at learning and well-being more holistically, and at the potential for possible breaches of confidentiality and data protection law when sharing information across services. Such issues can be lost when SENCos focus upon compliance and procedure without reflection and deeper analysis. Therefore, the opportunity afforded by this chapter is to take the information offered and use it to analyse practice in greater depth focusing upon the impact of procedure on individual learners.

Chapter 7 provides a similar opportunity for deeper professional reflection. Ostensibly focusing upon behaviour, Philip Garner and Barry Groom adopt a questioning approach to managing behaviour and managing the standards. As before, this chapter directly addresses a number of Professional Context Learning Outcomes, which include:

- teaching, learning and behaviour management strategies and how to select, use and adapt approaches to remove barriers to learning for pupils with SEN and/or disabilities;

- laws and associated guidance on SEN, including the policies and procedures set out in the SEN Code of Practice; their implications for the school, the SENCo and others; and how to put them into practice;
- effective practice in teaching pupils with SEN and/or disabilities;
- how to analyse, interpret and critically evaluate the relevant research and inspection evidence on teaching and learning in relation to pupils with SEN and/or disabilities and understand how such evidence can be used to inform personal practice and others' practice.

However, by problematizing the need for a knowledge base, the links between behaviour and the curriculum, and the professional dilemmas that surround this area of practice, the authors go beyond exemplification of these learning outcomes in order to encourage SENCos to develop a deeper understanding of practice in schools. What is evident, in this and each of the other chapters, is that deeper analysis of this nature not only evidences coverage of the standards but also positions the SENCo as an agent for change, reflecting on practice in order to develop a strategic vision.

The third chapter in this part is written by Peter Hick, Kath Kelly and Steve Tyler and uses two case study examples to critique assessment practices for learners with SEN and/or disability. Once again, this chapter directly addresses a number of Professional Context Learning Outcomes, which include:

- approaches, strategies and resources for assessment (including national tests and examinations) and how to select, use and adapt them to personalize provision and remove barriers to assessment for pupils with SEN and/or disabilities;
- the high incidence disabilities and the implications of these for teaching and learning and inclusive practice;
- how children's development can be affected by SEN and/or disabilities and a range of other factors including the physical and social environment in which they are taught.

The case studies in this chapter enable the reader to explore the potential of Assessment for Learning practices which move away from the traditional exclusionary forms of assessment that identify deficits, towards a deeper consideration of how assessment for learning can increase inclusion. The reflective questions that follow each case study enable the reader to apply the issues raised to their own practice in order to evaluate the strengths, and limitations, of assessment practices in their own setting.

In concluding this commentary, we would like to emphasize the overlapping and interactive nature of the NASC Learning Outcomes. While we have highlighted particular Learning Outcomes that are the focus for each chapter, this is not to ignore the ways in which each chapter also addresses Learning Outcomes within other sections of the Award, or the potential each chapter has to enable critical reflection of the role of the SENCo and the complex interplay between areas of SEN coordination that are addressed by the themed outcomes that inform the Award. For example, all three chapters in this part offer an insight into ways in which SENCos can develop, use, monitor and evaluate systems which relates to the theme of Coordinating Provision. In addition, these chapters seek to analyse practice in ways that might enable a SENCo to conduct a similar analysis on the Learning Outcomes that relate to Leading, Developing and Supporting Colleagues. Consequently, each of these chapters acts as a starting point for reflections on practice that might form the stimulus for further writing.

6

REASONS FOR UNDERACHIEVEMENT AND EVERY CHILD MATTERS

Janice Wearmouth

Introduction

Over the years, failure to learn or behave well in school has been explained as the result of a range of factors related to the pupil, the classroom/school or the wider context, for example:

- individual pupil deficiencies in learning and behaviour;
- inappropriate teaching methods, inadequate resources or inappropriate curricula and learning environment;
- the health and welfare of the child influenced, perhaps, by social circumstances outside the school including poverty and abuse within the family.

The *SEN Code of Practice* (DfES, 2001) focuses on the need to understand areas of learning and behaviour difficulties commonly seen in schools, and on ways in which the learning environment and particular pedagogies reduce difficulties. It can therefore be seen to combine the first two explanations into a conceptualization of difficulties as arising at the point of interaction between what the child brings to the learning and the requirements of the task, available resources, and so on. It is the third of these explanations, the concept of difficulties in learning as related to issues of well-being influenced by external social circumstances, that the approach outlined in the Code of Practice is less easily able to accommodate.

Particular views of difficulties and the interventions associated with them are often legitimated by the contemporary political context (Wearmouth, 2009). The introduction of various forms of consumer accountability into schools has tended to foster a preoccupation with internal school factors as the site of children's failure to learn and/or behave well rather than in the wider family and/or social context (Dyson, 1997), and with locating difficulties in the individual child's cognitive, sensory or physical attributes. The Code of Practice, for example, was designed as the accountability framework when hearing appeals about formal assessments at the special educational needs (SEN) tribunal system which itself was modelled on the industrial tribunal system (Wearmouth, 2000). Undoubtedly focusing on barriers to learning within schools has been beneficial for many individual pupils who experience difficulties. It has also meant, though, that until comparatively recently, there has been less emphasis on addressing broader issues of well-being that stretch beyond the school. In 2000, however, the tragic death of a young child brought welfare issues into sharp focus and highlighted the importance of viewing children's learning and well-being holistically and of more effective collaborative working between education, health and social services that might prevent such tragedies.

This chapter begins by examining the current special educational needs framework in schools. It discusses how the *Every Child Matters* (ECM) agenda that followed on from the death of Victoria Climbié in 2000 provoked a focus on a broader view of children's well-being, with learning closely linked to it, and highlighted inter-agency collaboration to safeguard young people and address issues such as the extremes of disadvantaged and abusive backgrounds. It concludes by discussing issues raised both by the ECM agenda itself and also by the requirement on schools to pay regard to both ECM and the conventional SEN framework.

Understanding the current legal position in schools

For many years, difficulties in learning and behaviour in schools, as well as motor and sensory difficulties, were conceptualized as disabilities of body and mind intrinsic to the individual – the so-called 'medical' or 'deficit model'. This saw some pupils who experienced cognitive difficulties being categorized as 'feeble-minded' and admitted to special schools or classes, others as 'imbeciles' and admitted to asylums, others as 'idiots' and classed as ineducable. Much later, at the end of the Second World War, the Handicapped Pupils and School Health Service Regulations 1945 developed a new framework of 11 categories including, for example, blind, deaf, epileptic, physically handicapped and aphasic. However, children with a 'severe mental handicap' remained the responsibility of health, not education, authorities.

Over the years that followed, a growing concern for social cohesion at large resulted in the establishment of comprehensive schools, the introduction of special classes and 'remedial' provision into mainstream and the integration of some pupils from special schools. In 1978, the Warnock Review replaced the previous description of 'handicapped by disabilities of body or mind' with a new concept of 'special educational needs'. The 1981 Education Act translated the Warnock Report into legislation with the view that a 'special educational need' exists if a child has 'significantly greater difficulty in learning' than peers, or a disability that hinders him or her from using educational facilities normally available in the local school.

Since 1981, there have been a number of amendments to the law, but the basic understanding of what constitutes a special educational need remains the same. In England and Wales, under the terms of Part IV of the 1996 Education Act a child 'has *special educational needs* if he or she has a *learning difficulty* that requires *special educational provision*' to be made. 'Statutory guidance' to schools in England and Wales about how to provide appropriate support to children with learning difficulties in the revised *Special Educational Needs Code of Practice* (DfES, 2001) suggests that children's learning needs may fall generally into four areas:

- *communication and interaction*: 'The range of difficulties will encompass pupils and young people with speech and language delay, impairments and disorders, specific learning difficulties, such as dyslexia and dyspraxia, hearing impairment and those who demonstrate features within the autistic spectrum; they may also apply to some children and young people with moderate, severe or profound learning difficulties' (para. 7:55).

- *cognition and learning*: 'Children who demonstrate features of moderate, severe or profound learning difficulties or specific learning difficulties, such as dyslexia or dyspraxia, require specific programmes to aid progress in cognition and learning. Such requirements may also apply to some extent to children with physical and sensory impairments and those on the autistic spectrum' (para. 7:58).

- *behaviour, emotional and social development*: 'Children and young people who demonstrate features of emotional and behavioural difficulties, who are withdrawn or isolated, disruptive and disturbing, hyperactive and lack concentration; those with immature social skills; and those presenting challenging behaviours arising from other complex special needs, may require help or counselling' (para. 7:60).

- *sensory and/or physical needs*: 'There is a wide spectrum of sensory, multi-sensory and physical difficulties. The sensory range extends from profound and permanent deafness or visual impairment through to lesser levels of loss, which may only be temporary. Physical impairments may arise from physical, neurological or metabolic causes that only require appropriate access to educational facilities and equipment; others may lead to more complex learning and social needs; a few children will have multi-sensory difficulties some with associated physical difficulties' (para. 7:62).

As the areas of Communication and Interaction and Cognition and Learning clearly overlap, these will be dealt with in concert in the next section.

Communication, language and cognition

Difficulties in the area of language acquisition may involve receptive (that is, limitations in comprehending what is said) or expressive (that is, difficulty in putting thoughts coherently into words) language impairments. Pupils who experience difficulty in expressing themselves need frequent opportunities for exploratory talk in every area of the curriculum in order to put new information and ideas into their own words and link subject matter to what they already know. Teachers might consider the following activities:

- Not always speaking in terms that are immediately understood by pupils or their language will never develop. Where children experience difficulties with understanding spoken language, they will often get the gist from non-verbal clues;

- Ensuring, whenever possible, that pupils who have a difficulty in language should have direct experience of a concept before it is used. Children learn by doing first;

- Allowing pupils plenty of time before expecting a response. With some, a teacher may wish to explain that s/he will be asking them a question in a minute or so;

- Organizing transitions between different activities and different parts of the class-room and school carefully. They should use visual timetables and schedules, prepare pupils by telling them when and where they are going to move, and go through the transition points in the day with them first thing. Support staff can make a great contribution to this;

- Ensuring pupils know they are being spoken to, and not posing a question in the middle of a string of less relevant talk;

- Not assuming one-to-one listening will generalize to listening to whole class instruction or during assembly. Specific teaching may be needed.

  (adapted from Primary National Strategy, QCA, 2005, ref 1235/2005)

Coping with written text

Commonly, difficulties in literacy may include problems in reading comprehension, accuracy and written expression, and/or difficulties of a dyslexic nature. It is impor-tant to consider carefully the level of difficulty of any text used in class as well as the interest level of the text and prior knowledge of the subject matter, sentence length and complexity, word length and familiarity and clarity of explanation of concepts (Wearmouth, 2009).

Teachers might foster pupils' reading comprehension by, for example, teaching pupils to think consciously about the text as they read: whether it fits in with what they already know, whether they have understood it, or what questions they might ask themselves about the meaning of a text as they read it through. Further examples might include: shortening the amount read before questions are raised; group reading; use of cloze; teaching pupils to scan the text before reading in depth, including focusing on pictures, diagrams, captions, subheadings and highlighted words.

Often pupils need to gain more experience in reading (reading 'mileage', Clay, 1979) for example by listening to word-perfect recordings of text while following the text with the eyes, 'paired reading' or 'reading buddies'.

Sometimes it can help to see the writing process as driven by a series of goals organized into a hierarchy (Flower and Hayes, 1980) of: planning the information, selecting what is relevant, converting the plan into text and revising and editing what has been written. Examples of effective interventions for the planning process are self-directed techniques for generating words relevant to the content of the script (Graham and Harris, 1993), the use of writing frames to generate and organize ideas (Lewis and Wray, 1997), and articulating 'process goals', that is the way in which the child intends to achieve the end product (Graham et al., 1989). Conscious reflection on the writing process is important at both the pre-writing and writing stage. Pupils can be encouraged to reflect aloud on ideas, sequences, starting and finishing points, as well as the information to be covered and the concepts to be incorporated in the text.

Some pupils experience a particular difficulty in reading individual words accurately, associating sounds and alphabetic symbols in words, in ordering letters correctly or in letter orientation. Whichever subject is taught, the teacher will need to show pupils *how* to learn to spell words through, for example, a multi-sensory approach, using auditory, visual, kinaesthetic and tactile senses simultaneously.

Dyslexia and literacy difficulties

'Dyslexia' is a psychological explanation of literacy difficulties that, most commonly, refers to the way in which individuals process information. The information-processing system of 'dyslexic' individuals is seen as different from that of non-dyslexics in ways which have an impact on a number of areas of performance, particularly reading and writing. The most common theory underpinning dyslexic-type difficulty suggests a phonological deficit (Snowling, 2000), a specific impairment in the ability to detect and process speech sounds. Co-ordination, personal organization, directionality, balance, and patterning may also be affected.

It may not be helpful for 'dyslexics' and 'ordinary poor readers' to be taught by different methods (Rice and Brooks, 2004). Specialist interventions for dyslexic people are well suited for mainstream teaching. For example, the processing difficulties experienced by dyslexic pupils may cause difficulties in mathematics including: the learning of number bonds and multiplication tables; the understanding of concepts involving directionality, time and space; sequencing activities; orientation, especially processing different operations in different directions; visual discrimination; and mental arithmetic.

The principles of multi-sensory teaching which apply to language work also apply to the mathematics field, for example, introducing new mathematical concepts and processes using concrete materials, diagrams, pictures and verbal explanation.

The example of 'autism'

A condition that is generally considered to affect communication, cognition and learning is that of autism coined by Kanner (1943), after the Greek 'autos' (self). Autism is characterized by:

- inability to relate to people and social situations from early life: marked by profound 'aloneness';
- failure to use language to communicate;
- anxious and obsessive desire to maintain sameness.

In addition, individuals with autism can demonstrate:

- over-sensitivity to stimuli;
- fascination for objects, which are handled with skill in fine motor movements;
- good rote memory;
- apparently good cognitive potential.

In 1944, Asperger described older children whose behaviour was in some ways similar, and identified a form of autism now commonly referred to as 'Asperger's

Syndrome' (cited in Frith, 1991). People with Asperger's Syndrome may find difficulty in social relationships and in communicating. This includes:

- social impairment – extreme egocentricity;
- speech and language peculiarities;
- repetitive routines;
- motor clumsiness;
- narrow interests;
- non-verbal communication problems.

Dumortier (2004) comments that many of the problems of a pupil on the autistic spectrum can be avoided by pre-planning so that pupils know well in advance what is going to happen, how, who is involved and so on. It can also be helpful to do the following:

- reduce extraneous material and help pupils to direct their attention in a pre-dictable physical environment where everything is in its place;
- provide work areas with limited visual distraction and sound-reduction options;
- organize a visual timetable and visual timer;
- teach pupils to recognize and name their own feelings and emotions, recognize these in others, and learn appropriate responses.

Above all, however, it is important to get to know the young person as an individual.

Having explored Communication and Interaction and Cognition and Learning as a single overlapping area, the next two sections deal separately with the remaining areas of need specified by the Code of Practice.

Behaviour, emotional and social development

Pupil behaviour does not occur in a vacuum. Difficult behaviour may be indicative of a range of contextual issues associated with the family, school, classroom, peer group or teacher, as well as the pupil. In the classroom, unacceptable behaviour is influenced by:

- inappropriateness of classroom tasks and activities (for example, reading materials that are too difficult);
- concepts that assume too much prior knowledge and understanding;
- the influence of the classroom peer groups;
- individual teachers' management of classes;
- teacher expectations that are too high or too low.

as well as by pupils' individual attributes (Wearmouth, 2009).

A few pupils may develop extreme behaviours, 'those that significantly and seriously disrupt the functioning and wellbeing of the pupil' (Dunckley, 1999: 12). Preventing this kind of behaviour from developing is preferable to intervening later on.

Prevention strategies may include:

- policies and practices that promote non-violence, mutual respect and respect for property;
- interesting programmes that are achievable for all;
- praise and positive reinforcement for effort;
- stable, predictable environments with familiar routines and consistent limits;
- positive environments;
- teaching that reinforces acceptable behaviour. Do not assume that this will be learned incidentally;
- defusing incidents through positive comments;
- giving choices;
- being aware of events that may be stressful for pupils and teachers. These situations cannot always be avoided, but careful management can reduce the risk of extreme behaviour;
- avoiding situations known to lead to extreme behaviour for individual pupils;
- early intervention. Don't ignore behaviours that are likely to become extreme.

(Dunckley, 1999: 13)

For a small minority of pupils whose behaviour continues to be a focus of teachers' concerns, it may be seen as appropriate to investigate learning and behavioural issues at the level of the individual. On occasion, pupils may be aggressive, out of control and a danger to themselves and others. Safety is a priority and the goal is to defuse the situation. Teachers should take great care to check the school policy on physical restraint.

Individual assessment might lead to the identification of syndromes such as Attention Deficit/Hyperactivity Disorder (AD/HD) described by Norwich et al. as:

[A] medical diagnosis of the American Psychiatric Association. It is characterised by chronic and pervasive (to home and school) problems of inattention, impulsiveness, and/or excessive motor activity which have seriously debilitating effects on individuals' social, emotional and educational development, and are sometimes disruptive to the home and/or school environment. Between two and five per cent of British school children are believed to experience this condition (BPS, 1996). The coming of this diagnosis has revived traditional conflicts between medical and educational perspectives on EBD, which affect the way in which practitioners approach problems surrounding childhood attention and activity problems . . .

(Norwich et al., 2002: 182)

The British Psychological Society (BPS) notes the 'defining features' of AD/HD as behaviour which 'appears inattentive, impulsive and overactive to an extent that is unwarranted for their developmental age and is a significant hindrance to their social and educational success' (BPS, 1996: 13). In Britain, the tradition has been 'to use the diagnostic systems of the International Classification of Diseases (ICD) published by the World Health Organisation' (1996: 13) and to assume a 'hyperkinetic disorder'. The strict requirement for 'pervasiveness and persistence' means that behaviour seen largely in one context does not constitute grounds for a diagnosis.

A medical diagnosis may result in a prescription for psycho-stimulant medication to encourage socially acceptable behaviour when combined with psychological, social and educational support. Of the three most commonly used psycho-stimulants, methylphenidate (Ritalin) is most widely prescribed (BPS, 1996: 50–2).

Sensory and/or physical needs

As noted already, 'There is a wide spectrum of sensory, multi-sensory and physical difficulties' (DfES, 2001, para. 7:62). Some of the principles for addressing sensory or physical needs might be exemplified by considering the advice from the Royal National Institute for the Deaf (RNID) (2004) about education in mainstream for pupils who are deaf or hard of hearing. Key to successful inclusion is the ethos of the school. Effective pedagogy for pupils who experience hearing difficulties is effective pedagogy for a whole range of other pupils also.

As the RNID (2004: 15) notes, in 2000 the vast majority of deaf children in English schools were reported to be using 'auditory-oral' approaches that do 'not use sign language or manually coded elements to support the understanding of spoken language'. Auditory-oral approaches require 'consistent, efficient use of individual hearing aids, radio aids and/or cochlear implant devices' (RNID, 2004: 15). The listening environment is a crucial consideration. Soundfield systems and acoustic treatment of teaching spaces can improve the listening environment for all pupils. Teachers should take care with the clarity of their spoken language, use natural speech patterns and not exaggerate lip movements or shout, highlight key terms and concepts and place themselves where pupils can lip read or benefit from a hearing aid where the maximum range is often 2 metres. Pupils may also need the support of visual and written forms of language. With video materials, deaf pupils – and others – might benefit with advanced access to a summary of the programme and new vocabulary and concepts explained, as well as subtitles.

Other pupils might use both signed and spoken English ('sign bilingual' approach) based on an understanding that deaf people are members of a minority linguistic and cultural group. Deaf children are therefore bilingual and bi-cultural and this must be reflected in the philosophy and structures of the school (RNID, 2004: 17, citing Pickersgill and Gregory, 1998).

Where pupils use sign bilingualism, classroom teachers have to become accustomed to communication support staff in their classes and the visual spatial nature of British Sign Language with syntax that is different from English.

Background to *Every Child Matters*

So far, discussion of provision for special educational needs and disabilities in schools has focused on within-child factors, and also on the immediate learning environment of the school as the source of children's difficulties in learning and behaviour. The conventional SEN framework is less concerned with issues related to the overall welfare and safety of the child. In the past it has often been quite difficult for schools to work closely with outside agencies to address welfare needs and/or protect pupils seen by teachers as at risk of injury or abuse (Roaf and Lloyd, 1995). In relation to Education, Health and Social Services, there have often been differences in priorities for policy, organizational structures, professional practice and financial arrangements and lack of clear structure to determine responsibilities in inter-agency working, a particular problem when resources are under pressure.

The problems associated with inter-agency work were brought to a head by the death of Victoria Climbié, in 2000, despite the fact that she was thought by her school to be at risk and was also known to social services. In 2003 the government published the Green Paper, *Every Child Matters* followed by the Children Act (2004) that gave legal force to five interdependent outcomes (DfES, 2004):

- Be physically, mentally, emotionally and sexually healthy.
- Stay safe from maltreatment, neglect, violence, sexual exploitation, accidental injury and death, bullying and discrimination, crime and anti-social behaviour in and out of school.
- Enjoy and attend school, achieve stretching national educational standards and personal and social development, and enjoy recreation.
- Make a positive contribution to the community and environment, develop positive relationships and self-confidence, deal successfully with significant life changes and challenges.
- Achieve economic well-being, engage in further education, employment or training on leaving school, live in decent homes and sustainable communities and have access to transport and material goods.

These outcomes link well-being and educational achievement in a way not apparent in the conventional SEN framework:

> Children and young people learn and thrive when they are healthy, safeguarded from harm and engaged. The evidence shows clearly that educational achievement is the most effective way to improve outcomes for poor children and break cycles of deprivation.
>
> (DfES, 2004, para. 2.2)

To achieve these outcomes, the Children Act highlights inter-agency working. The duty to co-operate is put into operation through the arrangements made for children's trusts which bring together in one area all services for children and young people. Trusts are governed by a statutory Children's Trust Board, comprising representatives of all statutory partners and other interests. From January 2010, schools have been 'statutory partners'.

A Common Assessment Framework (CAF) for use across the children's work-force has been developed to provide a shared framework for enabling decisions: 'about how best to meet [children's] needs, in terms of both what the family can do and also what services could be provided' (Children's Workforce Development Council, CWDC, 2009, para. 1.11).

CWDC (2009, para. 1.9) guidance suggests that the CAF might be used to identify needs associated with:

- disruptive or anti-social behaviour;
- overt parental conflict or lack of parental support/boundaries;
- involvement in, or risk of, offending;
- poor attendance or exclusion from school;
- experiencing bullying;
- special educational needs;
- disabilities;
- disengagement from education, training or employment post-16;
- poor nutrition or inadequate clothing;
- ill health;
- substance misuse;
- anxiety or depression;
- experiencing domestic violence;
- housing issues;
- teenage pregnancy and parenthood (including the risk of pregnancy and early parenthood, as well as actual pregnancies and parenthood among young people);
- young carers who exhibit additional needs which are as a direct result of their caring responsibilities, e.g. truancy/lateness, ill health, housing issues.

The assessment is holistic and includes:

- *development of the child or young person*: how well the child or young person is developing, including their health, emotional and social development, and progress in learning;
- *parents and carers*: how well parents and carers are able to support their child or young person's development and respond appropriately to their needs;
- *family and environment*: the impact of wider family and environmental elements on the child or young person's development and on the capacity of their parents/carers.

(CWDC, 2009, para. 5.2)

CAF information may be shared with other practitioners only with the consent of the child and/or his/her parents,/carers, unless, in the judgement of the professionals based on the facts of the case, there is sufficient public interest to share the information without consent. Paragraph 7.15 of guidance given by the CWDC (2009) clarifies this point:

> Where there is a clear risk of significant harm to a child or young person, or serious harm to adults, the public interest test will almost certainly be satisfied. However, there will be other cases where practitioners will be justified in sharing some confidential information in order to make decisions on sharing further information or taking action – the information shared should be proportionate.

As a result of the common assessment discussion, concerns about the child might be resolved, or particular actions for the professional undertaking the CAF and his/her service might be agreed with a date for review and monitoring progress. Alternatively, actions might be identified for other agencies. This will involve sharing the assessment with these agencies, subject to the appropriate consent of the child or young person/ family, and forming a team around the child (TAC) to support the child or young person. The actions needed would be agreed with the other agencies and a plan and responsibilities for delivering the actions recorded on the CAF form (CWDC, 2009).

Clearly, in the attempt to ensure the 'joined-up thinking' that is required by the 2004 Children Act and the ECM agenda in schools there is a potential overlap between assessment associated with provision for special educational needs and that carried out for the CAF. However, the CAF is not intended to replace other statutory assessments, but to complement or be integrated with them. The CAF is also not intended for assessment of a child where there is any suggestion of harm. Guidance given by the CWDC (2009, para. 1.4) states:

> The CAF is not for a child or young person about whom you have concerns that they might be suffering, or may be at risk of suffering, harm. In such instances, you should follow your Local Safeguarding Children Board (LSCB) safeguarding procedures without delay.

Early impact

So far there are mixed reports of the effectiveness of integrated children's services in addressing children's needs. In a study of 14 local authorities (Kinder et al., 2008), children, young people and parents reported a range of improvements in outcomes: getting on well with school work, feeling safer and feeling happier. Practitioners, however, raised a number of concerns, including:

- workload implications, especially in relation to the CAF which was seen to require 'extra paperwork', 'attendance at more meetings', 'balancing shared priorities' and an increased workload overall. Although the use of the CAF was felt to be 'useful' and 'comprehensive', it was also reported as 'long' and 'onerous';
- a reported lack of sign-up from some agencies, for example, schools and health;

- issues around communication and leadership;
- loss of professional identity and distinctiveness;
- resource issues and different service priorities that could inhibit or even undermine the embedding of integrated children's services in some instances.

In 2009, Lord Laming confirmed that significant problems remained in the 'day-to-day reality of working across organisational boundaries and cultures, sharing information to protect children' (Laming, 2009, para. 1.6). There were training issues still to be resolved and data systems to be improved (para. 1.5). Ultimately children's safety depends on individual staff having the time and the skill 'to understand the child or young person and their family circumstances', but:

> There are significant levels of concern that current practice, and in particular the pressure of high case-loads for children's social workers and health visitors, has meant that staff often do not have the time needed to maintain effective contact with children, young people and their families in order to achieve positive outcomes. In these circumstances professionals can find it very difficult to take the time to assess the family environment through the eyes of a child or young person. . . . Staff across frontline services . . . need to be able to notice signs of distress in children of all ages, but particularly amongst very young children who are not able to voice concerns and for whom bedwetting, head-banging and other signs may well be a cry for help.
>
> (para. 3.1)

At the same time, when children and families/carers did express their views and experiences, there was anxiety across all sectors about possible breaches of confidentiality or data protection law: 'The laws governing data protection and privacy are still not well understood by frontline staff or their managers. It is clear that different agencies (and their legal advisers) often take different approaches' (para. 4.6).

Conclusion

Overall, there is no golden formula for addressing the special learning and/or behaviour and welfare needs of every pupil. As noted by Wearmouth (2009: 17):

- every pupil who experiences difficulties is different;
- every situation is different.

Addressing difficulties is a question of problem-solving. In schools, teachers should find out about:

- the learner;
- the expectations/requirements of the particular curriculum area;
- the difficulties s/he experiences.

Then they should:

- think about the barriers to learning;
- reflect on what will best address those barriers to help the learner to achieve in the classroom.

Schools are legally obliged to take account of the approach to SEN and disabilities outlined in the 2001 Code of Practice, and also of the ECM agenda. These are rooted in different conceptualizations of the source of children's difficulties and, therefore, of appropriate interventions to address needs.

Common to both, albeit with differing emphases, is a need for teachers to work closely with other professionals. This is not easy, however, as long-standing problems associated with inter-agency working persist to some extent (Laming, 2009). Nevertheless, much is now known about effective inter-agency working. Policy-makers in the area of *Every Child Matters* might do well to look to the literature for guidance on the enablers associated with the development of integrated working (Robinson et al., 2008) if they are serious about supporting children holistically so that improvements in learning and behaviour are seen in the context of the whole child and his/her family:

- clarity of purpose with arrangements based on a coherent long-term vision and a focus in individual services on goals that are compatible across services;
- commitment at all levels to the vision and to ensuring adequate funding;
- strong leadership and management at all levels within services;
- trust and respect between partners that builds up over time;
- clarity of roles and responsibilities.

References

BPS (British Psychological Society) (1996) *Attention Deficit Hyperactivity Disorder (ADHD): A Psychological Response to an Evolving Concept.* Leicester: BPS.

Children's Workforce Development Council (2009) *The Common Assessment Framework for Children and Young People: A Guide for Practitioners.* London: CWDC.

Clay, M. M. (1979) *Reading: The Patterning of Complex Behaviour.* Auckland: Heinemann.

DfES (2001) *Special Education Needs Code of Practice.* London: DfES.

DfES (2004) *Every Child Matters: Change for Children.* London: DfES.

Dumortier, D. (2004) *From Another Planet: Autism from Within.* London: Paul Chapman.

Dunckley, I. (1999) *Managing Extreme Behaviour in Schools.* Wellington, New Zealand: Specialist Education Services.

Dyson, A. (1997) Social and educational disadvantage: reconnecting special needs education. *British Journal of Special Education,* 24(4): 152–7.

Flower, L. and Hayes, J. (1980) The dynamics of composing: making plans and joggling constraints, in L. Gregg and E. Steinberg (eds) *Cognitive Processes in Writing.* Hillsdale, NJ: Erlbaum, pp. 31–50.

Frith, U. (ed.) (1991) *Autism and Asperger's Syndrome.* Cambridge: Cambridge University Press.

Graham, S. and Harris, K. R. (1993) Teaching writing strategies to students with learning disabilities: issues and recommendations, in L. J. Meltzer (ed.) *Strategy Assessment and*

Instruction for Students with Learning Disabilities. Austin, TX: Pro-Ed MacArthur and Graham.

Graham, S., MacArthur, C., Schwartz, S. and Voth, T. (1989) Improving LD students' compositions using a strategy involving product and process goal-setting, paper presented at Annual Meeting of the American Educational Research Association, San Francisco.

Kanner, L. (1943) Autistic disturbances of affective contact, *Nervous Child*, 2: 217–50.

Kinder, K., Lord, P. and Wilkin, A. (2008) *Implementing Integrated Children's Services. Part 1: Managers' Views on Early Impact.* Slough: NFER.

Laming, Lord (2009) *The Protection of Children in England: A Progress Report.* London: HMSO.

Lewis, M. and Wray, D. (1997) *Writing Frames: Scaffolding Children's Non-fiction Writing in a Range of Genres.* Reading: Reading and Language Information Centre, University of Reading.

Norwich, B., Cooper, P. and Maras, P. (2002) Attentional and activity difficulties: findings from a national study, *Support for Learning*, 17(4): 182–6.

Pickersgill, M. and Gregory, S. (1998) *Sign Bilingualism: A Model.* London: LASER.

QCA (2005) *Primary National Strategy (PNS) Speaking Listening Learning: Working with Children Who Have Special Educational Needs* (Ref 1235/2005). London: QCA.

Rice, M. and Brooks, G. (2004) *Developmental Dyslexia in Adults: A Research Review.* London: NRDC.

RNID (2004) *Inclusion Strategies.* London: RNID.

Roaf, C. and Lloyd, C. (1995) Multi-agency work with young people in difficulty. *Social Care Research Findings*, No. 68. York: Joseph Rowntree Foundation.

Robinson, M., Atkinson, M. and Downing, D. (2008) *Supporting Theory Building in Integrated Services Research.* Slough: NFER.

Snowling, M. J. (2000) *Dyslexia.* 2nd edn. Oxford: Blackwell.

Warnock Report, The (1978) *Special Educational Needs: Report of the Committee of Enquiry into the Education of Handicapped Children and Young People*, Cmnd. 7212. London: HMSO.

Wearmouth, J. (2000) *Co-ordinating Special Educational Provision: Meeting the Challenges in Schools.* London: Hodder.

Wearmouth, J. (2009) *A Beginning Teacher's Guide to Special Educational Needs.* Buckingham: Open University Press.

7

MANAGING BEHAVIOUR, MANAGING THE STANDARDS

Philip Garner and Barry Groom

Introduction

This chapter explores the ways in which SEN coordinators (SENCos) manage and develop that aspect of their work which either relates directly to, or has a more general connection with, 'pupil behaviour'. That term is itself problematic, as most SENCos are inclined to ask the question 'When does inappropriate pupil behaviours signal or constitute a special educational need?' They may even query the efficacy of the official definition given to some of these pupils as experiencing behavioural, emotional and social difficulties (BESD) as indicated in the *SEN Code of Practice* (DfES, 2001) which offers an official working definition of BESD, stating that:

> Pupils with behavioural, emotional and social difficulties cover the full range of ability and continuum of severity. Their behaviours present a barrier to learning and persist despite the implementation of an effective school behaviour policy and personal/social curriculum. They may be withdrawn or isolated, disruptive and disturbing, hyperactive and lack concentration, have immature social skills or present challenging behaviours.
>
> (2001: 93)

These pupils are distinct from those learners who present only occasional 'behaviour problems' by virtue of the scale and longevity of their presenting behaviours. This is an important issue, and requires the SENCo to demonstrate considerable insight, judgement and understanding of causal factors and potential interventions and of the various responses of those who witness and are affected by the behaviour.

The *National Special Educational Needs Specialist Standards* (TTA, 1999) identifies three priority areas in which SENCos should generically demonstrate leadership. These refer to the establishment of a knowledge base, an emphasis on teaching and learning and the development of opportunities for professional enhancement in SEN-related topics. This section considers each of these in the light of references made to pupil behaviour in the *National Award for SEN Coordination* (TDA, 2010). This requires SENCos to 'have a critical understanding of teaching, learning and behaviour management strategies and how to select, use and adapt approaches to remove barriers to learning' (2010: 17), while acting to inform their colleagues about the 'learning needs, behaviour and achievement of pupils' (2010: 18). Moreover, they should be a source of help and support in assisting colleagues to 'have realistic expectations of behaviour for pupils . . . and set appropriately challenging targets for them' (2010: 18).

The section is divided into three parts, each of which is indicative of the pivotal position the SENCo needs to take in developing school provision for pupils experiencing BESD. In dispensing responsibilities in connection with this, a SENCo needs to have a *knowledge base* (an awareness of current guidance, legislation and available resources), *operational skills* (with a particular focus on linking behaviour and learning), and an *understanding* of the contested nature and controversies that continue to be part of any discussion regarding BESD in schools.

Developing a knowledge base: guidance, legislation and resources in BESD

Pupils experiencing BESD in schools continue to present significant professional challenges for teachers and others working in schools and settings. The most recent Statistical First Release (DCSF, 2010b) illustrates the overall numbers of pupils who present behavioural challenges, highlighting both the extent of the issue and the fact that the majority of such pupils are being educated within mainstream settings.

Because provision for managing problem behaviour in mainstream schools has been subject to considerable scrutiny and refinement over the past ten years, a diverse range of documents have emerged, to which SENCos need to have regard. These incorporate considerable emphasis on the capacity of SENCos to liaise effectively with the wider workforce, which in the case of BESD has become more diverse in terms of roles, involving professionals within and outside of the school.

As in other areas of SEN coordination, the principal document informing BESD practice in schools is the *SEN Code of Practice* (DfES, 2001). The Code states that pupils who have learning difficulties related to their 'behaviour, emotional and social development' can 'be withdrawn or isolated, disruptive and disturbing, hyperactive . . . lack concentration . . . [have] immature social skills; . . . [present] challenging behaviours arising from other complex special needs' (2001: 87). This terminology has been criticized because it is both too generic and can result in unintended labelling (Garner, 2010), an issue discussed elsewhere in this section. However, because of the need to recognize that all behaviours have to be viewed in context, this broad description does have the benefit of allowing individual schools to determine their own interpretations of what constitutes the varying levels of seriousness of problematic behaviour.

Other sources of guidance useful for policy formulation are easily accessible electronically (Behaviour4Learning, 2010). It is worth noting that these documents identify a broad emphasis on promoting positive approaches to pupil behaviour, and to defining measures by which learning and behaviour can be more closely linked. Among these the most relevant for SENCos is the *Behaviour and Attendance Strategy:*

Improving Behaviour and Attendance for All (DCSF, 2010b), which provides a range of guidance materials and resources.

The overall conclusions contained in the Steer Report (DCSF, 2009a) should also be essential reading for SENCos, although the report mainly places an emphasis upon non-ascertained behaviour problems in schools. In making 47 separate recommendations, the report highlights the centrality of the SENCo role emphasizing the importance of early intervention, professional development in behaviour management skills, effective whole-school procedures and policies, and liaison with parents, community and other professionals.

SENCos can also draw on a range of recent Ofsted reports which highlight effective practices in promoting positive behaviour and learning. These linkages are emphasized in *Managing Challenging Behaviour* (Ofsted, 2005) which confirms the relationship between behaviour and the curriculum and highlights the link between good behaviour and good teaching. It also reinforces the idea that curriculum adaptation is essential for some pupils and that insufficiently planned or differentiated curriculum may lead to behavioural problems from some pupils and exacerbate that of others. SENCos need to reinforce the view, expressed clearly in the report, that dealing with pupil behaviour in isolation is unlikely to achieve lasting results.

Nor should SENCos, in gathering advice and resources to assist in their leadership in this area, restrict themselves to official publications and protocols. There are important sources of information to be drawn from elsewhere. Two useful examples of this are those from the Scottish Executive (2006) and the Welsh Assembly Government (Estyn, 2006). Both illustrate elements of promoting effective pupil participation and contain numerous practice-related examples.

In many schools the SENCo will be viewed as a principal source of up-to-date information and advice regarding the management of pupil behaviour. For that reason one of the important dimensions of SENCo leadership is an awareness of current research across a range of SENs. Such is the diversity of challenging behaviours subsumed within the generic term BESD that it is impossible for a SENCo to be able to hold expertise or a knowledge base in every one. There are a number of comprehensive reviews and evidence bases to draw upon in BESD (Visser et al., 2001; Harden et al., 2003; Clough et al., 2005). Many of these are also accessible via electronic respositories.

By extending their personal knowledge base in BESD, the SENCo will then be in a good position to support other colleagues by providing leadership in this aspect of SEN provision through whole-school policies beyond those which specifically deal with 'behaviour'.

Operational skills: leading on pedagogy, curriculum and professional development

The SENCo needs to actively contribute to the way in which a school recognizes the link between behaviour and the curriculum. This connection, long recognized in the BESD literature (Bird et al., 1981), was amplified by Ofsted (2005) as a key factor in effective classroom management. It is therefore part of the SENCo's role, on a school-wide basis, to promote greater understanding of this link, by exploring innovative pedagogies, alternative curricula and by promoting staff development in these areas.

As previously noted, the most effective SENCo practice involves taking a major role in contributing to the development of a whole school approach to promoting positive behaviour. This is important and is a fundamental principle in the national policies; the *Key Stage 3 National Strategy* (DfES, 2005) states that, for example, the behaviour and attendance policy and the teaching and learning policies are mutually supportive. It follows, therefore, that the SENCo needs to adopt a critically reflective stance to aid pupil development, in part by asking the following questions:

- Are pupils offered an appropriate, broad and balanced curriculum?
- How effective is this in promoting positive behaviour and regular attendance?
- Do curriculum choices made about timetabling impact on pupils' motivation and learning?
- What are the strengths and weaknesses of curriculum design in each phase?

The *Primary National Strategy* (DfES, 2004) highlights the curricular dimensions of learning emphasizing the importance of effective pedagogy. It is here that a SENCo's background and experience can be a major source of modelling appropriate teaching for pupils who experience BESD. The Strategy offers insights into:

- how lesson structures can promote behaviour for learning;
- diverse teaching approaches and learning styles;
- the importance of classroom routines;
- strategies and techniques for explicitly teaching specific behaviours needed for learning;
- the impact of the classroom environment on behaviour.

SENCos can also take the lead in prompting discussion by those working in individual subject areas of the curriculum by linking what is being taught and how it is being taught to lesson structures. The most effective SENCos explore the nature of subject-specific behaviour management skills with specialist teachers in those areas. Might a teacher who works across both geography and mathematics, for example, have a different 'behaviour management' knowledge base, involving the exercise of differing skills and approaches, situated within each subject discipline? Would a teacher of English have a radically different approach to issues concerning behaviour than, say, someone teaching design technology or science?

One aspect of pedagogy, which greatly assists in the development of effective relationships is the so-called 'soft skill' dimension of teaching. Those SENCos who recognize that the basis of effective learning is to be found in a secure relationship between teacher, pupil and the curriculum, are well placed to provide insights to colleagues in this area.

Some teachers are outstandingly skilled in their interpersonal dealings with pupils who present behavioural challenges. Their classrooms are places where students are invariably polite, responsive and eager to learn and where their authority, which few are prepared to challenge, appears able to establish warm, caring relationships where students feel secure and supported. Such teachers invariably present a calm and unruffled demeanour, which gives a subtle message to the young people in the class that, in a very positive sense, 'their teacher is in control'. It is worth noting, in respect of pupils who present behavioural challenges, that they are inclined to immediately recognize the existence of these qualities in their teachers (Visser, 2005). They include such characteristics as good interpersonal skills, demonstrating respect for others, non-verbal approaches and motivational skills. Each has a substantial literature attached to it, which is based on a recognition by teachers that their own personality characteristics, beliefs and training have an impact on their classroom interactions with pupils.

Understanding: professional dilemmas in BESD

SENCos have an integral part to play in developing a school-wide understanding of BESD as an aspect of SEN which presents significant controversies and dilemmas. Within this short section there is insufficient space to explore all of the dilemmas that are likely to arise in this complex area of SEN. Those identified here have been highlighted by SENCos as part of on-line correspondence with SENCos participating in the SENCo Forum (BECTA, 2010).

Defining BESD

As noted elsewhere in this section, pupil behaviour in schools has long been a problematic issue. The term BESD is the most recent descriptor for pupils who have been variously defined in the past as disruptive, maladjusted, disaffected or as having challenging behaviour (Cooper et al., 1994). One of the main concerns about these terms is that they tend to place causal emphasis on the pupil. In other words, complex underlying issues are less obviously taken account of. Indeed, the widespread use of the expression 'disruptive pupils' in the 1970s and 1980s was a manifestation of an assumption that the principal determinant of the behaviour is the pupil himself (Saunders, 1979).

SENCos need to have very clear view of how BESDs are defined in their school, and should try to identify individual behaviours which might comprise each element of the term. This quest for specificity, moving away from a generic descriptor, is a vital element in the process of identification and assessment, leading to an appropriate intervention programme. For the SENCo – and for the pupil experiencing BESDs – the most problematic task is likely to be the quest for a consensus among teaching and other staff. But without a coherent and agreed understanding of what constitutes unacceptable behaviour, the process of determining whether it is an emerging SEN via systematic assessment cannot take place (Thomas and Loxley, 2001). It is important, therefore, that the SENCo participates in these professional discussions, thereby helping to raise levels of awareness among colleagues that a focus on concrete behaviours rather than a label has long been a prerequisite for effective intervention (Westmacott and Cameron, 1981).

Teacher attitudes and school effect

Pupil behaviour in schools evokes strong opinion and feelings, both from professionals and from the public. There is a tendency for some teachers to view BESD as a catch-all term for anti-social behaviour. Such views are amplified by the tendency to locate certain behavioural characteristics within 'syndromes', a phenomenon which arouses significant professional cynicism (Garner, 2010). It has, in consequence, been suggested that some teachers are what has been termed 'deviance provocative', in that their response to unacceptable behaviour actually becomes part of the problem (Reynolds, 1976). While in no way condoning the original unsatisfactory pupil behaviour, the SENCo is therefore required to adopt a sensitive middle ground, mediating between the needs of the pupil concerned and the professional standpoint of the teachers and the school.

This position is further amplified when an ecosystemic view is taken of BESD (Jones, 2003) which suggests that institutional factors within a school might be a contributory factor in BESD. In this there is an acceptance that, in the case of most instances of challenging behaviour, multi-factoral causes apply. Recognition of this, and an ability to address the tensions that arise from it, represent a sophisticated way of working, which requires the SENCo to utilize a wide range of interpersonal skills, as well as being assertive in offering guidance to colleagues.

Controversial interventions

In recent years there has been a tendency for the re-emergence of categorization in SEN, including BESD (Thomas and Loxley, 2001). This has undoubtedly brought with it a wide range of intervention strategies (Jones, 2003). Many of these are promoted commercially, and some are based on frail logic, inadequate field-testing and evaluation, and in some instances may even be invasive.

SENCos need to be aware of these tensions, which in part are prompted by an understandable professional desire to find a 'solution' to phenomena which have long been regarded as a structural feature of schools and of the school-age population (Furlong, 1979). Moreover, in a climate in which schools are increasingly placed under close official scrutiny, it is a natural response to seek instant solutions, even to pervasive and deep-seated problematic behaviour (Garner, 2010).

Given that there may be several underpinning causes for a given problematic behaviour, there is a strong recognition that interventions need also to be selected so that elements of different approaches can be incorporated in an overall strategy (Garner and Gains, 1996). Working closely with those colleagues who have school-wide responsibility for pupil behaviour, the SENCo must again ensure that the SEN within any behaviour plan is emphasized.

Liaison with parents and professionals

Making effective contact with parents of pupils experiencing BESD, and building this into a long-term relationship which can support the progress of the pupil, presents particular challenges for SENCos. In the case of BESD, there is a recognized correlation, evidenced by a significant body of research, between challenging behaviours and the social circumstances of the pupils exhibiting them (Jones and Smith, 2004). It is important to note that the disadvantages faced by many of their parents may result in ongoing difficulties in maintaining an effective working relationship with them. These parents will sometimes have had negative school experiences themselves, and feel marginalized by procedures and institutions when they focus on the unsatisfactory behaviour of their child (Daniels et al., 1998).

In consequence, the SENCo faces particular challenges, both in establishing a working relationship with parents and then maintaining this by providing an appropriate set of learning opportunities for the pupil.

Inclusion and exclusion

Perhaps the most contentious and institutionally problematic issue facing SENCos in respect of BESD is that of inclusion and exclusion. Pupils who present BESDs form a very high percentage of pupils who are excluded from schools (DCSF, 2010a) and are the least likely to be seen as potential candidates for a subsequent return to the mainstream. In the inclusion literature, relatively few texts focus on inclusion from the perspective of BESD (although one useful example is by Nind et al., 2003).

Each of the dilemmas facing SENCos require that a school-wide stance is taken, which is informed by developing skills, knowledge and understanding about pupils who experience BESD. A strong argument can be advanced that, as 'pupil behaviour' occurs across an extended continuum, and is irrevocably linked to issues of learning, curriculum access and co-morbid SENs, SENCos should be members of senior leadership teams in all schools.

References

BECTA (2010) SENCo Forum. Available at: http://collaboration.becta.org.uk/community/inclusion/senco-forum.

Behaviour4Learning (2010) Available at: http://www.behaviour4learning.ac.uk/Index.aspx (accessed 10 March 2010).

Bird, C., Chessum, R., Furlong, V. and Johnson, D. (1981) *Disaffected Pupils*. Uxbridge: Brunel University.

Clough, P., Garner, P., Pardeck, T. and Yuen, F. (2005) *Handbook of Emotional and Behavioural Difficulties*. London: Sage.

Cooper, P., Smith, C. and Upton, G. (1994) *Emotional and Behavioural Difficulties*. London: Routledge.

Daniels, H., Visser, J., Cole, T. and de Reybekill, N. (1998) *Emotional and Behavioural Difficulties in Mainstream Schools*. London: DfEE.

DCSF (2009a) *Learning Behaviour: Lessons Learned* (The Steer Report). London: DCSF.

DCSF (2009b) *Special Educational Needs in England: January 2009. Statistical First Release*. London: DCSF. Aavailable at: http://www.dcsf.gov.uk/rsgateway/DB/SFR/s000852/index.shtml (accessed 10 March 2010).

DCSF (2010a) *Permanent and Fixed Period Exclusions from Schools in England 2007/08*. Available at: http://www.dcsf.gov.uk/rsgateway/DB/SFR/s000860/index.shtml (accessed 2 March 2010).

DCSF (2010b) *Behaviour and Attendance Strategy: Improving Behaviour and Attendance for All*. London: DCSF.

DfES (2001) *SEN Code of Practice*. London: DfES.

DfES (2004) *The Primary National Strategy*. London: DfES.

DfES (2005) *Key Stage 3 National Strategy*. London: DfES.

Furlong, V. (1979) *The Deviant Pupil*. Milton Keynes: Open University Press.

Garner, P. (2010) SEBD; BESD; or even DEBS – descriptive or prescriptive. Labels and their contribution to good practice, keynote paper to 57th Annual SEBDA Conference, Manchester, 19 March.

Garner, P. and Gains, C. (1996) Models of intervention for pupils with emotional and behavioural difficulties, *Support for Learning*, 11(4): 141–5.

Harden, A., Thomas, J., Evans, J., Scanlon, M. and Sinclair, J. (2003) Supporting pupils with emotional and behavioural difficulties (EBD) in mainstream primary schools: a systematic review of recent research on strategy effectiveness (1999 to 2002), in *Research Evidence in Education Library*. London: Institute of Education.

Jones, J. and Smith, C. (2004) Reducing exclusions whilst developing effective intervention and inclusion for pupils with behaviour difficulties, *Emotional and Behavioural Difficulties*, 9(2): 115–29.

Jones, R. (2003) The construction of emotional and behavioural difficulties, *Educational Psychology in Practice*, 19(2): 147–57.

Nind, M., Sheehy, K. and Simmons, K. (eds) (2003) *Inclusive Education: Learners and Learning Contexts*. London: David Fulton.

Office for Standards in Education (2005) *Managing Challenging Behaviour*. London: Ofsted.

Reynolds, D. (1976) The delinquent school, in M. Hammersley and P. Woods (eds) *The Process of Schooling*. London: Routledge & Kegan Paul.

Saunders, M. (1979) *Class Control and Behaviour Problems*. Maidenhead: McGraw-Hill.

TDA (2010) *National Award for SEN Coordination*. Manchester: TDA.

Thomas, G. and Loxley, A. (2001) *Deconstructing Special Education and Constructing Inclusion*. Buckingham: Open University Press.

TTA (1999) *National Special Educational Needs Specialist Standards*. London: TTA.

Visser, J. (2005) Key factors that enable the successful management of difficult behaviour in schools and classrooms, *Education 3–13*, 33(1): 26–31.

Visser, J., Daniels, H. and Cole, T. (2001) *Children with Emotional and Behavioural Difficulties in Mainstream Schools*. Greenwich, CT: JAI Press.

Welsh Assembly Government (Estyn) (2006) *Behaviour in Wales: Good Practice in Managing Challenging Behaviour*. Cardiff: Estyn.

Westmacott, E. and Cameron, R. (1981) *Behaviour Can Change*. Basingstoke: Globe.

8

ASSESSMENT FOR LEARNING IN INCLUSIVE SCHOOLS

Peter Hick, Kath Kelly and Steve Tyler

Introduction

This chapter considers the role of 'assessment for learning', in developing more inclusive practices with children described as having special educational needs. 'Assessment for learning' is discussed critically in the current policy context and in relation to alternative approaches. Two case studies are presented, of a child described as having an autistic spectrum condition; and a child identified as having 'specific learning difficulties'.

Assessment for learning: a new approach to inclusive practice?

> Assessment for Learning is the process of seeking and interpreting evidence for use by learners and their teachers to decide where the learners are in their learning, where they need to go and how best to get there.
>
> (Assessment Reform Group, 2002: 2–3)

Paul Black and Dylan Wiliam produced an influential review of the evidence on *formative* assessment, which showed that 'formative assessment is an important aspect of teachers' classroom work and that attention to improving its practice can enhance the learners' achievements' (Black and Wiliam, 1998, 2006: 9). They pointed to key features, such as the active involvement of students in formative assessment; sharing criteria with learners; and the importance of teachers adjusting teaching and learning in response to feedback. In combination, these features are seen to build on practices such as promoting classroom dialogue, feedback through marking, peer and self-assessment, and the formative use of summative tests (Black and Wiliam, 2006). Arguably, teaching and learning practices that implement such principles may be effective in engaging a diverse range of learners; and schools that support such approaches may be well placed to develop more inclusive practices.

The 'Assessment for Learning Strategy' (AfL) was launched in 2008, and was promoted within the Inclusion strand of the National Strategies programme, with some £150 million allocated to training for teachers to support this development

(DCSF, 2008). Yet this strategy has been heavily criticized as presenting a narrow vision of assessment *of* learning, rather than assessment *for* learning:

> The AfL Strategy practically ignores the process and pedagogical essence of AfL, the nuanced interaction among pupils and teachers, the associated values and the underpinning principles. Rather it is dominated by an alignment with 'Assessing Pupils' Progress' and summative forms of assessment.
>
> (Swaffield, 2009: 13)

The implication is that inclusive approaches to assessment for learning require careful and critical thinking about the underlying purposes and values. Arguably assessment in special education has traditionally been an exclusionary process, underpinned by a medical model of disability, and with an underlying aim of identifying deficits within individual children as a means of allocating special school places, or rationing resources for support within mainstream settings. Assessment in relation to categories of special educational need can trace its origins to the development of IQ testing and special schooling, so that proponents of more inclusive practices have tended to look for more positive alternatives. For example, many educational psychologists draw on approaches such as dynamic assessment (Stringer, 2008), which focus on a child's potential for learning rather than aiming to measure innate or fixed abilities. Alternatively, could assessment processes be aimed at answering questions such as 'How can we include this child more?', or 'What would it take to achieve more inclusive outcomes with this student?'

Given the complex and contradictory roots of current policy initiatives on 'assessment for learning' in relation to children identified with special educational needs, how can SENCos respond, and navigate the competing demands they may experience? What kinds of assessment processes can SENCos contribute to, that can support their colleagues in developing more inclusive practices? In the following sections, Steve Tyler and Kath Kelly give case studies illustrating some of the ways in which these dilemmas can be played out in practice, in relation to children described as having autistic spectrum conditions and specific learning difficulties respectively. They give examples of elements of assessment that may form part of a process of *assessment for inclusive learning* for children with special educational needs. Each case study is followed by questions for the reader to consider, to which might be added the wider question of in what ways diagnostic assessment of special educational needs can be seen as 'assessment for learning'.

Assessment for learning: autistic spectrum conditions

Autistic spectrum conditions (ASC) are defined by differences in three areas of development relating to: (1) social understanding and social interaction; (2) all aspects of communication; and (3) flexibility of thought and behaviour (Jordan, 1999). In addition, young people with ASC may show other differences including atypical sensory responses, difficulties with motor coordination, and differences in attention control, although these do not currently form part of the diagnostic criteria (Roth, 2010).

Of greatest importance, however, when considering assessment for learning, is the evidence that young people with ASC tend to think and, therefore, learn in ways that are different from other pupils. These differences can lead to issues in group discussion; an inability to see how pieces of information relate to each other; difficulties with planning and organization; and the need for support to generalize learning from one context to another (Boucher, 2009; Roth, 2010). These differences, although sometimes subtle in presentation, may have a significant impact. However, it should also be recognized that young people with ASC may show strengths in a range of ways including a good ability to recall factual information, a depth of knowledge in particular areas of interest, an ability to persevere on a given task and conscientiousness in their approach to learning. Each young person will have a unique profile of strengths as well as weaknesses that needs to be identified and addressed through a process of detailed individual assessment and the formulation of targets that are shared with the young person in ways that they can understand and support.

Diagnostic assessment is normally undertaken by specialist teams, although schools may contribute observations that assist the process. Some young people may be undiagnosed and staff generally, and in particular SENCos, need to be aware of the patterns of behaviour that may be indicative of an ASC. It has been proposed that all schools should have specific policies on autism and take steps towards becoming more autism friendly (DfES, 2002; Roth, 2010). With regard to assessment for learning, there is a need to be clear about what is being assessed and what may contribute to a young person's difficulties in learning (Powell and Jordan, 1997). In particular, consideration needs to be given to the social and sensory contexts in which the young person is taught as well as to curriculum goals; to what motivates the young person, which may be different from the typical pupil; and above all to the impact of the process of assessment itself.

The difficulties that a young person with ASC may experience in learning in a social setting should be recognized. The pupil with ASC is effectively having to undertake a dual curriculum: the set curriculum and a social curriculum. In addition, young people with ASC may be hypersensitive to sensory stimuli or subject to sensory overload in particular environments, which needs to be considered as part of the assessment process (Attwood, 2006). Particular sensitivity may need to be shown when discussing problems that pupils encounter in learning as some young people with ASC may become excessively anxious or depressed about their inability to cope within the school setting. Personalized learning programmes need to reflect this, and targets should be shared with the young person in such a way that their self-esteem is maintained.

CASE STUDY 1

Jack is a Year 7 pupil who has recently joined the school and appears to have caused some concerns. His form tutor, Susan, has noticed that he has made no new friends in the form and appears to be very reliant upon another boy whom he knew at primary school. When Susan asks other staff about Jack, she gets mixed reports. While he appears to be coping well in Maths and Science, where he displays an advanced knowledge in certain areas, he is struggling in other subjects such as English and Religious Education. In all subjects, staff report that Jack often fails to hand in homework or that it is incomplete.

Susan talks to Jack about how he feels he is getting on in school. Jack seems ill at ease in talking to her, often glancing at a book he is holding rather than looking at her. He tends to reply to her questions with a simple 'yes' or 'no' and only offers information when they start to talk about how well he is doing in Science. At this point he talks at length about his interest in astronomy and the solar system, about which he seems to have a great deal of knowledge. When Susan changes the topic of the conversation, Jack reverts to his previous monosyallabic answers.

Susan discusses Jack with the SENCo who wonders whether Jack might have Asperger's Syndrome, a subtle form of autistic spectrum condition. The SENCo decides to ask other staff to report more formally upon Jack's progress. While some confirm Susan's initial impression that Jack is doing well in some subjects, others report that he is making little progress. In some classes Jack appears withdrawn and fails to contribute to class discussions, only answering questions that are posed directly to him. In other instances, he has become somewhat disruptive appearing to enjoy it when other pupils laugh at his interruptions. Some staff also note that he is often late for their lessons and appears to arrive in an agitated state. On the basis of this information, it is agreed by Susan and the SENCo that further assessment is required.

Questions for discussion

1   What further assessment might be undertaken?

2   How might Jack be enabled to participate in the process?

3   How might the SENCo use information gained to set targets and improve curriculum access for Jack?

4   How can Jack be supported to monitor his own progress?

Assessment for learning: specific learning difficulties (dyslexia)

Dyslexia has been defined as:

> A specific learning difficulty which mainly affects the development of literacy and language related skills. It is likely to be present at birth and to be lifelong in its effects. It is characterised by difficulties with phonological processing, rapid naming, working memory, processing speed, and the automatic development of skills that may not match up to an individual's other cognitive abilities. It tends to be resistant to conventional teaching methods, but its effects can be mitigated by appropriately specific intervention, including the application of information technology and supportive counselling.
>
> (BDA, 2009)

Current research suggests that in identifying dyslexia we need to assess a number of cognitive processes such as *phonological processing*, including letter sound knowledge, sound manipulation, rapid naming, and rhyme (McCrory et al., 2005; Hulme and Snowling, 2009); *visual processing* difficulties such as letters that appear to blur and move around when trying to read (Evans, 2001; Stein, 2003); *working memory* including the ability to follow verbal instructions, copy from the board, perform mental calculations and organize perceptual information (Baddeley, 2003; Gathercole and Pakiam-Alloway, 2008); *automaticity of learned skills* such as letter/sound knowledge and motor coordination needed for articulation, balance and handwriting (Reid, 2009; Nicolson and Fawcett, 2008, 2009); and *speed of information processing* (Tallal, 2007; Valeo, 2008).

Case Study 2 demonstrates a starting point in identifying the difficulties experienced by dyslexic learners through informal assessment:

CASE STUDY 2

Cassie had some concerns about a pupil in her class. Michael (age 8) was an articulate pupil who contributed well in discussions or question/answer sessions but produced very little written work and was reluctant to read. After consulting the school SENCo, Cassie decided to carry out some in-class observations.

She noticed that when he was asked to copy from the board he was painfully slow, mostly copying one letter at a time; inaccurate; and sometimes missed out words or lines.

In literacy lessons Michael often only produced one sentence and relied on finding words from classroom displays to support this. Cassie asked him to produce a piece of 'free writing' without the use of props and noticed that he knew very few keywords. Instead he attempted to spell words phonetically but frequently confused the vowel sound, omitted word endings or reversed letters. He seemed unsure of where to start and finish a letter. His writing was large and unevenly spaced.

In mental maths Michael struggled to recall number facts quickly but when Cassie gave him time to think he usually arrived at the correct answer (Cassie did observe him using his fingers to count on some occasions).

The teacher started to keep a running record when listening to Michael read and noted that he often misread words substituting them with words that had a similar meaning or started with the same letter. She noticed that he rarely tried to 'sound out' unknown words and that he used his finger to try to keep his place. She decided to ask the SENCo to carry out a miscue analysis of reading and to assess visual tracking skills for letters and words. The SENCo decided to carry out further assessment using a simple diagnostic Screening Test (2006, Ann Arbor), the Visual Stress pack (2007, Crossbow), the *Dyslexia Portfolio* (2006, GL Assessment) and the *York Reading Assessment* (2008, GL Assessment).

Questions for discussion

1   Which cognitive processes did Cassie assess herself?

2   Why do you think that she asked the SENCo to carry out further assessment?

3   How could she use this information to improve curriculum access and set learning targets?

Conclusion

Arguably assessment for learning is inherently more inclusive than summative assessment. Harlen (2006: 78) points out: 'The particularly serious impact of summative assessment and tests on lower achieving students results from their repeated experience of failure in comparison with more successful students.' However, recent reviews of the evidence for inclusive rather than *specialist* pedagogies raise questions about the role of diagnostic assessment in inclusive learning. Where diagnostic assessment takes an essentially summative approach to identifying deficits in abilities, this would not be seen as assessment that directly contributes to learning. Alternatively, where diagnostic assessment is focused on *how* a child learns, for example, through dynamic assessment or formative approaches to curriculum-based assessment, this is more consonant with the principles of assessment *for* learning.

What then would an inclusive approach to assessment for learning look like? If assessment for learning is understood as a 'process of seeking and interpreting evidence for use by learners and their teachers to decide where the learners are in their learning, where they need to go and how best to get there' (ARG, 2002), then this applies equally to all learners. The principles of universal design for learning should inform not only curriculum but also assessment planning, so that it becomes accessible for all. The Assessment Reform Group has proposed a set of key principles underpinning assessment for learning, which lend themselves well to this approach. An inclusive approach involves finding ways to support the achievement of all learners, through applying these principles of assessment for learning in ways that engage diverse learners. For example, questions of pupil involvement arise equally for children who have been identified as having special educational needs: how can they be involved in a process of assessing their learning? and how might they be supported to monitor their own progress? Here, there is no simple answer or toolkit that can be applied across educational settings. In this context, professional development for SENCos and their colleagues involves reflecting critically on current practices, to collaborate in developing more inclusive assessments with pupils identified as having special educational needs.

References

Assessment Reform Group (2002) *Assessment for Learning*. Available at: assessment-reform-group-org.

Attwood, T. (2006) *The Complete Guide to Asperger Syndrome*. London: Jessica Kingsley.

Baddeley, A. (2003) Working memory and language: an overview, *Journal of Communication Disorders*, 36(3): 189–203.

Black, P. and Wiliam, D. (1998) *Inside the Black Box: Raising Standards through Classroom Assessment*. London: King's College.

Black, P. and Wiliam, D. (2006) Assessment for learning in the classroom, in J. Gardner (ed.) *Assessment for Learning*. London: Sage.

Boucher, J. (2009) *The Autistic Spectrum: Characteristics, Causes and Practical Issues*. London: Sage.

British Dyslexia Association (2009) Definition of dyslexia. Available at: www.bdadyslexia. org.uk.

DCSF (2008) *The Assessment for Learning Strategy*. Nottingham: DCSF Publications.

DfES (2002) *Autistic Spectrum Disorders: Good Practice Guidance*. London: DfES.

Evans, J. W. (2001) *Dyslexia and Vision*. London: Whurr.

Gathercole, S. and Pakiam-Alloway, T. (2008) *Working Memory and Learning*. London: Sage.

Harlen, W. (2006) The role of assessment in developing motivation for learning, in J. Gardner (ed.) *Assessment and Learning*. London: Sage.

Hulme, C. and Snowling, M. (2009) *Developmental Cognitive Disorders*. Oxford: Wiley-Blackwell.

Jordan, R. (1999) *Autistic Spectrum Disorders*. London: David Fulton.

McCrory, E., Mechelli, A., Frith, U. and Price, C. (2005) More than words: a common neural basis for reading and naming deficits in developmental dyslexia? *Brain*, 128(2): 261–7.

Nicolson, R. I. and Fawcett, A. J. (2008) *Dyslexia, Learning, and the Brain*. London: MIT Press.

Nicolson, R. I. and Fawcett, A. J. (2009) *The Sage Handbook of Dyslexia*. London: Sage.

Powell, S. and Jordan, R. (eds) (1997) *Autism and Learning: A Guide to Good Practice*. London: David Fulton.

Reid, G. (2009) *Dyslexia: A Practitioner's Handbook*. Oxford: Wiley-Blackwell.

Roth, I. (2010) *The Autism Spectrum in the 21st Century: Exploring Psychology, Biology and Practice*. London: Jessica Kingsley.

Stein, J. (2003) Visual motion sensitivity and reading. *Neuropsychologia*, 41: 1785–93.

Stringer, P. (2008) Dynamic assessment for inclusive learning, in P. Hick, R. Kershner and P. Farrell (eds) *Psychology for Inclusive Education: New Directions in Theory and Practice*. London: Routledge.

Swaffield, S. (2009) The misrepresentation of Assessment for Learning – and the woeful waste of a wonderful opportunity. 'Work in Progress Paper' presented at the Association for Achievement and Improvement through Assessment National Conference, Bournemouth, 16–18 September.

Tallal, P. (2007) Experimental studies of language impairments: from research to remediation. Available at: http://en.scientificcommons.org.

Valeo, T. (2008) *Dyslexia Studies Catch Neuroplasticity at Work*. The Dana Foundation. Available at: www.dana.org.

Part III

Strategic development

Introduction to Part III

The chapters in Part III are positioned to address the three main themes included within the Learning Outcomes Section: Strategic Development of SEN Policy and Procedures.

In Chapter 9, Alison Ekins addresses the first of these, the need to work strategically with colleagues and governors. The chapter draws attention to the emphasis within the National Award on the strategic role of the SENCo as an agent of change, and links this to the legislative context, within the National Curriculum Inclusion Statement, for example. The need for an inclusive school ethos is examined, where the responsibility for meeting the needs of pupils is seen as a collaborative process. This is linked to a dynamic model, Inclusion in Action (Ekins and Grimes, 2009), that joins a number of systems, such as pupil tracking, intervention planning, and provision mapping that are widely used in current practice, to promote reflective and critical self-evaluation in schools. This material can be seen to exemplify the Learning Outcomes within the theme namely:

- to advise on and influence the development of an inclusive ethos, policies, priorities and practices;
- to ensure the objectives of the school's SEN policy are/can be reflected in the school improvement plan and self-evaluation form (SEF);
- to establish appropriate resources to support the teaching of pupils with SEN and/or disabilities, and the means of monitoring their use in terms of value for money, efficiency and effectiveness;
- to develop and provide regular information on the effectiveness of provision to inform decision making and policy review.

It should be noted that the chapter goes far beyond this narrow alignment with the Learning Outcomes (LOs), however, by inviting the reader to engage in reflection and deeper analysis. Three examples of this are particularly relevant; first, Alison discusses the need for reflection on what constitutes an inclusive school ethos, suggesting that this is a continuing and developing process. Second, the establishment of communities of practice to enable change is considered. Finally, the concept of 'principled interruptions' (Ainscow et al., 2006) is noted, and exemplified in two case studies, to illustrate the need to ensure that we do not simply perpetuate existing systems, but need to consider practice anew.

Chapter 10, by Pam Davies and John Hattersley, examines the change process undertaken by a Local Authority (LA) to improve inclusive practice in the area. The chapter clearly illustrates the second theme within this part, namely strategic planning in relation to finance, budget management and the use of resources. An evaluative model of the change process is offered, outlining three stages in the development. In Stage 1, the small-scale project used to begin change is examined; in Stage 2, the extension of this model to all provision in the LA is described, and in Stage 3, the LA review of SEN provision that followed is considered. A case study is provided for each Stage, to aid reflection on the change process as it relates to specific examples in schools or settings. In providing this material, Pam and John have explored many features of the three Learning Outcomes in this theme, which are:

- the ways in which funding for pupils with SEN and/or disabilities is provided to schools, including local funding arrangements, and, where appropriate, how to obtain additional resources;
- how funding for pupils with SEN and/or disabilities is used in their school;
- how to manage and make best use of available financial, human and physical resources, including how to use tools to plan, evaluate and improve provision for pupils with SEN and/or disabilities, including identifying ineffective or missing provision.

A number of concepts are developed further in the chapter through the adoption of a critical approach to the material. An exploration of the need to accept that attitudes will exist at the beginning of a change process that might inhibit that change is offered; the appointment of change 'champions' acting as advocates is noted as an outcome of this recognition. The chapter notes that change may require a new conceptualization of leadership and management, with an attendant need to support this within the change process. Closely linked to this, is that change has unintended consequences as well as those planned, and constant evaluation is required to prevent these acting as potential blockages to the process. Most significantly, perhaps, is the need to establish accountability procedures when initiating change; in this case, at both the level of the schools involved, but also at the Local Authority level, by commissioning an action research project with a local university.

In the third chapter in Part III, Angharad Beckett considers improving outcomes for young people, dealing particularly with addressing stereotyping. The chapter is themed around the results of a Research Project undertaken by Angharad and her team, to establish whether non-disabled young people exhibit evidence of what is termed *disabling* attitudes. In three sections, consideration is given to the historical movement towards the inclusion of pupils with SEN and/or disabilities within mainstream culture; to evidence that shows the presence of a disabling attitude; and to the challenges that exist for teachers in addressing these attitudes. A close link is established with the third theme, Strategies for improving outcomes for pupils with SEN and/or disabilities, in which the SENCo should:

- have a sound understanding of strategies for removing barriers to participation and learning for pupils with SEN and/or disabilities;

- know strategies for addressing stereotyping and bullying related to SEN and disability;

- draw critically on relevant research and inspection evidence about effective practice in including pupils with SEN and/or disabilities to inform practice in their school.

In reporting the research, Angharad locates her material within a framework that is developed by critically evaluating and analysing further aspects of the subject. The legislative framework that has been developed to establish disability rights is examined, and consideration is given to the need for further developments, both in changing the law, but more importantly, in changing attitudes. Stereotyping is examined, and evidence of the existence of the stereotypical classification of the disabled by non-disabled pupils is examined. The lack of resources showing positive images of disability, and the difficulty in ensuring interaction between those with disability and those without are also discussed.

It is perhaps obvious that in meeting the aims of the Section: Strategic Development of SEN Policy and Procedures, the contributors of the three chapters have shown a considerable overlap within the themes included. For example, the chapters emphasize that the strategic development of inclusive practice involves a continuing process, rather than a goal to be obtained. Similarly, all three chapters note the need to change attitudes as a necessary pre-condition to changing practice strategically.

It is our contention that this can be taken further, with the suggestion that each of these chapters as written could be used to demonstrate requirements within other Learning Outcomes, or could have been developed to do so, by further elaboration of the principles included in the writing. For example, there is an undoubted synergy between the material in Chapter 9 and the themes contained in Part IV: Coordinating Provision, that talk about using classroom data; planning interventions; and assessing the effectiveness of provision. Chapter 10 might be seen to address the theme of the same part, on making flexible and innovative use of the available workforce, or of that contained within the theme: Leading, Developing and Supporting Colleagues, which talks of the SENCo taking a lead in developing workplace policies and practices. Finally, Chapter 11 illustrates the importance of using evidence to inform practice, a key point within the theme: Professional Context. By suggesting these links, it is hoped that the aim set out in the Introduction to Part II is being illustrated; that the reflective and evaluative examination of practice can be used to evidence the completion of a number of the NASC Learning Outcomes without the need to produce separate material for each one.

References

Ainscow, M., Booth, T. and Dyson, A. (2006) *Improving Schools, Developing Inclusion*. Abingdon: Routledge.

Ekins, A. and Grimes, P. (2009) *Inclusion: Developing an Effective Whole School Approach*. Maidenhead: Open University Press.

9

DEVELOPING A JOINED-UP APPROACH TO STRATEGIC WHOLE SCHOOL PROCESSES

Alison Ekins

Introduction

It is now essential that the SENCO is enabled and supported to develop a strategic role within the school setting. The role has changed significantly in recent years, moving from a situation where the SENCO was seen to independently coordinate systems around SEN (DfES, 2001) to current legislation which emphasizes the role of the SENCO as a strategic leader within the school setting (TDA, 2009); this is implicit in the Learning Outcomes for the National Award for SEN Coordination.

This is significant and the SENCO, both new to the role and established within the school setting, will need to develop effective ways for managing this wide-ranging role to best meet the needs of all within the school: colleagues, pupils, parents and other professionals supporting the school.

The SENCO as strategic leader: enabler, facilitator and supporter

SENCOs now need to be very clear about the nature and scope of their role. We have moved away from a model which has seen the SENCO as the person taking on the responsibility for all SEN identification, planning and, often, teaching. Instead, notions based on the National Curriculum Inclusion Statement (DES, 1999) need to be emphasized. This statement clearly set out the statutory duty of every teacher to directly ensure that they meet the needs of *all* pupils within the classroom by:

- setting suitable learning challenges;
- responding to pupils' diverse learning needs;
- overcoming potential barriers to learning and assessment for individuals and groups of pupils.

While it is the responsibility of the class teacher to meet the needs of every pupil within their class on a day-to-day basis, the SENCO has a role to provide the support and advice required to assist each class teacher in fulfilling their statutory duties. The

SENCO therefore needs to develop a clear role as facilitator, enabler and supporter to work with teachers to discuss, reflect upon and develop their skills, to meet the day-to-day challenges of working with these pupils.

Inclusive school cultures: shared commitment and responsibility

This cannot happen overnight, and therefore such an approach needs to be embedded within an inclusive whole school ethos. SENCOs will find that their schools are at different stages in the development of effective inclusive cultures, and will need to consider how to work strategically with other leaders within the school to develop an approach to working which ensures the involvement of all in the discussion and agreement of shared inclusive values and principles.

Booth and Ainscow (2002) emphasize the importance of developing cultures that share inclusive values, to enable the effective removal of barriers to learning and participation. This is clearly a central aim for pupils with SEN. Structured opportunities for reflective and collaborative discussions about such a concept will help all staff to understand that there is a need to look past the individual difficulties experienced by the pupil, to a consideration of the barriers to learning and participation inherent within school-based systems and processes. This will help to initiate a move to a whole school approach that is creative, flexible and responsive, and which enables individual teachers to take responsibility and ownership for their practice, in ensuring full access and participation for all pupils.

This is not an easy task, and to change a school culture, and its values and practices, takes some considerable amount of time, often with resistance on the way (Harris, 2007). Indeed: 'Change is a double-edged sword . . . Change arouses emotions, and when emotions intensify, leadership is key' (Fullan, 2004: 1). Time must therefore be given to ensuring that values and practices are discussed and agreed; that there is shared understanding of issues; that adequate support is given to staff members in changing aspects of their practice, and that there is clear strategic leadership.

The SENCO will not be able to work strategically until there is a fully embedded approach towards collective responsibility for meeting needs, and this is therefore the first step in working towards developing strategic practices within the school.

Linked to this are two central principles: collaboration and communication. In order to be able to work strategically, the SENCO must look broadly at the roles and responsibilities of other colleagues, particularly those within senior leadership positions, and consider ways that collaboration can occur, to share information and ideas about moving practice forward. This is about collaborating with a range of different people, including pupils and parents as well as teaching staff. Ways must then be found to plan a strategic whole school response to meeting identified needs across the school.

Communication skills within this process are key, and the SENCO should be considering ways to ensure that messages are shared, to reinforce the importance of a strategic rather than reactive approach to meeting the needs of all pupils. The notion of 'communities of practice' fostering collaborative opportunities to engage in shared professional dialogue are therefore central (Durrant and Holden, 2006).

The importance of developing joined-up systems

It is important to ensure that staff members are not overburdened by a range of new initiatives and approaches. Staff will not respond positively to changing established practices if:

1   They do not understand the reason for change.
2   They think that the change simply leads to extra workload for themselves without clear gain or benefit.

One way to approach this may therefore be through a critical analysis and review of existing school systems and processes to establish how these support staff in better meeting the needs of all pupils through inclusive principles and values.

Key systems currently used in the majority of schools to review and respond to pupil needs include:

- Pupil tracking
- Data analysis
- Intervention planning
- Provision mapping
- Target setting.

Embedded in all of these should be self-evaluation: not self-evaluation solely for the purposes of Ofsted inspections, but ongoing reflective and critical self-evaluation involving a wide range of stakeholders to consider and challenge existing practices to ensure that they continue to remain effective and meaningful.

The processes and systems listed above will not be new. They are key processes introduced over recent years through DfES (2004, 2006), DCSF (2007) and Ofsted (2006) guidance, and developed within schools to track and respond to pupil progress. However, they are systems and processes which have often become meaningless: bureaucratic pieces of paper filed in dusty files on a top shelf to prove to external bodies that pupil progress is being considered. There is a need to reconsider the effect and impact of such processes within the busy school setting: to re-evaluate the purpose and values of the education that we are providing to the pupils within our schools, and how those processes are currently contributing to the development and evaluation of practices and experiences which are enhancing our pupils' lives and enabling them to make progress and achieve in the broadest, most holistic, sense of the term.

Ainscow et al. (2006) use the notion of providing 'principled interruptions' within our thinking and practice in order to ensure that we do not simply perpetuate existing systems for the sake of it. Instead, we need to stop and look at the purpose and efficiency of the systems that we are using: to check that the hours that we spend filling in forms is impacting directly, relevantly and effectively to enhance the day-to-day teaching and learning experience of each child. If they are not doing this, then there is a need to stop: to challenge existing practices, and to return to a consideration of the underlying values, culture and practices within the school.

The systems, when used effectively, are extremely powerful and valuable tools within the school context. It is therefore worth investing time into setting up an overall approach to the use of them which involves everyone and which can support class teachers in meeting the needs of all pupils within their class (Ekins and Grimes, 2009).

The systems are also processes central to the role of the SENCO, in the effective management of resources and support to meet the needs of pupils with SEN within the school. However, to make these systems as effective as possible, there should be whole school understanding and ownership of the processes, which should be joined together in a dynamic way to ensure that each is meaningfully linked to direct action and support within the school. The SENCO should therefore reconsider the use of those processes and systems and start to consider not only how they are used from an individual SEN perspective, but more broadly, how they can be used and developed to enable a more strategic approach to SEN practice and provision across the whole school setting.

In the Inclusion in Action model (Ekins and Grimes, 2009), a different way of conceptualizing the systems is offered, which moves away from each system being seen as a separate component, towards a model in which all systems are dynamically linked to inform strategic development of practices across the whole school.

With the new direction of the SENCO role, reflecting the strategic, enabling, facilitating nature of the role, SENCOs can use and adapt the model to introduce and establish joined-up, meaningful strategic approaches to meeting needs within the school, in which all staff are involved and take responsibility.

To support the SENCO in developing a more strategic approach to key aspects of their role around coordinating provision and meeting needs, two case studies are presented below to highlight the different stages in development and practice at which schools may be operating.

CASE STUDY 1

In this school, individual members of staff have been identified to be allocated key areas of responsibility. They carry out their responsibilities with little communication with each other, and do not plan time to analyse patterns and trends which may arise from the data and information that they are responsible for, or to share information more widely with the individual class teachers involved.

Different processes are scheduled to happen at different times of the school year. This has been planned so as not to overburden staff, although some class teachers feel that there is an overlap in information systems because the key information that needs to be gathered to input into the range of processes required has not been identified.

The SENCO works hard to identify and understand the needs of pupils with SEN within the school. She sets up intervention groups and independently sets IEP targets to ensure that the primary needs of all pupils with SEN in the school are addressed through clear targets.

Time has not, however, been provided to enable effective discussion of those targets and intervention groups between the SENCO and the individual class teachers, and understanding of them across the whole school is therefore inconsistent.

The SENCO does not have a clear overview of assessment data and trends emerging from this across the school, as this is collated and filed by the Assessment Coordinator.

At times there is a conflict between intervention groups introduced by key curriculum coordinators and those set up by the SENCO. The setting-up of interventions is based upon knowledge of new programmes rather than any scrutiny of need within the school or cohort. Interventions therefore do not always fully meet the needs of pupils who are underachieving. The progress of pupils on interventions is not monitored or evaluated, so once pupils are identified and placed in an intervention group, they often remain in that group for the rest of their time at the school.

CASE STUDY 2

In this school there is an embedded understanding of the need for a whole school strategic approach to coordinating provision and meeting the needs of all pupils. Time has been set aside to ensure that all staff are enabled to contribute fully and effectively to Pupil Progress Review Meetings three times a year. These meetings provide an opportunity to consider the needs and progress of individual cohorts of pupils, and to draw on the expertise and ideas of a range of staff within the school to develop a more flexible and creative approach to responding to individual needs.

These meetings are prioritized within the school context, and it is important for key strategic leaders to be present to support the discussion of each cohort. The Headteacher, Assistant Headteacher, SENCO, Family Liaison Officer and Learning Mentor support each Pupil Progress Review Meeting, along with the class teacher (as well as the receiving class teacher at the end of the year) and teaching assistants where appropriate.

As a result of the presence of strategic leaders at every meeting, whole school trends and patterns of progress or underachievement can easily be identified. These are recorded, and then explored and addressed through a range of strategic processes, with the SENCO taking a central role in supporting and facilitating the development of effective discussions. To achieve this:

1   the Senior Leadership Team (including the SENCO) critically explore the identified issue from a range of perspectives, drawing on their individual expertise and knowledge of practice in different areas of the school;

2   a focus for development is identified to explore more fully with all staff. This is achieved through a staff meeting at the beginning of term to raise the issue and explore different perceptions of it, including new ways forward in

addressing it, with follow-up focus slots (10–15 minutes) during every staff meeting to review progress towards addressing the issue;

3   a learning wall is set up in the staffroom to help staff to focus upon the strategic issue being addressed and to aid the sharing of good practice and potential barriers. It is seen as a collaborative problem-solving resource;

4   significant issues are identified to be included in the School Development Plan, with a wider strategic response including pupils and parents planned to explore and address the issue.

Conclusion

Two very different approaches to the SENCO role are evidenced within the case studies above. Within one, the SENCO role, and SEN issues generally, are seen as very separate to other whole school practices and systems. The SENCO therefore works separately, reacting to situations as they arise, while trying to understand and meet the needs of pupils with SEN more fully. In the other, the issues and systems around SEN have become fully embedded within a whole school approach to meeting the needs of all pupils, and to identifying and addressing progress and underachievement strategically and systematically through a unified whole school approach.

SENCOs and schools cannot easily be expected to 'jump' from one approach to the other. Rather, a significant amount of work needs to be put into developing an underlying understanding of the need to link systems and processes together to more fully support a strategic approach to meeting the needs of all pupils.

The SENCO may therefore find it helpful to consider the Reflective questions below as a starting point to reviewing and evaluating existing practices within their school context.

Reflective questions

- Which case study most closely represents existing practices within your school setting?
- What values inform the existing culture within your school?
- How could good practice be developed strategically within your school setting?
- What may be the barriers in your school that prevent strategic development?
- What/who could be the supporters/resources that you could use to develop a more effective approach to removing barriers to learning and increasing participation for all learners?

References

Ainscow, M., Booth, T. and Dyson, A. (2006) *Improving Schools, Developing Inclusion.* Abingdon: Routledge.

Booth, T. and Ainscow, M. (2002) *Index for Inclusion: Developing Learning and Participation in Schools,* rev. edn. Bristol: CSIE.

DCSF (2007) *Primary National Strategy: Pupil Progress Meetings, Prompts and Guidance.* London: The Stationery Office.

DES (1999) *The National Curriculum Key Stages 1 and 2.* London: DES.

DfES (2001) *Special Educational Needs: Code of Practice.* London: DfES.

DfES (2004) *Using Curricular Targets.* London: DfES.

DfES (2006) *Leading on Intervention.* London: DfES.

Durrant, J. and Holden, G. (2006) *Teachers Leading Change: Doing Research for School Improvement.* London: Paul Chapman Publishing.

Ekins, A. and Grimes, P. (2009) *Inclusion: Developing an Effective Whole School Approach.* Maidenhead: Open University Press.

Fullan, M. (2004) *Leading in a Culture of Change.* San Francisco: John Wiley & Sons.

Harris, B. (2007) *Supporting the Emotional Work of School Leaders.* London: Paul Chapman Publishing.

Ofsted (2006) *Best Practice in Self Evaluation.* London: Ofsted.

TDA (2009) *The Learning Outcomes for Those Successfully Completing Nationally Approved Training for SENCOs.* London: TDA.

10

MANAGING FINANCIAL AND PHYSICAL RESOURCES

Pam Davies and John Hattersley

Introduction

Competition between schools, a lack of clear vision for inclusion and not knowing how to include some very complex or challenging children into schools led one Local Authority to take an approach which successfully developed culture, attitudes and practice. Case studies exemplify the importance of building change in the learning and experience of people 'doing the job' and the need for a courageous senior management to allow such an organic process of change.

Step One: changing the attitude and practice of established and respected practitioners and winning their advocacy

Beginning with an understanding that a 'long view' is required to change attitudes and culture, the first required step is captured by a recognition of the need to change but a lack of understanding as to how to go about it.

Inclusion was not viewed positively by most teachers, schools and local authority officers in January 2001 in the Local Authority (LA) in which these case studies are based. Some viewed it with suspicion, some with a deep sense of protectiveness, and others held a view that while it may be the right thing to do, it was not a realistic or practical approach to meeting the needs of children with SEN. Some mainstream colleagues felt fear and inadequacy, while SEN colleagues felt their own specialist status might be under threat. This range of arguments was echoed by parents who were on the extremes of a continuum for and against inclusion. At the end of debate we heard the following question in the background; 'But how do we do it?'

There was an absence of practical day-to-day understanding of how to include. A culture where anything which might reflect badly on standards was feared and the deep-seated attitudes of SEN being the preserve of the specialist needed to be changed.

Any change generates stress, fear and resistance. If the consequences of getting it wrong is damaging the welfare of children and teachers, then resistance is understandably greater. To change attitudes and practice across over 350 schools and a large children's service this fear needed to be understood. The voice of people involved at the point of delivery, the children, the parents and the teachers all needed to be heard and responded to.

To address these fears and find out what worked, a small-scale project with 25 very different schools; primary, secondary, special; leafy lane, urban, rural; top of the league table and bottom were invited to explore a simple question: 'OK, we know we should be inclusive, but how do we do it in the classroom every day with ordinary teachers and very few teaching assistants?' These schools identified 'champions', some experienced, some NQTs, who would research inclusive practice, trial it in their classrooms and model it on a day-to-day basis demonstrating the real benefits, or otherwise, for all children.

Action research gave a framework for teachers to explore and reflect upon their own practice and with a model of coaching and mentoring, these became the main tools supporting change. Teachers quickly found they were challenging their own practice using a new vocabulary of learning.

Other teachers, and parents, could quickly see how successfully children with significant, and in some cases very complex needs could be included and thrive but also bring benefit to the rest of their class and school. Action research in every school showed that rather than a negative impact on standards, there was a positive impact by removing barriers to learning for the most vulnerable.

The 'lead learners', as they were designated, became advocates who were passionate about inclusion and felt there was a reality to 'learning to learn'. These champions became the vanguard to change practice, attitude and culture of their school and showed what was practically possible to others.

Key messages from the first phase were:

- Understand what inclusion is and isn't! Why are we saying it is important? What is the evidence that it is a good thing?

- The teacher is the adult, therefore must continually build and rebuild a relationship with a vulnerable and challenging child despite daily rejection and setback.

- The teacher is as much a learner as the children. When the children are asked how the teacher could teach better, they know. The children are the experts, not the teacher.

- Leadership which gives permission to fail is essential. Teachers need to know their leadership supports and understands inclusion.

- A 'long view' needs to be taken when considering the benefit and success of the inclusion of a child in a school.

- Systems and structures (alongside poorly managed emotional exchanges) are often what lead to exclusion and alienation. We seem to think that to be fair we must treat every child the same. To be truly fair we need to treat every child in a way which will bring the best out in them.

- Partnership in the staff room is as important as between schools, services and parents. Teachers need to open their classroom door.

CASE STUDY 1

Primary school

The project
The funding received enabled the whole school to look again at inclusion with a much broader vision and scope, not solely looking at including children with Moderate Learning Difficulty (MLD) but identifying the different learning styles that can give every child in the school success.

The goals
- To identify multiple learning processes.
- To identify existing good practice.
- To develop and incorporate good practice in every classroom.
- To motivate and celebrate each member of staff.
- To maintain good practice and whole school inclusive awareness through and beyond the period of the project.

The process
- Whole school in-service training day.
- Lead learner working in every classroom with each member of teaching and non-teaching staff.
- Planning sessions with all teams – Foundation Level, Key Stage 1, Key Stage 2 – Lower Junior and Upper Junior.
- Video snapshots and display.
- Presentation to parents and governors.

Who was involved?
Families, staff, governors and the children of this primary school.

Impact
- The children (and staff) recognized their own intelligences and talents.
- A raised awareness of inclusion by all staff – that it is for all children not only those with statements.
- Resources were effectively mobilized including parent helpers and support from the local high school.
- Following the introduction of daily exercise sessions for children with dyspraxia or immature co-ordination, the educational psychologist noted the marked improvement in learning.
- Commitment to continued development of inclusive practice.
- Celebration of the collaborative development of a school for all.
- School awarded Inclusion Charter Mark.

Stage Two: partnerships between schools to develop inclusion

Schools in competition will never be able to take responsibility for every child in their community without being worried about their position in the community and in the eyes of the parents who are interested in 'league tables'. The benefits of a higher education partner as a critical friend, and local leadership and decision making are critical to the long-term success but the key was to use the expertise of practitioners not 'experts'.

The local authority now had 25 schools and 50+ teachers, across all age ranges, subjects and communities that had moved their practice towards being more inclusive. There was a real understanding and passion, based upon evidenced action research, that inclusion was beneficial to all children in the school. In fact, many lead learners found that inclusive practice made life easier and they rediscovered the delights of teaching. These schools and teachers became the core of a team enabled to share practice more widely.

To build partnerships where there were none began with incentives. Every school was offered funding to develop inclusive practice but only if they did this in partnership with other schools.

Over 350 schools joined with partners to make 19 'Inclusion Clusters'. At times, difficult negotiations, conflicts and unrealistic plans looked likely to de-rail the initiative but simple solutions at a practical class teacher level provided the route to success. Health, social care, parents, children, local politicians and school-based ancillary staff were all included in development activities where they could consider what inclusion was, why it was important and how they could do it on the ground.

Success varied far more than with the first stage of the project. Giving choice and ownership to the clusters meant less control by the local authority. Professionals were encouraged to explore their own solutions which generated a culture of learning, exploration and sharing their own good practice. There was an explicit intent to build the professionals own judgement and reflective behaviour rather than give them a 'handbook' based upon the previous project.

As each partnership developed, clear differences in the activities and philosophy of clusters emerged. Of the 19 Inclusion Clusters, 16 were described as successfully impacting on the confidence of staff to include SEN children and positive outcomes for vulnerable children could be identified. The less successful tended to be those with over-complicated, aspirational plans. They focused less on what matters to individual practitioners in the classroom and listened less. Typically there was an imposed top-down strategy with a strong leader in the partnership.

Obeng (1997) argues that in periods of rapid change an organization needs to learn new ways of doing things faster than they can manage. Obeng suggests that a rigidly hierarchical organization can be limited by the rate of learning of those at the top.

Schools and teachers were being asked to manage huge change from all directions but senior managers, who had little experience of inclusion, had to create an environment where their practitioners could learn how to do it.

The successful Inclusion Clusters were able to bring forward significant leaders who may have been relatively inexperienced but were willing to trial, explore and share new approaches to problems. Rather than a hierarchically driven model for change, we saw a more networked leadership model with different leaders coming forward for different parts of the programme. Above all, people were willing and enabled to take risks.

Some rigour and quality assurance were introduced as schools were supported to self-evaluate using an Inclusion Charter Mark and their success was celebrated in whole cluster events where children, parents, teachers and teaching assistants from all the schools in the partnership came together to share best practice and celebrate inclusion.

The University of Manchester evaluated the success of the project. Two strengths were identified: the impact on classroom practice and the collaboration between schools:

> There has been a significant impact on inclusive classroom practice and on the creation of inclusive solutions to the challenge of the diversity of learners . . . the idea of school-to-school collaboration is well established and developing in ways that should have a longer term impact.
>
> (Ainscow et al., 2005)

Lessons learned

- To form partnerships where there is a history of conflict, incentives need to be high.
- A focus on simple, practical projects where success can be experienced quickly builds trust and communication.
- People working with children from a range of services can collectively share their expertise leading to better outcomes.
- Leadership is not always from 'the top'. Practitioners working together to solve practical problems generate high levels of ownership, engagement and solutions which work.

CASE STUDY 2

Small cluster

The initial difficulties encountered in this compact cluster of eight primaries feeding into their local high school were due to the historic competition between the primaries and the lack of trust in the equitable use of central funding held by the high school. Initially the schools had wanted to divide the funding nine ways but it soon became apparent that by keeping the funding centrally they would have far more buying/brokering power.

The goals
- To establish a steering group to develop an action for cluster development.
- To develop a cluster-wide Inclusion Policy.

- To provide a range of CPD for teachers in response to need.
- To extend and develop inclusive classroom practice.
- To improve outcomes for children and young people with a range of learning difficulties and disabilities.

Who was involved?

It was agreed that the steering group would be more effective if not made up of Headteachers. The group was comprised of Deputy Heads and/or SENCOs and was led by the Deputy Head from the high school, with administrative support.

The process

An initial action plan was drawn up for joint CPD which looked at 'Levers for Inclusion'. A pattern of breakfast meetings was established where representatives from the nine schools were able to share concerns in an atmosphere of mutual support. The LA Inclusion Facilitator supported these meetings and the cluster moved forward delivering the following initial training:

- 1 day CPD on Circle of Friends – Peer Support.
- 1 day CPD on Peer Mentoring – Peer Listening Service.
- 1 day CPD on Restorative Justice – Relationship Mending.
- Established working group for Gifted and Talented Programme.
- Cluster Conference with range of inclusive workshops.
- Joint Arts Project.

Impact

- Schools have well-established Peer Mentoring systems.
- Professionals work across schools with work shadowing and team teaching.
- Effective use of art therapy.
- Introduction of counselling service for parents and children.
- Employment of CAMHS worker.
- Schools awarded the county's Inclusion Charter Mark.
- Clusters have developed into effective Education Improvement Partnerships.

This cluster of schools has, following a very shaky start, been successful in delivering improved outcomes for all pupils and improved confidence for teachers and teaching assistants in a range of schools serving a diverse population.

Stage Three: the SEN review

Changing structures for SEN is fraught with risk and challenge. There can be families arguing for total inclusion whatever the complexity, sharing a consultation table with someone who feels that Special School provision is the right thing for almost every child with special needs. SEN reviews are thought of as a synonym for closing a school where there are children, families and teachers who will be justifiably proud of provision.

The natural focus will be to engage with families and schools but focusing entirely on families and schools can backfire. Equal attention must be given to local authority services which work with the children.

The inclusion programme has changed attitudes and the face of provision for SEN. Children with complex SEN and/or disability were in mainstream classes, units and special schools, most achieving well whatever the type of setting.

The SEN review began with an audit, giving a profile of current provision; the effectiveness of this; predicted future trends and population needs; costs; budget and national and local drivers.

The review led to a 'redesignation' of special units in primary schools as 'resourced provisions'; a closure by any other name but with less controversy perhaps? Secondary school units were closed and the funding distributed to every school to build their own 'resourced provision' to cater for all the children with SEN and/or disability in their community who did not need a special school placement.

Parents whose children were currently in a particular type of provision were assured their children would complete their education where they were. However, professionals working within or with specialist provisions could sense threat to their own position. Colleagues from other services such as health and social care had little engagement other than at a strategic level and therefore little understanding about the rationale behind the new provisions. Even officers working within the LA felt 'in the dark'. In short, by focusing on the confidence of families and schools, the local authority service teams were lost.

The implementation plan embedded this problem by once again focusing on schools and families. Each school knew and understood its local population and community. They had children with different needs, accommodation and staff. Consequently each school developed a 'resourced provision' which was right for their community and bespoke support was provided. Again local authority teams were not part of this process and so alienation and resentment built.

Lessons learned

- Every stakeholder is vital.
- Failure to engage key partners can lead to losing momentum.
- Families can be very supportive through a significant review if they are engaged throughout and do not experience any surprises or threats to what they value.
- Families, and their children, often have the answers before people supporting them do. They are waiting to be asked.

CASE STUDY 3

Resourced primary school

The primary school in this case study applied for Resourced Provision status and funding to develop a service for all the schools in the cluster (seven primaries and one high school). Some LA officers were sceptical that the 'Outreach Model' would be a token gesture and not actually provide any improved outcomes for children in any school.

The project

To develop an effective outreach model of support to develop effective inclusive practice in all schools in the cluster.

The goals

- To provide support and advice for teachers in mainstream schools to meet the needs of children with a range of learning difficulties and disabilities.
- To provide practical support – in class.
- To provide help with ensuring that planning is inclusive.
- To provide improved outcomes for children.
- To provide parent/carer support.

Impact

- Provision launched through SENCO Network.
- Established parent/carer 'drop-in' facility.
- Established social skills and Safe Space sessions in all schools.
- Advice for teachers on assessment methods, formulation of IEPs, IBPs.
- In-class modification/alternative strategies and team teaching.
- Advice to High School re-inclusion of pupils working significantly below age-related national levels.
- Positive feedback from all stakeholders to Resourced Base Team.
- Continuity of swift response service with an easy referral system to all schools in the cluster.
- Pupils happy and making progress.

Editors' note: The Local Authority explored in this case study has undergone considerable change which is explored more fully in the evaluative report produced by the University of Manchester (Ainscow et al., 2005).

References

Ainscow, M., Fox, S. and Francis, A. (2005) *Evaluation Report: Outcomes of the Inclusion Cluster Programme in Cheshire*. Manchester: University of Manchester.

Obeng, E. (1997) *New Rules for the New World*. Oxford: Capstone Publishing.

11

CHALLENGING DISABLING ATTITUDES AND STEREOTYPES

Angharad E. Beckett

Inclusive Education is increasingly being seen as being about more than 'mainstreaming' alone. It is also about ensuring that schools become truly 'inclusive' environments with associated values and ethos (Sapon-Shevin, 2005; Armstrong and Barton, 2007). Addressing disabling attitudes is an important part of building inclusive school communities that are supportive of disabled young people (Beckett, 2009). Encouraging non-disabled children to befriend disabled children and eliminating bullying of disabled children are crucial to developing inclusive communities. This chapter argues that efforts need to go beyond this, however, to promote positive attitudes towards *all* disabled people, i.e. disabled people *beyond the school gates*. This is important because if we are concerned about the life-chances of our disabled pupils, then we will want to do our best to foster an inclusive and enabling society.

The broadening of the concept of Inclusive Education is mirrored in policy and legislation, most crucially the introduction of the Disability Equality Duty (DED) (2006) and its application to schools. The DED involves duties to 'eliminate harassment' and to 'promote positive attitudes towards disabled people'.[1] Schools are now legally required to become proactive about changing attitudes towards disabled people. This is clearly an issue for Headteachers and governing bodies.

SENCOs have not, to date, been officially allocated responsibility for developing schools' strategies regarding the DED, but it is likely that they will often be/have been delegated or involved in this task. If SENCOs represent the teachers most committed to the philosophy of Inclusive Education, then this must be a good thing. SENCOs can do no more, however, than co-ordinate a strategy that must be supported by all school staff. It is the argument here that before embarking on a process of developing this type of strategy, SENCOs may find it helpful to consider three issues in particular: first, the justification for promoting positive attitudes towards disabled people; second, the evidence surrounding non-disabled children's attitudes towards disabled people; third, the challenges that schools/teachers may face, or believe that they face, when seeking to promote positive attitudes towards disabled people. The remaining sections of this chapter will consider each of these issues in turn.

What is the justification for these strategies?

Struggling under the weight of league table pressures (Lowe, 2007) and an arguably 'over-stuffed' curriculum (Peters, 2002), some teachers may feel that duties under the DED are simply an expectation too far. The presence of a legal requirement may not be enough to convince everyone of its importance. In an effort to convince colleagues that their school really has a vital role to play in challenging disabling attitudes, it may be helpful for SENCOs to remind them that the DED arises from many years of campaigning and struggle on the part of disabled people and their organizations (DPOs).

In 1979, the Union of People with Impairments Against Segregation (UPIAS) defined 'disability' as being the result of society's failure to address the needs of people with impairments, effectively excluding them from mainstream economic and community life. The UPIAS definition of disability influenced the development of the Social Model of Disability by Oliver (1990). It distinguishes between barriers facing individuals associated with their impairments (e.g. a mobility impairment) and those that result from the ways in which society is organized (e.g. a lack of access, employment discrimination) which bring about disability. The model does not deny the reality of impairment or minimize the impact that this has upon an individual's life, but states that the causes of disability lie beyond the body of an individual, within a 'disabling society' (Barnes et al., 2002).

Over the past 20 years, there have been improvements to the position of disabled people in the UK, but there is ample evidence that the disabling society remains. Disabling barriers continue to be documented within education and employment, transport and the built environment, and independent living and leisure activities (see Miller et al., 2006). To this evidence should be added the rise in 'disability hate crime'. Such is the extent of the ongoing injustice, the charity Scope recently sought to introduce the term 'disablism'.

Disabling attitudes and stereotypes are embedded within the dominant culture, acting to maintain the disabling society. Many attempts have been made to describe and understand these attitudes. A useful starting point is Clark and Marsh's (2002: 1) statement that:

> If [people] behave as if the problem is with the individual, they will take a different approach than if they regard the problem as being with the attitudes, systems and practices that create disabling barriers.

Many disabled people report that disabling attitudes can act as a greater barrier to their achievements than the difficulties that may be associated with their particular impairment.

Stereotyping disabled people is a form of disabling attitude. Employing false social constructs in this way de-humanizes and removes the individuality of disabled people. The subjects of stereotyping often experience name-calling, bullying and even violence. Disabled people have consistently identified ten common stereotypes (Biklen and Bogdana, 1977; Barnes, 1992). Disabled people are seen as:

1   pitiable or pathetic (reduced to being the objects of 'charity');

2   objects of violence ('dependent' and 'helpless', unable to fight back);

3   sinister and evil (the 'baddy' in many media portrayals);

4   a curio (as having 'freakish' impairments);

5   an object of ridicule (the 'hapless fools');

6   the 'supercripple' (having to 'over-achieve' in order to be considered worthy of respect);

7   their own worst and only enemy ('self-pitiers' who need to 'stop feeling sorry for themselves');

8   a burden (e.g. on a family);

9   a perpetual child (asexual);

10   incapable of fully participating in everyday life (left out/sidelined).

These stereotypes do not just exist within the 'adult' world, but have also been identified, for example, within children's literature (Quicke, 1985; Rieser and Mason, 1990; Beckett et al., 2010a).

In the same way that implicit or explicit racist or sexist attitudes are acquired through the learning process, so too are disabling attitudes. As Rieser and Mason (1990: 7) state children are not born with negative attitudes towards disabled people 'but acquire them from adults, the media, and the general way in which society is organised'. As children grow up, to a greater or lesser extent and consciously or unconsciously, they perpetuate these attitudes, and ultimately, maintain the disabling society. The impact of disabling attitudes justifies any efforts to challenge them. Many institutions, from families to the media, have responsibilities here, but so too do schools, which are well placed to play an important role in this regard.

Is there any evidence that non-disabled children express disabling attitudes?

To date, this question has received insufficient attention from researchers. In 2007, however, the ESRC funded a study, led by the author, to explore primary-age non-disabled children's attitudes towards disabled people.[2] The study concluded in 2009 and findings suggested that many non-disabled children *do* express attitudes that, no matter how naïvely articulated, are, or have the potential to be, disabling (Beckett et al., 2010b).

The research revealed that children, like many adults, tend to view the body as the site or source of the 'problem' of disability and seldom articulate anything that approximates to a social model of understanding. Exceptions were the attitudes of children in a school where the social model of disability informs the school's approach to disability awareness. There was some evidence of the 'curio' stereotype within children's attitudes, with both age groups finding the idea of 'different bodies' fascinating and frightening. For some children this was reinforced by their viewing of 'Body Shock'-type TV programmes,[3] which generated both fearful and somewhat voyeuristic responses.

Evidence of the 'incapable' stereotype was also found within children's views. Many children were uncertain whether disabled people could work, have relationships or marry. Children also perceived disability to be a personal tragedy (the 'pitiable and pathetic' stereotype), referring to incidents of bullying of disabled people and describing the lives of disabled people as 'hard', 'horrible' and 'lonely'. At first glance this may not, and probably *is* not, the most worrying of the children's attitudes – it was clear, for example, that they thought that bullying was a 'bad thing'. This tragedy approach, however, is rejected by many disabled people because it is all too often associated with sentiments of pity and a distant, charitable response, rather than the preferred empathetic and empowering approach (French and Swain, 2004). The personal tragedy model also underlies assumptions that a 'disabled life is not worth living', an idea expressed by at least one child.

So far, this may appear to be a gloomy appraisal of the attitudes of non-disabled children. Findings were not all so pessimistic. Many children were clearly thinking about how 'we' (non-disabled people) ought to treat disabled people, stressing the importance of treating disabled people *kindly* or *fairly* and not bullying them. This is encouraging. Further, evidence suggests that children's attitudes towards disabled people are not always intractable and that they can/do respond positively to accurate information. Children who had been encouraged to think about disabling attitudes and barriers were more likely to express some more positive attitudes towards disabled people. These were the children most likely to state, giving examples, that the position of disabled people in society is not always 'fair'.

What was clear, however, was that none of the children interviewed had received much information about the lives of disabled people. This is significant because according to a classic definition (Allport, 1954), prejudice exists when people continue to hold negative attitudes even when new knowledge, that should challenge those attitudes, is introduced. If children have not received sufficient knowledge about the lives of disabled people, then it becomes difficult to say for certain whether they are exhibiting prejudice 'proper' against disabled people. Arguably, however, although interesting, firming up this distinction is somewhat less important than acknowledging that the answer to the question 'is there any evidence that non-disabled children express disabling attitudes?' is 'yes', however these attitudes are understood.

What challenges do teachers believe they face when seeking to address disabling attitudes and stereotypes?

The ESRC-funded study referenced above also explored this question (Beckett et al., 2010b). As part of the research, a survey of English primary schools investigated what, if anything, schools are doing to promote positive attitudes towards disabled people and what, if any, challenges they face when seeking to achieve this. Before considering the findings of this survey, it may be of interest to the reader to know that 57 per cent of respondent schools admitted that they 'could do more' in this regard.[4]

In terms of perceived challenges, 'finding time' was an issue for some schools: 45.4 per cent of schools stated that there is inadequate time within the existing teaching framework to implement relevant strategies.[5] Interestingly, however, the schools that stated that time was not a problem/challenge, were more likely to report that they brought disability into the wider curriculum.

Schools also reported difficulties in accessing suitable teaching and learning resources. For example, 32 per cent of schools stated that they had no inclusive-type books[6] (books that convey positive messages about disabled people). Good quality resources of this type are available,[7] however, and there is persuasive evidence that inclusive literature can impact positively upon non-disabled children's attitudes towards disabled peers and others (e.g. Umerlik, 1992; Heim, 1994; Andrews, 1998, and others). In total, 21 per cent of schools reported that they had no resources of *any kind* (e.g. books, lesson plans, action packs, DVDs, etc.) that facilitated teaching and learning about disability and those with a high proportion of pupils who have 'special educational needs' were the least likely to have any resource. This is a worrying finding, not least because if disabled children are to develop positive self-images, it is important that they see/are able to access positive images and ideas about 'people like me'.

Concerns also relate to one possible explanation for this situation. Several respondent schools indicated that they believed that their 'best resource' is their disabled pupil or pupils and suggested that if disabled children are present within a school, no additional resources are required. This type of thinking is not supported by research evidence. Doubts have consistently been raised about whether, without any additional intervention or resource, proximity between disabled and non-disabled children is sufficient to break down disabling attitudes – on the whole, evidence suggests that it is not (e.g. Shapiro and Margolis, 1988; Umerlik, 1992).

During interviews with teachers in a sub-sample of schools that had responded to the survey, teachers were also asked about the message that they believed they should be conveying to non-disabled children about disability and the lives of disabled people. Views expressed ranged from an approximation of a social model approach described earlier, to other, considerably less progressive understandings and those that indicated both confusion and uncertainty about how disability should be approached. Underpinning many responses was a sense – expressed forcefully in some cases – that teachers lack sufficient knowledge about disability politics (please note the small 'p' here), particularly the appropriate use of language, to feel entirely confident about approaching the issue.

Several teachers stated that it was important that children had positive encounters with disabled people, including disabled adults. As previously mentioned, research supports the idea that meeting disabled adults and hearing about the barriers that they have encountered is a valuable learning experience (Beckett et al., 2010b). Nevertheless, in the majority of cases, teachers emphasized the difficulties involved in arranging these encounters. It need not be difficult to arrange, however, because there are many local disabled people's organizations that work with schools and could be approached about school visits. There are also disabled-led arts organizations like Shape and theatre companies such as Graeae and other inclusive drama companies that offer training and workshop experiences for schools, for example, Chicken Shed and Deafinitely Theatre.

What these research findings suggest, therefore, is that it is important that SENCOs explore both the well-founded and, sometimes, less well-founded concerns of colleagues. One place to start when developing a strategy to challenge disabling attitudes would be to determine whether all members of teaching staff feel confident that the following is the case: first, that there is sufficient time, space and opportunity within the school year to approach this issue proactively; second, that sufficient resources are available to facilitate relevant teaching and/or learning activities; third, that they are sufficiently knowledgeable about disability politics, are aware of the common stereotypes about disabled people, understand the impact of disabling attitudes and know what 'message' disabled people would like to be conveyed to non-disabled children.

Conclusion

As educators from pre-school to HE (i.e. this applies to the author as much as to the likely reader), we all need to play our part in dismantling the disabling society. Challenging disabling attitudes and stereotypes is key to achieving this and evidence relating to the attitudes of non-disabled children suggests that there is work to be done in this regard. It is not enough for us to be 'nice' people ourselves and to expect our values automatically to transfer to our students – if only it was this easy! We need to be adequately informed and have the confidence to talk to our pupils/students about disability and the lives of disabled people and to encourage them to develop positive attitudes towards disabled people. In short, it is important that schools (together with other educational establishments) establish proper teaching and learning strategies in this area.

Notes

1   Full list of DED requirements available at: http://www.teachernet.gov.uk/wholeschool/disability/disabilityandthedda/requirementsofschoolsunderthedda/ (accessed 20 February 2010).
2   ESRC RES-062-23-0461. For full details of this study including methodology, see the Final Report, downloadable at: http://www.sociology.leeds.ac.uk/research/projects/deeps.
3   Programmes referred to by children included *Half Man Half Tree*, shown during a series entitled 'My Shocking Story' (Discovery Channel) and *Extraordinary People* (Channel 5) and *The Girl with Eight Limbs*, part of Channel 4's 'Body Shock' series. This type of programme has widely been termed contemporary 'freak-show TV'.
4   500 schools surveyed. 137 responses.
5   97 per cent response rate to question. 44.6 per cent 'there is adequate time', 10 per cent 'unsure'.
6   79 per cent response rate to question.
7   See leaflet 'Inclusion Literature: a guide to books for disability awareness', download-able at: http://www.sociology.leeds.ac.uk/assets/files/research/deeps/inclusionlitera-tureguide.pdf (accessed 20 February 2010).

References

Allport, G. W. (1954) *The Nature of Prejudice*. Cambridge, MA: Addison-Wesley.

Andrews, S.E. (1998) Using inclusion literature to promote positive attitudes toward disabilities, *Journal of Adolescent and Adult Literacy*, 41(6): 420–6.

Armstrong, F. and Barton. L. (2007) Policy, experience and change and the challenge of inclusion, in L. Barton and F. Armstrong (eds) *Policy, Experience and Change: Cross-Cultural Reflections on Inclusive Education*. Dordrecht: Springer.

Barnes, C. (1992) *Disabling Imagery and the Media: An Exploration of the Principles for Media Representations of Disabled People*. Halifax: BCODP and Ryeburn Publishing.

Barnes, C., Oliver, M. and Barton, L. (eds) (2002) *Disability Studies Today*. Cambridge: Polity Press.

Beckett, A. E. (2009) 'Challenging disabling attitudes, building an inclusive society': considering the role of education in encouraging non-disabled children to develop positive attitudes towards disabled people, *British Journal of Sociology of Education*, 30(3): 317–29.

Beckett, A. E., Ellison, N., Barrett, S. and Shah, S. (2010a) 'Away with the Fairies?' Disability within primary-age children's literature, *Disability and Society*, 25(3): 373–86.

Beckett, A. E., Ellison, N., Barrett, S., Shah, S., Buckner, L. and Byrne, D. S. (2010b) *Disability Equality in English Primary Schools*. ESRC Final Report. Available at: http://www.sociology.leeds.ac.uk/research/projects/deeps (accessed 31 March 2010).

Biklen, D. and Bogdana, R. (1977) Media portrayal of disabled people: a study of stereotypes, *Inter-racial Children's Book Bulletin*, 8(6 and 7): 4–9.

Clark, L. and Marsh, S. (2002) Patriarchy in the UK: the language of disability. Disability Archive, University of Leeds. Available at: http://www.leeds.ac.uk/disability-studies/archiveuk/Clark,%20Laurence/language.pdf (accessed 20 February 2010).

French, S. and Swain, J. (2004) Whose tragedy?: towards a personal non-tragedy view of disability, in J. Swain, S. French, C. Barnes and C. Thomas (eds) *Disabling Barriers – Enabling Environments*, 2nd edn. London: Sage.

Heim, A. B. (1994) Beyond the stereotypes: characters with mental disabilities in children's books, *School Library Journal*, 40(9): 139–42.

Lowe, R. (2007) *The Death of Progressive Education: How Teachers Lost Control of the Classroom*. London: Routledge.

Miller, P., Gillinson, S. and Huber, J. (2006) *Disablist Britain: Barriers to Independent Living for Disabled People in 2006*. London: Scope.

Oliver, M. (1990) *The Politics of Disablement*. Basingstoke: Macmillan.

Peters, L.C. (2002) Reflections from across the Atlantic: What can we (and the U.S. Governors) learn from the U.K. education reform experience? *Curriculum Inquiry*, 28(2): 259–62.

Quicke, J. (1985) *Disability in Modern Children's Fiction*. London: Croom Helm.

Rieser, R. and Mason, M. (1990) *Disability Equality in the Classroom: A Human Rights Issue*. London: ILEA.

Sapon-Shevin, M. (2005) Ability differences in the classroom: teaching and learning in inclusive classrooms, in D. Byrnes and G. Kyger (eds) *Common Bonds: Anti-Bias Teaching in a Diverse Society*, 3rd edn. Olney, MD: ACEI.

Shapiro, A. and Margolis, H. (1988) Changing negative peer attitudes toward students with learning disabilities, *Reading and Writing Quarterly*, 4(2): 133–46.

Umerlik, A. (1992) Fostering an understanding of the disabled through young adult literature, *School Library Media Activities Monthly*, 8(9): 35–6.

PART IV
Coordinating provision

Introduction to Part IV

The three chapters in Part IV are designed to address the section contained within the Learning Outcomes framework, Coordinating Provision. This is made up of three themes, which deal with assessment and accountability, data collection and analysis, and staff deployment and resource management.

Chapter 12, by Cathy Svensson and Bridget Middlemas, focuses on Assessment and the development of a dyslexia-friendly primary school. It is written as a case study, which considers a number of elements of the strategic vision needed to fulfil this aim, including staff training, Assessment for Learning (AfL), the need to focus on all achievements, and the development of high expectations for all. The strategic role of the SENCo is examined, as a member of the Senior Leadership Team in the school, in a wider Local Authority role, and in Continuing Professional Development. The major steps in developing the dyslexia-friendly school are seen to include more flexible groupings; multi-sensory learning, based on assistive ICT; improved pedagogic practice; embedded AfL practices, and responding to pupil voice. This content has applicability to the Learning Outcomes contained in the theme 'Developing, using, monitoring and evaluating systems', which include:

- identifying pupils who may have SEN and/or disabilities (using classroom observation, data, assessment and other forms of monitoring);
- helping colleagues to have realistic expectations of behaviour for pupils with SEN and/or disabilities and set appropriately challenging targets for them;
- planning approaches and interventions to meet the needs of pupils with SEN and/or disabilities, geared to removing or minimizing barriers to participation and learning;
- recording and reviewing the progress of pupil with SEN and/or disabilities towards learning targets;
- assessing the effectiveness of provision for pupils with SEN and/or disabilities.

Two particular reflective elements are developed further in the chapter. The way in which dyslexia is understood, and the educational implications that stem from this, are drawn from British Dyslexia Association resources. The chapter acknowledges that there is contention around these understandings, and notes that dyslexia is a contested concept; the need to consider the strengths that the condition might bring is stressed. The chapter also highlights the need to consider further the link between important elements that are fundamental to the development of a dyslexia-friendly school; these include personalized learning, formative assessment, provision mapping, and target setting.

The next contributor, Bob Franks offers a critique of data gathering, in Chapter 13. The main part of this chapter deals with three important benchmarking instruments: CASPA, RAISEonline, and the National Strategies Progression Guidance; these are described and evaluated in tabular form. In the early part of the chapter, consideration is given to the need for data gathering, in setting SMART targets and in providing baseline assessments, and some weaknesses of current diagnostic tools are identified, in particular their lack of linkage to current curricula. The critique is developed by an examination of what constitutes good progress, and at what levels expectations should be set. An extensive review of other available resources is given, including a selection of e-resources. The chapter can be seen to be representative of the Learning Outcomes contained within the theme 'Using tools for collecting, analysing and using data', which should enable SENCOs to:

- know how school, local authority and national data systems work, including RAISEonline;
- analyse and interpret relevant, local, national and school data to inform policy and practices, expectations, and targets for improving the learning of pupils with SEN and/or disabilities.

In Chapter 13, Bob develops two themes that require an evaluative and reflective approach. In the first, a number of key factors associated with achievement for pupils with SEN are suggested, including non-linear progress, the difficulty of making secure judgements of very small step progress, and socio-economic and well-being factors that may make achievement problematic. Two further contentious issues within this theme are identified; prevailing attitudes that produce variable expectations of success; and the need to consider progress for pupils who experience a lack of a stimulating learning environment tailored to their needs.

The second theme broadens the first into a discussion around what constitutes good progress for pupils with SEN and/or disability across the full range of Key Stages. This is heightened by the wide variability both within, and across categories of SEN, making comparability in achievement difficult to assess. This, in turn, makes it hard to judge the best interventions at Wave 2 and Wave 3.

Chapter 14 is written by Gill Richards, Alison Patterson and Linda Lyn-Cook, and describes practice in a Local Authority in the Midlands, designed to increase participation and decrease bureaucracy. The model adopted by the Local Authority has removed Statements from procedures and practice in the area. This change occurred in response to a recognition that the Statementing process, while conceived as good practice, had become drawn out, bureaucratic and costly. It also gave rise to inequalities of provision, often based on where the young person lived, rather than on their needs. The account describes how this process was simplified, by delegating responsibilities, and finance, to School Families; the assessment of need to establish resource allocation has become something that the Family has a vested interest in getting right, with fairness and equity paramount. That this is tied to the pre-specification of aims and outcomes, rather than deciding these after the allocation of resources, is seen as an added bonus. This case study is seen to demonstrate the Learning Outcomes in the theme 'Deploying staff and managing resources', which should enable SENCOs to:

- delegate tasks appropriately, deploy and manage staff effectively to ensure the most efficient use of teaching and other expertise;
- make flexible and innovative use of the available workforce.

The area offering greatest scope for reflection and critical analysis centres on the flexibility offered but seldom utilized within systems. The requirements laid down in legislation such as the SEN and Disability Act (SENDA) (2001), the Disability Discrimination Act (DDA) (2005), while statutory, give flexibility in making provision, and this flexibility has been used by the LA to focus funding at the point of need, and in so doing reduce costs, and speed up the impact of resourcing.

In giving examples of coordinated provision, the chapters in this part, while focusing on a theme, have implicitly evidenced Learning Outcomes from the other themes in the Section. Assessment has featured in each chapter, and the inter-relationship of assessment processes, data recording and analysis, and target setting is discussed in all three contributions. Similarly, it is possible to develop the emergent themes outlined in the contributions by linking them to other Sections of the Learning Outcomes Framework. The influence of legislation, and the presence of statutory frameworks, makes up the first theme within the Section Professional Context, for example. The third theme within that Section, 'Using evidence about learning, teaching and assessment to inform practice', would seem to align strongly with the subjects dealt with in the chapters in Part IV. Further examples of this cross-realization of Learning Outcomes would include examples from 'Strategic financial planning, budget management and use of resources' (Section 2 Strategic Development of SEN Policy and Procedures), and from 'Promoting professional direction to the work of others' (Section 4 Leading, Developing and Supporting Colleagues).

This again invites the comment that an evidential basis for demonstrating the Learning Outcomes is not dependent on an approach based on meeting each one singly. The richness and variety that come from evaluating and critiquing practice seem to afford the opportunity of developing a much more grounded and holistic approach to this task, as suggested by these contributions.

12

ASSESSMENT FOR EFFECTIVE PRACTICE
Cathy Svensson and Bridget Middlemas

Introduction

The *Code of Practice on the Identification and Assessment of Special Educational Needs* (DfE, 1994) and later the *Revised Code* (DfES, 2001) have both contributed to a major policy development relating to the education of children with special educational needs (SEN). The publications were influential for a number of reasons, not least because the professional status and strategic role of the SENCO were highlighted, and the critical role of assessment in making effective provision for *all* pupils was endorsed.

The importance of assessment is also reflected in the *National SEN Specialist Standards* (TTA, 1998). Standards linked with assessment are considered to be key elements of a SENCO's professional knowledge and understanding, and each standard clearly underpins the strategic direction and development of SEN provision in schools and colleges (TDA, 2009). More widely, the assessment of pupils with SEN is regarded as essential in promoting teaching and learning (DfES, 2010b) and the SENCO role is viewed as strategic to that endeavour.

The dyslexia-friendly primary school

This chapter highlights the role of a particular primary school SENCO and her colleagues in facilitating educational inclusion and participation for all pupils, including pupils with dyslexia (a high incidence SEN which is also categorized as a *specific learning difficulty*). We will explore the ways in which the progress of pupils with dyslexia in the primary school might be assessed. In so doing, the chapter adopts a position which proposes that provision for pupils on the dyslexic continuum in primary school is not only contingent on an effective assessment policy, but also demands a commitment to wide-ranging teaching methodologies, and the dedication of the whole school community to becoming a dyslexia-friendly school (Rose, 2009). The DfES states that: 'One of the basic principles of becoming a dyslexia-friendly school is the expectation that teachers take immediate action when faced with learning needs, rather than refer for assessment and wait for a "label" ' (2005: 24).

Dyslexia typically affects between 4 and 8 per cent of pupils (Snowling, 2008) and is described as one of the least understood disabilities (Reid, 2006). If unidentified, it is believed to be a major cause of 'educational failure' (BDA, 2009: 1). The numerous and varied definitions of dyslexia do little to dispel the concerns of those who challenge its existence (Elliot, 2005) or who seek a rigid set of defining characteristics. However, some key agreements emerge which are identified below:

- Dyslexia is strongly associated with a difficulty in reading and spelling.
- It has been traditionally associated with a discrepancy between a pupil's performance and reasoning abilities.
- It manifests itself in various ways in different pupils.
- It is underpinned by a cognitive difficulty frequently associated with phonological processing.

(Reid, 2009)

Many of the understandings of dyslexia and its educational implications are captured in this definition:

> Dyslexia can be described at neurological, cognitive and behavioural levels. It is typically characterised by inefficient information processing, including difficulties in phonological processing, working memory, rapid naming, and automaticity of basic skills. Difficulties in organisation, sequencing and motor skills may also be present.
>
> (Task Force for Dyslexia, 2001: 28)

While this definition identifies the multi-faceted nature of dyslexia, it does not acknowledge the potential strengths associated with the condition, nor the potential learning and teaching issues that may either impact negatively or positively on a pupil's learning potential. This chapter raises these wider issues, and posits the necessity of adopting a whole-school, inclusive approach to assessment (DCSF, 2008).

Hypothetical case study: Whistledown Primary School

Whistledown Primary School is a two-form entry school in a suburban area, which enjoys a good reputation as a friendly, well-run establishment. There are 320 pupils, from a range of socio-economic backgrounds. Some 18 per cent of the children at Whistledown are identified as School Action or School Action Plus (DfES, 2001), and 24 per cent receive free school meals. Two children have statements for specific learning difficulties. The school works closely with outreach teachers from the Special Literacy Unit which is in the borough. Whistledown is also working towards achieving dyslexia-friendly school status (BDA, 2010) which the school believes will benefit all the children, not only those who are on the dyslexic continuum.

The school's strategic vision

The school's strategic vision for an inclusive, accessible learning and teaching environment is closely aligned to the SENCO standards and actively shared with all stakeholders. The Headteacher is working towards improving inclusive SEN and disability provision at Whistledown, and with the senior leadership team is making good use of the *School Improvement Planning Framework* (TDA, 2008) to guide discussions, while concurrently embedding the dyslexia-friendly school agenda.

Whistledown School has agreed the following priorities for development:

- to create a well-trained and motivated staff, who engage in regular CPD opportunities to meet the needs of all pupils with SEN;
- to be recognized as a dyslexia-friendly school with an ethos and culture where assessment for effective learning (*Assessment for Learning Strategy*, DCSF 2008) is fundamental to pupil entitlement;
- to promote an optimal learning environment for all pupils: where children can celebrate their strengths and improve on their weaknesses.

The School Development Plan embodies these priorities: it emphasizes the importance of a whole-school inclusive approach to SEN provision as well as a culture of high expectation for all. It recognizes the fundamental role of assessment for learning as the basis for meeting these priorities (DCSF, 2008). The senior leadership team is in agreement that:

- the child's learning needs are central to this endeavour;
- clearly informed assessment is always the starting point in creating barrier-free provision;
- the links between effective personalized learning, formative and summative assessment, provision mapping and target setting need to be recognized as fundamental to meeting school development aspirations;
- the focus needs to be on *how* pupils learn rather than *what* they learn.

The senior leadership team also recognizes the relationship between school effectiveness and the dyslexia-friendly schools' agenda.

The strategic role of the SENCO

As a member of the senior leadership team, the SENCO endeavours to provide advice and support to staff in their efforts to remove barriers for learning for pupils with SEN/disability (DfES, 2001). She works closely with the Deputy Headteacher, the SEN Governor and the specialist dyslexia teacher to discuss whole-school SEN and assessment issues. She also meets regularly with SENCOs from local cluster schools with a view to sharing expertise and discussing effective practice. She contributes to the borough's multi-professional planning meetings (MPPMs), which have a focus on ensuring that the child and the family remain at the heart of the decision-making process (DfES, 2004).

The SENCO is actively engaged in her own continuing professional development (CPD) and is a regular contributor to the SENCO Forum discussion list (BECTA, 2010). The SENCO's CPD has already impacted on:

- her confidence in contributing to the strategic vision of the school as a member of the senior leadership team in Whistledown School;
- the quality of the advice and guidance she can now offer to staff and the wider school community;
- the strategic direction she can now take the SENCO role, and her vision for enhancing pupil provision.

Around 60 per cent of the SENCO's time is taken up with administration and liaising with outside agencies, and she frequently struggles to maintain a good balance between her four main roles (see Figure 12.1).

In keeping with the devolving of aspects of SEN to the specialist dyslexia teacher class teachers, and the higher level classroom assistants, the SENCO has set up a rota of classroom observations, which enables her to observe SEN provision in each class.

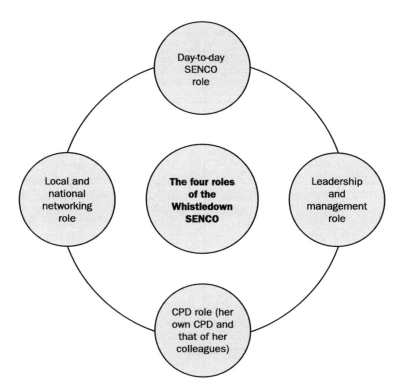

Figure 12.1 The four roles of the Whistledown SENCO

and also supports her in getting to know each pupil personally. The insights gained from her observations support her in planning for CPD and in identifying the assessment priorities for implementing personalized learning initiatives, which ultimately inform school target setting and in turn the School Development Plan.

Embedding assessment for effective practice

Through a series of CPD workshops supported by the local university and the BDA, Whistledown staff have been sensitized to the identification of dyslexia, its strengths and potential weaknesses, and the implications for professional practice. They understand that the central characteristics associated with dyslexia relate to literacy, and the fact that literacy acquisition may pose real challenges for some pupils. They have discussed the potential impact of difficulties with phonological and visual processing, and understand how this may impact in different curriculum areas. Teachers have engaged fully with the challenges presented by the CPD workshops.

Following the workshops, Whistledown teachers were in agreement about the necessity to do the following:

- adopt more flexible pupil groupings, based on finely tuned assessment evidence;
- identify opportunities for multisensory and ICT learning opportunities in all classroom planning;
- plan for pupils' language development;
- use real-life scenarios to inform their own pedagogic practice;
- embed both formative and summative assessment as routine in their practice, enriched with informal data from pupils, parents, carers and staff.

The rota of classroom observation which the SENCO and the specialist dyslexia teacher have established allows them to monitor the quality of SEN/Disability provision across the whole school; to manage the deployment of higher level teaching assistants in the classroom; and to highlight priorities for future CPD (see Figure 12.2 for Whistledown's own way of working).

Example of working strategically in the classroom: making effective use of ICT

The SENCO and the specialist dyslexia teacher are working with the ICT Co-ordinator to promote the potential of ICT to underpin inclusive teaching and learning. The promotion of flexible pathways to personalized learning goals is high in the school's pursuit of excellence, and reflects the dyslexia-friendly ethos. The classroom staff have all been supported in making effective use of assistive technology, including the specialist dyslexia software which is available on the school intranet (DfES, 2005; BECTA, 2010). The SENCO promotes the BDA's belief that:

> ICT is a key tool to help dyslexic learners in the classroom in both learning and teaching experiences as well as accessing or recording written information. Many

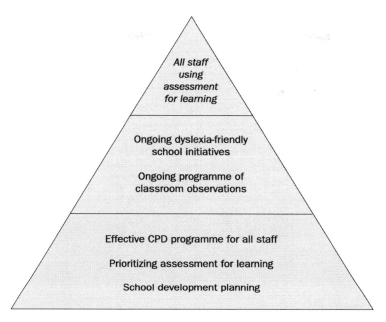

Figure 12.2 The Whistledown pyramid: embedding assessment for effective practice

of the learning differences experienced when reading, writing, spelling, accessing the curriculum, learning vocabulary, improving phonic skills and assisting recording and presentation, become a smaller problem when ICT is used.

(BDA, 2010)

Support staff regularly attend SEN/dyslexia ICT training provided by the local authority. One of the learning support assistants (LSAs) says that:

> It is really important to investigate and invest in technology that can assist children with specific learning difficulties to maximize their potential. Sometimes the class teachers don't have the time to look at all the software available, so we can help to make them more aware of what works and what doesn't.

The SENCO encourages the two LSAs to share their ICT expertise with other staff and parent helpers. In so doing she can organize SEN provision in a more strategic way with particular groups of children. For example, a small group of children with dyslexia from Key Stage 2 needed some additional input for their science topic work on Life Cycles. One of the LSAs used specialist concept-mapping software, which not only enabled the group to successfully complete their science projects, but also gave them enough confidence to present their work in a whole school assembly. Low self-esteem and other affective issues are often evident in children with dyslexia (Rose, 2009) and this type of initiative helps to build self-confidence and verbal skills.

Listening to the pupils' voices

The involvement of the school community is as important to the dyslexia-friendly ethos as it is to the principles of AfL. Not only does the SENCO regularly involve parents in discussions about their child's provision but she proactively empowers pupils to engage in their own learning. Through the insights offered by both pupils and parents she is then able to use the data to contribute to Whistledown's day-to-day recording and reviewing of pupil progress (DCSF, 2008).

For example, when reviewing the use of concept mapping software, children made comments such as these in their group discussion:

> JOHNNY (*Statemented pupil*):   I like it . . . because . . . you know, when I write . . . I sometimes forget things . . . and this way . . . I remember everything, because that programme really helps you.
>
> SAJIDA (*on School Action Plus, awaiting a statement*):   Yeah, like . . . you know . . . sometimes when you are writing, and you get some new, like different ideas . . . and then . . . you forget them . . . and you're thinking, oh, what was that? But, when you plan it on this programme, you can see it all in front of you!

These comments were then fed back to the class teacher, and she is now using the software with the whole class, for a wide range of different learning and teaching activities.

Discussion: assessment for effective practice

Knowing how pupils learn and how we respond to their learning are essential components of effective classroom practice. Assessment, in all its varied forms, needs to be at the heart of teachers' professional practice, underpinned by the adoption of a whole school approach to learning, teaching and assessment. The involvement of all stakeholders is vital in order to achieve an inclusive, accessible learning environment, where learners are equally aware of how they learn and what they are learning.

The process of learning has to be in the minds of both the learner and the teacher when assessment takes place, and when the evidence is interpreted. We need to remember that pupils may appreciate being treated as participants in the learning process – as one of the Whistledown children commented: 'Miss, it's great that you're asking us *how* we learn – this is the first time I've ever really thought about it!'

Acknowledging that adults are learners too is also important. An effective school will ensure that staff are engaging in their own learning, and assessing their own professional practice, as well as making sure that they are able to use assessment processes to ensure that all children in their school are able to achieve their true academic potential.

References

BDA (2009) *No to Failure Project: Overview and Interim Report.* Available at: http://www.notofailure.com/media/downloads/articles/2-no_to_failure_interim_report_mar08.pdf.

BDA (2010) *Dyslexia Friendly Schools*. Available at: http://www.bdadyslexia.org.uk/quality-mark-and-accreditation.html.

BECTA (2010) SENCO Forum List. Available at: http://lists.becta.org.uk/mailman/listinfo/senco-forum.

DCSF (2008) *The Assessment for Learning Strategy*. Nottingham: DCSF Publications.

Department of Education (2001) *Report of the Task Force on Dyslexia*. Dublin: Government Publication Office.

DfE (1994) *Code of Practice on the Identification and Assessment of SEN*. London: DfE.

DfES (2001) *SEN Code of Practice*. Nottingham: DfES.

DfES (2004) *Removing Barriers to Achievement. The Government's Strategy for SEN*. Nottingham: DfES.

DfES (2005) *Learning and Teaching for Dyslexic Children*. Nottingham: DfES.

Elliot, J. (2005) Dispatches, Channel & Television, 8 September.

Reid, G. (2006) *Dyslexia and Inclusion: Classroom Approaches for Assessment, Teaching and Learning*. London: David Fulton Publishers.

Reid, G. (2009) *Dyslexia: A Practitioner's Handbook*. Chichester: John Wiley.

Rose, J. (2009) *Identifying and Teaching Children and Young People with Dyslexia and Literacy Difficulties*. London: HMSO.

Snowling, M.J. (2008) *Dyslexia*. Paper prepared as part of the Foresight Review on Mental Capital and Wellbeing, available at: http://www.foresight.gov.uk/OurWork/ActiveProjects/Mental%20Capital/ProjectOutputs.asp.

TDA (2008) *School Improvement Planning Framework*. London: TDA.

TDA (2009) *Standards for National Award for SEN Coordination*. London: TDA.

TTA (1998) *National Standards for SEN Coordination*. London: TTA.

13

A CRITIQUE OF DATA GATHERING
Bob Franks

Introduction

Experienced SENCOs are well versed and skilled in the process of setting and review-ing SMART targets for pupils with SEN. Many hours of SENCO time can be spent immersed in activities such as writing personalized targets for Individual Education Plans (IEPs), Personal Learning Plans (PLPs) and more recently Group and Individualized Provision Maps. One important outcome, regardless of the particular personalized target setting approach being used, is the expectation that pupils will make some level of progress as a direct result of being actively engaged in an inter-vention activity. The teacher's judgement about the level of progress each pupil makes is often problematical. One of the reasons for this has been the lack of reliable SEN benchmarking instruments. This chapter will attempt to illuminate the strengths and weaknesses of three important benchmarking instruments: RAISEonline (Ofsted, 2006), New National Strategy Progression Guidance (DCSF, 2009a) and CASPA (Comparison and Analysis of Special Pupil Attainment – SGA Systems, 2010).

Within the process of reporting on the progress of learners with SEN there is the need for all schools to have secure and reliable assessment procedures that enable teachers to identify 'good' academic and social progress. Although diagnostic tools such as reading tests and non-verbal IQ tests are used regularly in schools to inform decisions on aspects of subject and cognitive abilities, they are not always directly related to the school's curriculum.

It is commonly accepted that the first assessment tool a teacher should use to assess a pupil's ability is the curriculum. However, our current reporting processes concentrate on the priority core subjects of English, Mathematics and Science, despite the intention stated in the National Curriculum Inclusion Statement to pay heed to Equalities, Diversity and Inclusion (QCDA, 2010).

A central concern in the process of accurate assessment is the choice of assessment tool that will enable attainment to be accurately identified and from that point, allow formative and summative assessment points to demonstrate progress. In the case of pupils with complex special needs, the choice of assessment tool should be sensitive enough to reflect the pupil's current attainment levels, even at the very lowest levels of core subject academic abilities (e.g. CAN Do's at P1i). If the assessment tool selected for baseline attainment does not facilitate assessment opportunities at different time intervals, to demonstrate small step progress, schools may not have a secure evidence base to demonstrate that pupils are making progress related to where they fit on a continuum of academic ability.

However, before outlining the key elements of each benchmarking tool it is worth briefly commenting on some important contextual issues that are likely to impact on the validity of any judgements connected with making accurate and reliable judgements about individual pupil progress.

Key factors associated with the academic and social achievement of pupils with SEN

The progress of pupils with SEN depends on a variety of reasons, such as:

- teacher insecurities about selecting reliable assessment methods, which can result in teaching staff not being able to accurately identify individual progress using appropriate diagnostic tools and reliable benchmarking instruments;
- inconsistencies in the implementation of assessment, recording and reporting policies, which result in insecure judgements about the progress of all pupils;
- an assumption that progression is linear, and continues to develop as an upward trend. This fails to acknowledge that progress targets for some pupils may be to maintain current levels of attainment, and for a very small number of children with extreme and complex needs, good progress targets might be to minimize regression.
- variable expectations of achievement evidenced by teachers setting under- and over-challenging targets;
- a lack of stimulating learning environments, that can de-motivate pupils regardless of ability;
- prevalent socio-economic factors and within-child factors, that have a direct impact on pupils making different levels of expected progress;
- complex issues related to personal, social and emotional development, and well-being, that restrict pupils with SEN from accessing their full curriculum entitlement.

In addition to the above, many SENCOs and special school staff have raised questions associated with SEN target setting processes and making judgements of 'good' progress. In essence, four questions appear to dominate these concerns:

1   What constitutes 'good National Curriculum progress' for SEN children across Key Stages?

2   How do I know if my IEP targets are challenging?

3   How can I find out if the social and academic progress of my pupils is the same as that of other SEN children of a similar starting point and age?

4   What are the best interventions, at Wave 2 and 3, to accelerate the progress of SEN/LDD pupils?

In the process of deciding what is good progress, it is evident that one has first to be clear about what is expected progress for all children. The commonly accepted view of national bodies like Ofsted, HMI, DCSF and the National Strategies is that most children with SEN and/or disabilities are expected to reach national expected levels regardless of their particular SEN area of need. For clarity, I have included the full reference from the National Strategies which states nationally expected attainment levels.

> Most pupils with special educational needs, learning difficulties and disabilities (SEN/LDD), including those in special schools, are able to reach national expected levels. For the majority of those who do not, National Curriculum levels and sub-levels still offer a suitable framework for assessment, planning and the evaluation of attainment and progress. For a much smaller number of pupils working below level 1 of the National Curriculum, the use of P levels (along with other assessment/planning frameworks linked to the Every Child Matters (ECM) five outcomes) enables schools to measure progress, set targets and evaluate the impact of their provision for these pupils.
>
> (DCSF, 2008)

Many SENCOs may feel that the commonly held national perspective is unrealistic. They may find the process of deciding on and writing realistic and achievable targets extremely challenging for the most complex pupils with SEN (e.g. at School Action Plus and Statemented). Current progress judgements for this group of children, across all schools, appear variable across different years groups and very often appear to be based on school-specific subjective criteria.

At this point I would like to stress the need for all SENCOs to write SEN targets which have been rigorously scrutinized to ensure they have an appropriate level of challenge within them. The new Progression Guidance cites two local authorities, Leicestershire (Key Stages 1 to 4) (Leicestershire County Council, 2008) and Kent (Secondary) (Kent County Council, 2007) as having addressed the challenge of deciding on good progress indicators across a range of Key Stages. It is often the judgement of Ofsted inspectors that pupils who are set challenging targets make good progress and those that have aspirational targets make outstanding progress.

In the absence of a detailed knowledge of appropriate benchmarking instruments like RAISEonline; Fischer Family Trust (FFT, 2010), PIVATs (Lancashire County Council, 2010), CASPA; the new NS Progression Guidance, staff should make effective use of the school's historical data in core subject attainment to set realistic and challenging targets for pupils with SEN. Accurate historical data may also be used to provide evidence of significant progress where current benchmarking tools appear to have specific weaknesses, namely, to provide comparative data for Early Years settings, at the end of Key Stage 3 or for pupils in Sixth Form environments (such as special schools).

The data sets within NS Progression Guidance (DCSF, 2009a) begin to quantify pupil progress by using age and prior attainment as the starting point for developing expectations of pupil progress. The guidance encourages schools to set targets in line with the highest performing learners. By this I assume it means the top 25 per cent of learners which on close analysis of the data sets often refers to pupils making at least two levels progress (often three) over a Key Stage. The Progression Guidance does not make it explicit whether judgements about pupils making 1, 2 and 3 levels progress over a Key Stage can be considered as being unsatisfactory, satisfactory or good and outstanding. However, it does enable the analysis of end of Key Stage attainments for pupils with SEN to be categorized as in line with lower, median and upper quartile NC levels of attainment. This an extremely useful analysis tool that can assist all staff in the process of setting realistic and challenging SEN targets.

In the process of setting progress indicators for all pupils with SEN, schools need to be aware of the latest guidance, and the most appropriate SEN interventions and strategies for accelerating social and academic progress.

Recent initiatives, such as the Making Good Progress (MGP) pilot (DCSF, 2010a) and the Inclusion Development Programme (DCSF, 2007a) have been introduced to increase rates of pupil progress and improve the effectiveness of quality first teaching for all pupils, especially the most vulnerable. In addition, new LA and school guidance has been published to support all schools in setting appropriate targets for all children (DCSF, 2010b). Finally a new DCSF website, What Works Well (DCSF, 2010c), has been created to enable teachers to share effective practice to improve learning for all children, including those with SEN.

Further information is available. In 2003, the DfES produced guidance to support pupils with significant literacy difficulties (DfES, 2003), and followed this in 2005 with guidance in the Primary National Strategy in the form of Leading on Inclusion materials. This suggested a way of analysing the progress of vulnerable learners (see 2003: 159) and gave several ideas for different types of Provision Maps (DfES, 2005: 190–210). Secondary SENCOs will find the Leading on Intervention materials of particular use (DfES, 2005). This was followed with an additional comprehensive resource in 2007 (DCSF, 2007b).

Finally, it is worth noting three very important SEN and Disabilities (SEND) e-learning resources, produced to support pupils with SEN to maximize their learning. All SENCOs should encourage staff and parents to use these materials, to improve knowledge, confidence and expertise. The sources are: Leading on Inclusion – understanding and using data sections 1 and 2 together with the information booklet on maximizing progress for pupils with SEN (DCSF, 2005); SEN/LDD Progression Guidance – in particular National and Local Data, Determining Good Progress and Setting Targets (DCSF, 2010d) and the Inclusion Development Programme with regard to online training modules in Dyslexia, Speech Language and Communication Needs, Autism and Behaviour (DCSF, 2009b).

Three key SEND benchmarking tools

1 CASPA

Name of resource: CASPA – Comparison and Analysis of Special School Attainment

Target audience	Special Schools; Resourced provision, Pupil Referral Units
Target pupils	School Action Plus/Statemented
Good and outstanding progress indicators	Pupil Progress data is represented in percentile graphs for all national curriculum subjects. Graphs are plotted as coloured trend lines that represent different centile values. The top 25 per cent correlate with pupils attaining above the 75th centile and the lowest 25 per cent of pupils would be linked to those pupils achieving below the 25th centile. Wherever practicable, and depending on the pupil's starting point, the aspiration would be to set targets in line with the NC values associated with the highest attainers.
Age range covered	Reception (age 4) to Year 13 the end of Key Stage 5 (age 19)
Main approach	Database uses as its main source *SEN type of primary need* in line with school census categories.
What CASPA can do	• Set individual trajectory targets for pupils that are one and two years ahead. • Allow examples of pupils' achievements to be electronically clipped to pupils' individual records, illustrating pupil progress over different periods. • Plot year-on-year progression across all NC subjects using CASPA percentile graphs. • Plot progress in the difference of percentile ranking between start and end points. • Plot overall pupil progress in a traffic light graph, showing the percentage of pupils making below and above expected progress.
Additional points to consider	• Currently CASPA only compares progress by using one primary need. Pupils with complex additional needs that impact on their progress might have inaccurate expected rates of progress. • CASPA expected rates of progress do not contain a 'challenge' factor.

2 RAISEonline (RoL)

Name of Resource: RAISEonline – Reporting and Analysis for Improvement through Self-Evaluation

Target audience	Mainstream Primary, Secondary and Special schools, where the latter cater for pupils performing within the expected age-related attainment range
Target pupils	End of Key Stages 2 and 4

Name of Resource: RAISEonline – Reporting and Analysis for Improvement through Self-Evaluation

Good progress indicators	• The overall Contextual Value Added (CVA) score for the school, and also for Mathematics, English and Science. • Whether the CVA score is significantly higher or lower compared to the national mean for the whole school, Mathematics, English and Science. • Progress measures from KS2 to KS4 in the form of: charts that show relative attainment and CVA for all subjects; charts that compare predicted vs actual attainment for individuals; progress measures for the proportion of students achieving Grade C or above in Mathematics, English and Science Judgements about progress are colour coded. If attainment is judged as being statistically significantly above average (sig+) it is coded green and for below average (sig–) it is coded blue
Age range covered	10 to 16
Main approach	Database
What RAISEonline can do	As well as detailed individual reports, it is possible for RoL to produce summary reports. The summary report has three main sections: • A summary of the context of the school including SEN and FSM data, attendance data and some other socio-economic data • Progress (CVA) data and judgements for the headline figures, groups of pupils and individual students including data in English and maths • Attainment information comparing examination/test results with national averages
Additional points to consider	• KS3 data analysis has been suspended due to the abolition of KS3 tests. This may be replaced by moderated judgements based on Assessing Pupil Progress (APP) activities • RoL can be used to predict set targets and possible outcomes for similar pupils and groups • When looking at individual school data it is evident that many pupils exceed their expectations, some by a considerable margin, while others do not • It is intended to include P Level progression data in the future. However, for a small minority of pupils working at the lower end of the P scales, it is unlikely to be finely tuned enough to report very small step progress

3 The new National Strategy Progression Guidance 2009–2010

Name of Resource: The new National Strategy Progression Guidance

Target audience	Mainstream and Special schools, in making their own judgements about pupil progress. These materials set out the evidence of progress being made by learners with special educational needs, learning difficulties and disabilities (SEN/LDD). The intended audience is: teachers; school leadership teams; Governors; LA officers, School Improvement Partners (SIPs) and National Challenge Advisers (NCAs); Ofsted inspection teams; (and) other interested parties, including parents and children and/or their supporters, who are interested in the use of data to raise expectations and improve outcomes for learners with SEN/LDD
Target pupils	Pupils working well below age-related expectations in Key Stages 2, 3 and 4.

Good progress indicators	Using mainstream data sets to attain within higher quartile (top 25 per cent):
	KS 1–2 English 2/3 NC levels of progress (often 3);
	        Maths, mainly 2 NC levels of progress.
	KS 2–3 English and Maths mainly 2 NC levels.
	KS 3–4 English W/E, 1-F, 2F,3-E;4-D,5-C;6-B,7-A*;
	        Maths W-F, 1-G, 2-F,3-F, 4-E, 5-C,6-B,7-A,*-A.
	Using P-scale data sets for P1–P3 see PG data KS1-2 and KS2-3 with sub sets P1–P8
	KS1-2 English – often 3 levels,
	        Maths – often 3 levels;
	KS 2–3 English and Maths often 2 levels

Age range covered	5 to 16
Main approach	Age and prior attainment are the primary starting points for developing expectations of pupil progress

What the progression guidance can do	The guidance can be used in a variety of ways:
	• *Tracking and evaluation of progress*
	  In providing national data sets to support tracking and the evaluation of progress by introducing benchmarks against which the achievement of individuals and groups can be compared
	• *Target setting*
	  In providing a framework for schools to judge the degree of ambition in the proposed targets
	• *School improvement*
	  In adding to the information that LAs and schools use when planning and evaluating additional resources for pupils with SEN/LDD
	• *Related work*
	  In providing the basis for developing a wider understanding of the use of data for learners working below age-related expectations (LAs, schools and other interested groups)

Additional points to consider	• It may be argued that this approach does not fully take into account the personalized learning needs of the child but it can be used effectively with other evidence about the child's teaching and learning needs
	• It assumes that progression is linear
	• In the first year of implementation, data sets are small
	• Full analysis can only be done online by downloading current data sets
	• Progress is at end of Key Stages, not year on year; however, some schools may want to disaggregate data

Conclusion

Whichever SEND benchmarking instruments a school uses to set targets, national expectations of attainment data are there to inform rather than to dictate the process of personalized target setting. The analysis of what constitutes progress for a pupil with SEND has to be informed by teacher knowledge of overall ability. The school will need to carry out an accurate baseline identification and assessment of social and academic need, using assessment instruments that demonstrate what the pupil 'Can DO'. Good progress, for all children, will be dependent on staff demonstrating high expectations of achievement.

What is of paramount importance is the ability of a school to make use of assessment data to implement reasonable adaptations that reflect individualized learning needs. In the process of trying to determine what is a reasonable adaptation to make for any individual pupil with SEN, I use a simple question – If this pupil was *my child* what would I expect the class teacher to do to ensure my son or daughter made good progress during their lessons?

References

DCSF (2005) *Maximising Progress: Ensuring the Attainment of Pupils with SEN*. Nottingham: DCSF.

DCSF (2007a) *Primary and Secondary National Strategies, Inclusion Development Programme*. Available at: http://nationalstrategies.standards.dcsf.gov.uk/node/116685.

DCSF (2007b) *Primary and Secondary National Strategies: What Works Well for Pupils with Literacy Difficulties*. Available at: www.standards.dcsf.gov.uk/phonics/downloads/gregbrooks.pdf.

DCSF (2008) *Primary and Secondary National Strategies: Attainment and Progress for Pupils with SEN/LDD*. Available at: http://nationalstrategies.standards.dcsf.gov.uk/node/123037?uc=force_uj.

DCSF (2009a) *The National Strategies, Progression Guidance 2009–2010*. Available at: http://nationalstrategies.standards.dcsf.gov.uk/node/190123.

DCSF (2009b) *Primary and Secondary National Strategies: The Inclusion Development Programme*. Available at: http://nationalstrategies.standards.dcsf.gov.uk/node/116691.

DCSF (2010a) *Evaluation of the Making Good Progress Pilot*. Available at: http://www.dcsf.gov.uk/research/programmeofresearch/projectinformation.cfm?projectid=15619&resultspage=1.

DCSF (2010b) *Guidance for Local Authorities and Schools on Setting Education Performance Targets for 2011.* Available at: http://www.standards.dfes.gov.uk/ts/informationcentre/news/?newsID=971511.

DCSF (2010c) *What Works Well (database).* Available at: http://whatworkswell.standards.dcsf.gov.uk/.

DCSF (2010d) *Leading on Intervention Materials.* Available at: http://nationalstrategies.standards.dcsf.gov.uk/search/results/%22leading%20on/%Intervention%22.

DfES (2003) *Targeting Support: Choosing and Implementing Interventions for Children with Significant Literacy Difficulties.* Available at: http://nationalstrategies.standards.dcsf.gov.uk/node/8523.

DfES (2005) *Leading on Inclusion.* Available at: http://nationalstrategies.standards.dcsf.gov.uk/node/116685.

Fischer Family Trust (2010) *Guidance for Schools.* Available at: http://www.fischertrust.org/downloads.aspx?area=1&country=en&filter=training and support.

Kent County Council (2007) *Pupil Achievement Review and Target Setting (Secondary).* Canterbury: KCC.

Lancashire County Council (2010) *PIVATS, Assessment of Learning, Performance Monitoring and Effective Target Setting for All Pupils.* Available at: http://www.lancashire.gov.uk/corporate/web/?PIVATS/14585C).

Leicestershire County Council (2008) *What is Good Progress for Children and Young People with Special Educational Needs in English and Maths?* Leicester: LCC.

Ofsted (2006) *RAISEonline, Reporting and Analysis for Improvement through School Self-Evaluation.* Available at: https://www.raiseonline.org/login.aspx?ReturnUrl=%2findex.aspx.

QCDA (2010) *New Primary and Secondary Curriculum.* Available at: http://curriculum.qcda.gov.uk/new-primary-curiculum/equalities-diversity-and-inclusion/including-all-learners/index.asp.

SGA Systems (2010) *CASPA, Comparison and Analysis of Special Pupil Attainment.* Available at: http://www.sgasystems.co.uk/.

Further reading

DCSF (2007) Use of Data in Special Schools by School Improvement Partners. Available at: http://nationalstrategies.standards.dcsf.gov.uk/node/154554.

DfEE (2001) *Supporting the Target Setting Process.* Available at: http://www.teachernet.gov.uk/_doc/3965/targetsetting%5B1%5D.pdf.

Ofsted (2003) Good Assessment in Secondary Schools. Available at: http://www.ofsted.gov.uk/layout/set/print/Ofsted-home/Forms-and-guidance/Browse-all-by/Other/General/Good-assessment-in-secondary-schools.

Ofsted (2004) *Setting Targets for Pupils with Special Educational Needs.* Available at: http://www.ofsted.gov.uk/layout/set/print/Ofsted-home/Forms-and-guidance/Browse-all-by/Other/General/Setting-targets-for-pupils-with-special-educational-needs-Glossy-pdf.

14

INCREASING PARTICIPATION, DECREASING BUREAUCRACY

Gill Richards, Alison Patterson and
Linda Lyn-Cook

Introduction: a costly and bureaucratic process?

While most pupils with special educational needs (SEN) have their support needs assessed and routinely met within mainstream schools, a small number have a statutory assessment that leads to a Statement of Special Educational Need (Wearmouth, 2009). This assessment has often been criticized by parents and professionals for its failure to respond quickly to provide the support required. In 2002, the Audit Commission described statutory assessment as 'A costly, bureaucratic and unresponsive process . . . which may add little value in helping meet a child's needs' (2002: 3). Furthermore, it argued that 'Statements' provided little assurance to parents due to weak monitoring arrangements and subsequently led to inequitable distribution of resources for support (2002: 3). Later in 2004, Ofsted suggested that schools rarely evaluated their provision of SEN so were unable to establish whether it was effective or value for money (2004: 5) and in 2006, the House of Commons stated that 'While some local authorities have made good progress in managing SEN in recent years, there remains much variation in performance and some poor practice (2006: 46). This was followed by the Audit Commission's (2007) continued criticism that many LEAs did not know if the money spent on SEN 'out of county placements' represented value for money.

These concerns suggest a climate of an *intention* for good quality provision that has not been matched by national practice. Additionally, when differences in the numbers of pupils receiving a Statement of Special Educational Need and the types of school in which they were educated can be seen across local authorities, producing a suggested 'postcode lottery' (Rustemier and Vaughan, 2005; House of Commons, 2006; DCSF, 2009), this raises further questions about the impact of localized ideology, responsibilities and assessment processes.

Simplifying the process?

Local Authorities and schools have specific duties under the Special Educational Needs and Disability Act (2001) and the Disability Discrimination Act (2005) to ensure that pupils' special educational needs are assessed and supported. Within statutory requirements, there is flexibility for local authorities to develop systems with schools that manage special educational needs provision in ways that suit the local context (Implementation Review Unit, 2007).

One local authority, with a strong commitment to inclusive education, decided that its schools should not need to be reliant on a Statement of Special Educational Need to access additional resources, including funding. It structured its schools into 'Families', each including a secondary school and its feeder primary schools: the SENCOs within each school receive support from an allocated experienced 'Family SENCO' leader. Funding for pupils with special educational needs is then allocated into three funding blocks (levels).

The first level, 'Additional School Need' (ASN) requires schools to assess the pupil and use their school budget to ensure that appropriate support is provided to remove barriers to learning – this would typically involve a few hours support a week. If this strategy proves unsuccessful, schools move to the next level, 'Additional Family Need' (AFN). This involves an application to the Family of schools for additional support funding from the Family's annually allocated AFN budget. The application requires a bid under one of four areas of need – cognition, sensory, behaviour or communication. The school must justify the support requested against specific indicators that have been drawn up by the local authority. It must clarify what level a child is working towards and identify any additional barriers to learning. It must also be clear what the funding will be spent on and how this will match with the identified barriers to learning. Schools are required to demonstrate that they have used their ASN funding effectively for the pupil and will continue to do so. The AFN level of funding is typically divided into three levels – low, middle and high.

The final level, 'High Level Need' (HLN) involves completion of the same form as for the AFN, but requires agreement from the SENCOs for the particular Family of schools that additional funding is needed. The application then proceeds to be considered at a Local Authority panel, which meets once a term to review county-wide submissions. This panel requests a report from the relevant support service worker for consideration at the review meeting. If the application is turned down by the panel, the pupil automatically receives the highest level AFN funding.

These procedures mean that a 'Statement' is not required to ensure provision of appropriate support for pupils with special educational needs. Although there is an opportunity within the application forms to indicate that a child has a Statement of Special Educational Need, the actual document is not attached so that all children have equal access to funding based on their needs. This ensures parity between local children and those coming into the county from other authorities that may award 'Statements' more routinely. Where a pupil moves into the county with a Statement of Special Educational Need, s/he is usually moved onto the county funding system after an annual review.

The whole process is supported by structured provision from SENCOs and advisory teachers within the Local Authority's Inclusion Support Service and the Educational Psychology Service. The school SENCO is responsible for writing bids for funding support, working closely with teachers, teaching assistants and the Family SENCO leader. Advice and support are provided by the Local Authority through advisory teachers specializing in the inclusion of pupils with cognition, sensory, behaviour or communication needs. This support is available from early years through to post-16, and involves school visits, meetings with parents and provision of training courses, some of which are accredited at Master's level with a local university.

Underpinning principles

The Local Authority developed this process to replace the need for 'Statements' so that it could utilize all of its funding for support rather than on expensive statutory assessment, a major concern of the Audit Commission which estimated that £90 million was spent at that time on this 'costly bureaucratic and unresponsive process' (2002: 3). Its intention was that children would no longer be reliant on 'Statements' to access resources and so to facilitate this, statementing and additional funding systems were separated.

The bid process requires specific details on what the money will be spent on, for example, 5 × 10 minutes a day working on *additional* and *specific* fine motor skills. This means that the bid is thorough and specific; in effect it has devised a detailed programme of support for the child. This has the benefit of schools having to think support through in advance of funding approval, rather than deciding on provision once resources have been allocated to them.

There was a strong belief within the Local Authority that with appropriate support, pupils' needs could be met within mainstream schools, and subsequently the focus became on whole school development. The importance of pupil voice within the process was recognized and SENCOs were provided with training to support them as they developed strategies to include this within assessment. The focus also remains on achievement for all children, with high expectations for pupils based on individual progress. Schools and local authority staff have become more confident in interrogating data, looking in depth at outcomes for children and challenging underachievement. This has led to more robust systems for collecting evidence and measuring impact, enabling them to address the concerns expressed within the Ofsted (2004) and House of Commons (2006) reports.

Conclusion

It is possible to meet the needs of pupils with special educational needs in mainstream schools (even when those needs are severe and complex), without the need for a 'statement'. The processes described in this chapter offer particular advantages for schools and their children. First, they give more ownership of funding at a local level. This does, however, also require more responsibility to be taken; accountability is more localized as the funding 'pot' belongs to the Family of schools. Second, the Support Service usually has a good overview of the pupils with special educational needs across any one particular family and so can give advice on the relative needs of children from different schools. This helps to smooth out any inequalities that might arise if some SENCOs are more skilled at bid writing than others. Third, to write a good bid, the SENCO needs detailed information from the class teacher. This means that some responsibility for funding remains with the class teacher, as they are directly involved in the process.

Although generally positive, the system does have some frustrations. As in many Local Authorities, there are concerns about there being enough money to provide for *all* support requirements, particularly if a child suddenly arrives from another Local Authority, and the school's 'Family' have to find the funding themselves to meet any additional needs. This difficulty can be alleviated by centralized (Local Authority) funding for any child identified as having a High Level Need, or who has hours written into a 'statement' from his or her previous Local Authority.

All Local Authorities have a duty to provide for the support requirements of pupils identified as having special educational needs. The bureaucracy involved with this can create much frustration and take up considerable resources, all impeding a swift and positive outcome for the child and his or her school. The system and processes described in this chapter offer one possible solution to empower schools and SENCOs as they move towards more inclusive education provision.

References

Audit Commission (2002) *Statutory Assessment and Statements of SEN: In Need of a Review?* Wetherby: Audit Commission.

Audit Commission (2007) *Out of Authority Placements for Special Educational Needs.* London: Audit Commission.

DCSF (2009) *Special Educational Needs in England. Statistical First Release.* London: DCSF.

House of Commons, Education and Skills Committee (2006) *Special Educational Needs. Third Report of Session 2005–06.* Vol. 1 HC478-1. London: The Stationery Office.

Implementation Review Unit (2007) *IRU Statement on SEN and Disability: Meeting Need, Minimising Bureaucracy.* Available at: www.dfes.gov.uk/iru.

Ofsted (2004) *Special Educational Needs and Disability: Towards Inclusive Schools.* London: Ofsted.

Rustemier, S. and Vaughan, M. (2005) *Are LEAs in England Abandoning Inclusive Education?* Bristol: CSIE.

Wearmouth, J. (2009) *A Beginning Teacher's Guide to Special Educational Needs.* Maidenhead: Open University Press.

Part V

Leading, developing and supporting colleagues

Introduction to Part V

The following four chapters are designed to explore the themes, and Learning Outcomes, that relate to Leading, Developing and Supporting Colleagues.

In Chapter 15, Hazel Lawson and Tricia Nash address the potentially pivotal nature of the SENCo role in Initial Teacher Education; an area that will be unfamiliar territory for many serving SENCos. Hazel and Tricia argue that the work-based element of teacher education leaves much to be desired in terms of preparing aspiring teachers for diverse classrooms. In particular, this chapter examines the impact of the SEN Personalized Learning Task (Golder et al., 2005) in Initial Teacher Education. In doing so, this chapter attends to a number of Learning Outcomes within two of the themes that comprise this section. The first of these is the Leadership and Deployment of Staff:

- support and train trainee and beginner teachers and higher level teaching assistants, where appropriate, in relation to relevant professional standards;
- model effective practice and coach and mentor colleagues.

Additionally, this chapter addresses Learning Outcomes from the allied theme of 'Providing professional direction to the work of others', namely:

- to take a leadership role in promoting a whole school culture of best practice in teaching and learning in relation to pupils with SEN and/or disabilities;
- to promote improvements in teaching and learning, offering examples of good practice for other teachers and support staff in identifying, assessing and meeting the needs of pupils with SEN and/or disabilities.

Hazel and Tricia discuss the experiences of trainee teachers and schools engaging with this task, calling for increased levels of 'practical theorizing' in order to open up boundary spaces between educational stakeholders.

Chapter 16, written by Rachel Barrell, considers the complexity of interpersonal relationships between SENCos and the teachers and teaching assistants to whom they might give feedback. As before, this chapter explores Learning Outcomes across two themes: 'Leadership and development of staff' and 'Providing professional direction to the work of others'. Specifically, this chapter offers an insight into how:

- to give feedback and provide support to teaching and non-teaching colleagues on effective teaching, learning and assessment for pupils with SEN and/or disabilities;
- to model effective practice and coach and mentor colleagues;
- to promote improvements in teaching and learning, offering examples of good practice for other teachers and support staff in identifying, assessing and meeting the needs of pupils with SEN and/or disabilities.

Drawing on a contextualized learning event, Rachel highlights the often fragmentary nature of provision for learners with SEN and/or disabilities, pointing out that the opportunity to give meaningful feedback to colleagues depends upon the existence of a collaborative ethos. This chapter offers a challenge to SENCos to examine whether practice in their own settings encourages seamless dialogue between teachers, teaching assistants and SENCos.

Chapter 17, authored by Niki Elliot, analyses collaboration and dialogue further by examining how SENCos might enable negotiation and the building of consensus. Focused on fictional 'critical incidents', this chapter addresses Learning Outcomes within the theme 'Providing professional direction to the work of others', specifically:

- to take a leadership role in promoting a whole school culture of best practice in teaching and learning in relation to pupils with SEN and/or disabilities;
- to help staff to achieve constructive working relationships with pupils with SEN and their parents/carers.

The critical incidents are framed by a number of reflective questions to assist the readers' understanding of how SENCos might build partnerships with hard-to-reach learners and their parents. In these rich descriptions, Niki emphasizes the interplay between culture, attitudes and practices and the need to value the knowledge held by all stakeholders. In this way, the critical incidents could serve as a starting point for SENCos wishing to question claims to collaboration, inclusivity and negotiation within their own practice.

The final chapter in this part, written by Sue Pearson, analyses the role of the governing body in general and that of the SEN Governor in particular. While this chapter has clear resonance with Section Three of the NASC Learning Outcomes 'Strategic development of SEN policy and procedure', a major theme of which relates to 'Working strategically with senior colleagues and governors', it resides in this part of the book as a focus on the untapped resource of the governing body. It has clear implications for two of the Learning Outcomes within this section:

- to lead on developing workplace policies and practices concerning pupils with SEN and/or disabilities and promoting collective responsibility for their implementation;
- to encourage all members of staff to recognize and fulfil their statutory responsibilities towards pupils with SEN and/or disabilities.

Indeed, Sue draws attention to the statutory obligations of the governing body in monitoring workplace policies and practices, pointing out that in recent years governing bodies have acquired specific responsibilities towards the SENCo (DCSF, 2008). With reference to the Lamb Inquiry (2009) and research commissioned by nasen (Pearson, 2008), Sue highlights the need for SENCos to work closely with the governing body alongside the need for role clarification and collaborative and creative communication strategies. The reflective questions interspersed throughout this chapter act as a catalyst for the reader to reflect upon how SENCos might build constructive relationships with the governing body in their own school.

As in the previous three parts of this book, each of the chapters discussed here, while focusing on different aspects of 'Leading, developing and supporting colleagues', could equally be used to exemplify and explore other Learning Outcomes within the National Award. For example, Chapter 15 raises issues relating to 'Statutory and regulatory frameworks and relevant developments' in terms of current developments in Initial Teacher Education. Likewise, by analysing interpersonal relationships, Chapter 16 lends itself to further exploration of 'Working in partnership with pupils, families and other professionals'.

In an examination of negotiation and consensus building, Chapter 17 relates both to 'Strategic development of SEN policy and procedures' and, as with Chapter 16, 'Working in partnership with pupils, families and other professionals'. Finally, while the links made between Chapter 18 and Learning Outcomes relating to 'Working strategically with senior colleagues and governors' have already been stated, this chapter could also be used as a vehicle to examine the 'Coordination of Provision'.

In this way, the writing in this part offers a focused insight into particular aspects of practice that could be viewed via a different lens in order to examine all aspects of the SENCo role.

References

Golder, G., Norwich, B. and Bayliss, P. (2005) Preparing teachers to teach pupils with special educational needs in more inclusive schools: evaluating a PGCE development, *British Journal of Special Education*, 32(2): 92–9.

Pearson, S. (2008) Deafened by silence or by the sound of footsteps? *Journal of Research in Special Educational Needs*, 8(2): 96–110.

15

SENCOs: A PARTNERSHIP ROLE IN INITIAL TEACHER EDUCATION?

Hazel Lawson and Tricia Nash

Introduction

The need for education and training of teachers with regard to special educational needs has long been recognised (Warnock Report, DES, 1978), but provision for this aspect of initial teacher training has frequently been limited. The permeation of special educational needs across the general parts of a course can become invisible and therefore difficult to monitor (Mittler, 1992). However, reliance on school placement for training in this area leads to considerably varied provision (Ofsted, 2008). Through the illustration of a practical school placement teaching task carried out under the guidance of the school's special educational needs coordinator (SENCO), this chapter explores the possible role for SENCOs in initial teacher education.

Background: special educational needs within initial teacher education

The framework for professional standards in teaching (TDA, 2007a) states that in order to gain qualified teacher status, trainee teachers should:

Q19: Know how to make effective personalized provision for those they teach, including those for whom English is an additional language or who have special educational needs or disabilities, and how to take practical account of diversity and promote equality and inclusion in their teaching.

Q20: Know and understand the roles of colleagues with specific responsibilities, including those with responsibility for learners with special educational needs and disabilities and other individual learning needs.

Q25: (a) use a range of teaching strategies and resources, including e-learning, taking practical account of diversity and promoting equality and inclusion.

In this way, all teachers are arguably considered to be 'special education teachers' (Garner, 2000), required to have the skills and confidence to support children with special educational needs in reaching their potential (DfES, 2004). However, the area of special educational needs has long been highlighted as being inadequately covered through initial teacher education (ITE) (Garner, 2001; Golder et al., 2005; Ofsted, 2009; House of Commons, 2010). Hodkinson's recent review (2009) suggests that the training of pre-service teachers with regards to special educational needs has changed very little since the 1970s, although educational practice has changed considerably, particularly in relation to broader drives towards inclusion. Trainee teachers and recently qualified teachers similarly express dissatisfaction with the special educational needs input in their ITE courses (Winter, 2006; Nash and Norwich, 2008).

A distinction may need to be made between different types of ITE provision. Training and Development Agency (TDA) materials have been piloted and published for use in both primary and secondary ITE undergraduate programmes (TDA, 2007b, 2009b) and special school or resourced unit placements can more easily be built into these longer ITE programmes (TDA, 2008, 2009a; Golder et al., 2009). Resources have also recently been published for use in the one-year PGCE programmes (TDA, 2009c). These resources have been produced in an attempt to partially address the concerns about inadequacy of provision with regard to special educational needs. Their impact is not yet known.

In this chapter, we explore the possible role of the SENCO within ITE partnerships. First, we briefly examine the notion of partnership and the involvement of schools in ITE considering where and how special educational needs and SENCOs can be located within such partnerships. Second, we illustrate a special educational needs focused practical teaching task carried out by trainees on their school placement under the guidance of the SENCO. Finally, we consider the potential for the contribution of the SENCO in ITE.

Initial teacher education partnerships: special educational needs and SENCOs

Partnership arrangements between Higher Education Institutions (HEIs) and schools for the initial training of teachers have been a requirement since 1993. The active involvement of schools, and coordinated consistent training with continuity across the different HEI and school contexts, are emphasized (DfES, 2002). A central aspect of preparing teachers is through school placements. Trainee teachers spend a significant proportion of their training in schools gaining practical classroom experience with the support of school-based teacher-mentors. With regard to special educational needs, however, this school-based preparation may not necessarily provide the required coverage and, being dependent on the specific provision within the school, experiences may be very variable (Ofsted, 2008). The role of the SENCO in this school-based work is sometimes referred to in course documentation in relation to specific school-based sessions (for example, on the implementation of the SEN Code of Practice in the school), but rarely in relation to any wider role in the preparation of trainee teachers.

Dart (2006) proposes three elements to a special educational needs awareness course in ITE. It should enable trainee teachers to develop professionally: (1) in *attitudes*, affecting how they view disability; (2) in *educational practice*, giving them skills to enable them to support pupils with special educational needs in the classroom; and (3) in *knowledge* gained through courses and teaching practice. In HEIs, course input generally takes the form of a discrete course or unit, permeated or embedded content (whether explicit or implicit) or some combination of the two (Winter, 2006). It is generally hoped through this input to provide knowledge, influence attitudes and give some introduction to practice (Lambe, 2007; Mintz, 2007). Teachers' beliefs and attitudes are also influenced by the norms and cultures of a school (Jordan and Stanovich, 2003) and shaped by their interactions with teachers in schools through their school placements (Pearson, 2009), so attention to special educational needs is important in school placements as well as in HEIs.

The SEN Personalized Learning Task

For several years, the University of Exeter PGCE programmes have used and developed a practical school placement teaching task, called the SEN Personalized Learning Task (Golder et al., 2005). This involves all primary and secondary teacher trainees having direct experience of working over a period of time with an individual pupil who has an identified special educational need, under the guidance of the school's SENCO.

The specific aims of the task are for trainees to develop their practical knowledge, skills and positive attitudes by teaching a pupil with special educational needs, to learn to relate effectively with teaching assistants and SENCOs, and to extend their knowledge and understanding of this aspect of inclusive teaching and learning. Liaising with the SENCO and class teacher, trainees focus on an individual pupil. They are expected to spend 6 to 8 hours on the task in total. This includes: collecting information about the pupil through reading pupil records; observing the pupil in various teaching and learning contexts; meetings with the SENCO and/or class teacher; perhaps direct assessment; planning; consultation with the pupil; providing personalized learning opportunities; and recording. The teaching part of the task can be completed in class, in small group work, in a withdrawal setting or in some combination of these. Trainees write a report describing their background research and teaching, appraising their teaching and reflecting on their professional learning.

In evaluation, SENCOs reported that the activity supported students in learning about the special educational needs framework and understanding the educational needs of those with SEN (Golder et al., 2005). One suggestion for improvement from this initial study was in relation to creating better HEI–school links, so that SENCOs were better informed about the nature of the task and their role in it.

This task has been further trialled and evaluated at Exeter as well as across other universities nationally during 2007–8 (Nash and Norwich, 2008). This evaluation involved short feedback forms from Exeter trainees as well as more lengthy surveys and interviews with trainees and HEI and school staff involved in the trial of the task both in Exeter and nationally. At Exeter, the experience of trainees undertaking the task was also evaluated in 2009 through short feedback forms. The findings from all sources will be amalgamated here.

Once again it was found that some partnerships did not adequately inform the SENCOs in schools about the task, what was expected of trainees in undertaking the task and the SENCO's role within this. This led in several cases to trainees not feeling able to complete the task:

> I mean, I suppose if people like the SENCO, if I had had more support myself, maybe we would have been able to put in place more specific action to the task and maybe I would have chosen a pupil who wouldn't have minded so much having some specific attention put on him. I mean, I think you know if the SENCO had known, then she could have picked a child and then made sure I teach that child and then they have my timetable when I come here and it's all much more organized and you know who you're going to be following.

The importance of the ITE coordinator in schools in handing over the task-briefing materials from the HEI to SENCOs appeared to be instrumental to trainees receiving adequate support with the task. Too often it was reported that this was not happening, a factor acknowledged by this PGCE course director:

> And part of the problem is this channelling of everything through the ITE coordinator, which we have to do on partnership grounds and we can't have multiple access points to school, but because we go through the ITE coordinator, it gets stuck at that level too often.

In many cases trainees across all the HEIs involved did receive some support from the SENCO, although this varied from a quick meeting to much more substantial support. Examples of support included: the trainees spending time with the SENCO in the SEN department of the school in order to understand the support provided for pupils defined as having special educational needs; being given access to school policies; helping trainees identify a suitable pupil and providing access to their IEP; and offering support as the trainee undertook the task. One SENCO in a primary school outlined the support she had provided:

> Well, I began by meeting with them together and just talking generally about special needs within the school, and then we had a talk about the children that they were going to specifically work with. They talked about children on the special needs register and from that they had identified two children that they'd got a particular interest in. And then we talked briefly about those two children, and then I arranged a time to meet with them again and go through the file in more detail with each of them and to talk about the individual children. And just to talk about sort of strategies and a little bit about the conditions.

Other SENCOs gave less support, for instance, in primary schools where there was only a part-time SENCO or in secondary schools with multiple trainees: 'The SENCO had a 20-minute meeting with all 10 trainees about it, then we were left to our own devices.' In the latter situation, however, some SENCOs still managed to offer adequate support to a large number of trainees by arranging group meetings and supervision as well as involving the support of teaching assistants to trainees.

The evaluations indicated that when trainees received adequate support from the SENCOs with the task, it was completed very successfully. A primary trainee in a small rural school reports:

> Straightaway as soon as I talked about doing this task, he straightaway suggested this child and said how that would be the perfect child to do it with and talked me through a bit of background. Obviously, you know it was quite confidential and things but he told me the basics and he gave me lots of kind of background information to have a look at like . . . funding reports and things from meeting that they'd had, the kind of provision that they were given at the moment, his IEPs and things like that, so he really set me up and I talked to him at the end as well.

Similarly many secondary trainees praised the support received from SENCOs in their feedback about their experience of the task:

> Had a meeting with the SENCO where she spoke about how pupils were identified in the school and what strategies could be put in place. We were provided with CAT [cognitive abilities test] scores for our chosen pupils and IEPs for the whole school. She helped to proofread my final report and gave me guidance on how to improve. I was very impressed with the support.

This intensive and extensive evaluation has led to further development and improvement of the task which is now promoted by the TDA for use by PGCE programmes across England (TDA, 2009c).

The task is only one aspect of the provision about special educational needs and disabilities. However, Ofsted (2008) noted that the most effective ITE providers in their survey extended their provision beyond generic issues to such additional, specifically focused work.

Role of the SENCO in initial teacher education: reflections

The TDA SENCO Learning Outcomes, published as part of the specification for the National Award for SEN Coordination (TDA, 2009d), include general outcomes relating to the leadership, development and support of colleagues, for example, 'provide professional direction to the work of others' and 'model effective practice and coach and mentor colleagues'. They also include a specific outcome with regard to teacher trainees: 'support and train trainee and beginner teachers . . ., where appropriate, in relation to relevant professional standards'.

Despite wide variations in the role, and perceptions of it (Kearns, 2005; Szwed, 2007), the position of SENCO is generally regarded as complex and demanding (Mackenzie, 2007). Issues around identity (Pearson and Ralph, 2007), status, time and workload (Pearson, 2008) are frequently raised. To include another element to the role, that of supporting trainee teachers, might seem onerous. However, if the

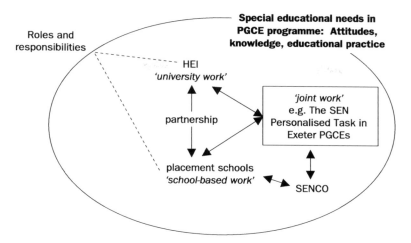

Figure 15.1 Special educational needs: university work, school-based work and joint work

SENCO's role can be envisaged as an agent of change in relation to vision and values and as a within-school advocate for children with special educational needs (Cole, 2005), then greater scope would seem to exist for the involvement of SENCOs in ITE. This is particularly important when it is argued that 'whatever is achieved in the university, the teaching practices and attitudes that student-teachers usually learn to adopt are those currently dominant in the schools' (McIntyre, 2009: 602). Further, Furlong et al.'s (2006) research indicates that ITE partnerships tend to be rather superficial, operating within a technical–rationalist environment: the lead provider becomes the 'agent' for delivery of the programme; content and structure are defined by the government; and schools become sub-contractors, agreeing to deliver their part as set out in the partnership agreement. The complexities of pupil learning and of professional education are generally not confronted and teacher performance rather than pupil learning is frequently the focus (Edwards, 2002, in Wilson, 2004). It is argued that the school-based work in ITE needs to go beyond 'largely incidental learning' (McIntyre, 2009: 606) and provide planned diverse learning experiences. In order to promote 'practical theorizing', such experiences need to be seen as more than university work (McIntyre, 2009).

The SEN Personalized Learning Task, used as an example in this chapter, has the potential for opening up 'boundary spaces' (Edwards and Mutton, 2007) where the HEI and the school, specifically the SENCO, can participate in joint work (see Figure 15.1). In spending specific time focusing on a pupil it is hoped to introduce the trainee to the relational nature of the teacher–learner relationship, to view greater complexity in the pedagogical event, beyond an often 'mechanistic and piecemeal' curriculum coverage approach (Wilson, 2004). Trainees regard the school placement as the most important aspect of their PGCE for learning about special educational needs (Nash and Norwich, 2008). There is potential here for SENCOs to support practical theorizing, bringing together theoretical and practical knowledge as part of a planned school-based programme.

References

Cole, B. (2005) Mission impossible? Special educational needs, inclusion and the re-conceptualisation of the role of the SENCO in England and Wales, *European Journal of Special Needs Education*, 20(3): 287–307.

Dart, G. (2006) 'My eyes went wide open' – an evaluation of the special needs education awareness course at Molepolole College of Education, Botswana, *British Journal of Special Education*, 33(3): 130–8.

DES (1978) *Report of the Committee of Enquiry into the Education of Handicapped Children and Young People* (The Warnock Report). London: HMSO.

DfES (2002) *Qualifying to Teach: Professional Standards for Qualified Teacher Status and Requirements for Initial Teacher Training*, Circular 2/02, London: DfES.

DfES (2004) *Removing Barriers to Achievement: The Government's Strategy for SEN*. Nottingham: DfES.

Edwards, A. and Mutton, T. (2007) Looking forward: rethinking professional learning through partnership arrangements in Initial Teacher Education, *Oxford Review of Education*, 33(4): 503–19.

Furlong, J., Campbell, A., Howson, J., Lewis, S. and McNamara, O. (2006) Partnership in English Initial Teacher Education: changing times, changing definitions: evidence from the Teacher Training Agency National Partnership Project, *Scottish Educational Review*, 37: 32–45.

Garner, P. (2000) Pretzel only policy? Inclusion and the real world of initial teacher education, *British Journal of Special Education*, 27(3): 111–15.

Garner, P. (2001) Goodbye Mr Chips: Special needs, inclusive education and the deceit of initial teacher training, in T. O'Brien (ed.) *Enabling Inclusion: Blue Skies . . . Dark Clouds?* London: The Stationery Office.

Golder, G., Jones, N. and Eaton Quinn, E. (2009) Strengthening the special educational needs element of initial teacher training and education, *British Journal of Special Education*, 36(4): 183–90.

Golder, G., Norwich, B. and Bayliss, P. (2005) Preparing teachers to teach pupils with special educational needs in more inclusive schools: evaluating a PGCE development, *British Journal of Special Education*, 32(2): 92–9.

Hodkinson, A. (2009) Pre-service teacher training and special educational needs in England 1970–2008: is government learning the lessons of the past or is it experiencing a ground-hog day?, *European Journal of Special Needs Education*, 24(3): 277–89.

House of Commons Children, Schools and Families Committee (2010) *Training of Teachers, Fourth Report of Session 2009–10*, Vol. I. London: TSO.

Jordan, A. and Stanovich, P. (2003) Teachers' personal epistemological beliefs about students with disabilities as indicators of effective teaching practices, *Journal of Research in Special Educational Needs*, 3(1): unpaginated.

Kearns, H. (2005) Exploring the experiential learning of special educational needs co-ordinators, *Journal of In-service Education*, 31(1): 131–50.

Lambe, J. (2007) Northern Ireland student teachers' changing attitudes towards inclusive education during initial teacher training, *International Journal of Special Education*, 22(1): 59–71.

Mackenzie, S. (2007) A review of recent developments in the role of the SENCO in the UK, *British Journal of Special Education*, 34(4): 212–18.

McIntyre, D. (2009) The difficulties of inclusive pedagogy for initial teacher education and some thoughts on the way forward, *Teaching and Teacher Education*, 25: 602–8.

Mintz, J. (2007) Attitudes of primary initial teacher training students to special educational needs and inclusion, *Support for Learning*, 22(1): 3–8.

Mittler, P. (1992) Preparing all initial teacher training students to teach children with special educational needs: a case study from England, *European Journal of Special Needs Education*, 7(1): 1–10.

Nash, T. and Norwich, B. (2008) *Adaptation of ITT Resources Relating to Teaching Pupils with SEN/Disabilities*. London: TDA.

Ofsted (2008) *How Well New Teachers Are Prepared to Teach Pupils with Learning Difficulties and/or Disabilities*. London: Ofsted.

Ofsted (2009) *The Annual Report of Her Majesty's Chief Inspector of Education, Children's Services and Skills 2008/09*. London: Ofsted.

Pearson, S. (2008) Deafened by silence or by the sound of footsteps? An investigation of the recruitment, induction and retention of special educational coordinators (SENCOs) in England, *Journal of Research in Special Educational Needs*, 8(2): 96–110.

Pearson, S. (2009) Using activity theory to understand prospective teachers' attitudes to and construction of special educational needs and/or disabilities, *Teaching and Teacher Education*, 25: 559–68.

Pearson, S. and Ralph, S. (2007) The identity of SENCOs: insights through images, *Journal of Research in Special Educational Needs*, 7(1): 36–45.

Szwed, C. (2007) Remodelling policy and practice: the challenge for staff working with children with special educational needs, *Educational Review*, 59(2): 147–60.

TDA (2007a) *Professional Standards for Teachers in England: Qualified Teacher Status*. Available at: http://www.tda.gov.uk/upload/resources/pdf/s/standards_qts.pdf.

TDA (2007b) *SEN and Disability Materials for Primary Undergraduate ITT Providers*. Available at: http://www.ttrb.ac.uk/ViewArticle2.aspx?Keyword=sen&SearchOption=And&SearchType=Keyword&RefineExpand=1&ContentId=14307.

TDA (2008) *SEN and/or Disabilities: A Guide to Extended Placements in Special Provision: Primary Undergraduate Courses*. Available at: http://sen.ttrb.ac.uk/attachments/ff142ba2-f0a0-4ab8-84cb-533989e213ca.pdf.

TDA (2009a) *Secondary Undergraduate Courses: A Guide to Extended Placements in Special Provision*. Available at: http://sen.ttrb.ac.uk/attachments/8faea634-9991-4404-96f5-128078b8e2e0.pdf.

TDA (2009b) *Special Educational Needs and/or Disabilities: A Training Resource for Secondary Undergraduate Initial Teacher Training Courses*. Available at: http://sen.ttrb.ac.uk/ViewArticle2.aspx?anchorId=14612&selectedId=18276&menu=17918&ContentId=15481.

TDA (2009c) *Special Educational Needs and Disability Training Resources for Post-graduate Certificate in Education Programmes*. Available at: http://www.tda.gov.uk/teachers/sen/training_resources/pgce_programmes.aspx.

TDA (2009d) *Specification for Nationally Approved Training for Special Educational Needs Coordinators (SENCOs) New to the Role, Leading to the Award of the National Award for SEN Coordination*. Available at: http://www.tda.gov.uk/upload/resources/pdf/s/national_senco_training_specification.pdf.

Wilson, E. (2004) Using activity theory as a lens to analyse interaction in a university–school initial teacher education and training partnership, *Educational Action Research*, 12(4): 587–612.

Winter, E. C. (2006) Preparing new teachers for inclusive schools and classrooms, *Support for Learning*, 21(2): 85–91.

16

THE IMPORTANCE OF INTERPERSONAL SKILLS

Rachel Barrell

Introduction

The aim of this chapter is to evaluate and reflect on the importance of communication skills when giving feedback and support to teaching and non-teaching colleagues. The focus is on the relationship between the class teacher, teaching assistant and special needs co-ordinator (SENCO) in providing high quality teaching and learning to children with special educational needs and/or disabilities in a mainstream context. The chapter will also describe a contextualized learning event which analyses the impact this feedback can have on each party and will highlight implications for the SENCO through staff development, training and deployment.

The role of the teaching assistant in removing barriers to children's learning is pivotal to ensuring inclusive practice in the modern classroom. This is reflected in the way teaching assistants are being used; from the stereotypical 'helper' model where they may have heard readers, changed books and helped with classroom organization to one where they may be trained in specific areas of expertise to help support the teaching and learning of all children. It has been recognized (DfES, 2003) that teaching assistants have skills that may not be recognized by the class teacher and thus be under-used, particularly when working with children with SEN and/or disabilities. This shift in support provision has developed alongside the rapidly changing models of integration and inclusion of children with special educational needs (SEN) and/or disabilities into mainstream provision.

With the publication of recent government legislation such as *The Children's Plan* (DCSF, 2007) and *21st Century Schools: A World Class Education for Every Child* (DCSF, 2008a), removing barriers to learning through personalized provision, intervention, and a shift in societal attitudes, has been highlighted as essential for meeting the needs of individual children. The DCSF publication, *Personalised Learning* (DCSF, 2008b) outlines the key features necessary to ensure that high expectations for every child are set and achieved. Clearly, this will have an impact on the ways in which teaching assistants are used in the classroom. These are likely to include focused assessment, intervention, target setting and tracking, and pupil groupings.

However, research into the use of teaching assistants in supporting children with SEN and/or disabilities shows that they are currently not being used or managed to maximum effect in the classroom (Gerber et al., 2001; Blatchford et al., 2003; Ofsted, 2006). Issues of over-dependency on support leading to reduced contact with peers, described by Gerschel (2005) as the 'velcro model', has meant that support by teaching assistants has had a varied impact on children with SEN and/or disabilities, particularly in relation to social inclusion. The Ofsted Report on Teaching Assistants (2002) made the following comment in light of the findings of school Inspections:

> Pupils with SEN depended on teaching assistants to break down the tasks further so that they could participate. In these lessons the focus of the teachers' planning was on how the pupils with SEN could be kept engaged, rather than on what the pupils needed to learn next.

> (para. 72)

The SEN Code of Practice (DfES, 2001: 15) states that 'All teaching and non-teaching staff should be involved in the development of the school's SEN policy and be fully aware of the school's procedures for identifying, assessing and making provision for pupils with SEN.' However, this frequently does not match what is actually happening in practice, and this places a considerable burden on the role of the special needs co-ordinator (SENCO) in ensuring that policy implementation occurs in all classrooms. It might also be that teaching assistants do not recognize this transformation in their role but still see themselves as 'carers rather than pedagogues' (MacBeath, 2009).

A main thread included in the outcomes for the new Post Graduate National Award for SEN Co-ordination is leadership and the deployment of staff. Training should enable the SENCOs to 'give feedback and provide support to teaching and non-teaching colleagues on effective teaching, learning and assessment for pupils with SEN and/or disabilities' (TDA, 2009).

Communication between a class teacher, teaching assistant and SENCO is crucial to ensure high quality teaching and learning for pupils with SEN and/or disabilities. Dyer (1996: 191) describes providing feedback as 'a glueing, quilting and genuinely cementing role'. However, for this relationship to be successful in practice, there needs to be a foundation of 'mutual respect and confidence and a shared purpose, which can only be achieved through joint planning and evaluation' (Rose, 2000: 194).

The SENCO needs to be able to implement a clearly defined co-ordinated approach, so that teaching assistants are clear on what their roles and responsibilities are, and so that they become 'increasingly knowledgeable in ways of supporting pupils . . . to help maximise their levels of achievement and independence' (Rose, 2000: 183). Research has shown (DfES, 2003: 65) that teaching assistants would value feedback on evaluating and assessing learning, methods of questioning pupils, encouraging independence of learning, scaffolding learning, and methods of explanation.

In practice, however, this can be problematic. Many schools try to assign a teaching assistant to a particular class to ensure this shared purpose through consistency and continuity between teacher and teaching assistant. However, in some cases support from a teaching assistant can be fragmented due to several classes 'sharing' support, which means that feedback through effective communication is often hindered due to time constraints (Ofsted, 2002: 13). An important aspect, therefore, for a SENCO would be to monitor the work patterns of these teaching assistants to assess both the quantity and quality of time spent supporting children with SEN and/or disabilities in each classroom. This may include initiating and developing formal procedures to monitor the impact that support is having on the progress and attainment of those children.

In light of the above discussion and research, a contextualized learning event was carried out to illustrate the importance of communication from three different perspectives: a class teacher, a teaching assistant and a SENCO.

The activity was carried out in a large urban primary school with identified pupils from Key Stage 2 classes who were supported in a socially speaking group (as part of a nurture group) for an hour each week. This continuity in classroom organization helped the teaching assistant work on routines and rules which pupils found difficult in the classroom environment. The pupils in the group had a range of needs including behavioural, social and emotional difficulties (BESD), speech, language and communication needs (SLCN), attachment disorder (RAD), and one pupil who was described as being on the autistic spectrum (ASD). This group was managed by a teaching assistant and took place once a week at the same time in the same room. All the children in the group (three boys and two girls) were on School Action Plus of the SEN Code of Practice (DfES, 2001).

Interestingly, the school's special educational needs co-ordinator (SENCO) had recently been given a senior management position in the school with responsibilities for the management and training of all the support staff in the school. This was a key development which built on the comments made by Ofsted in their school inspection findings: 'The team of talented teaching assistants provides effective additional support to teachers and pupils' (Ofsted, 2009).

The teaching assistant had been provided with both a group provision map and also an individual provision map for the pupil with ASD by the SENCO. These maps provided the teaching assistant with clear expected outcomes for the socially speaking group activities and also with interventions that could be transferred back into the classroom environment. The individual provision map also had links to outside agencies detailed, although targets were not identified on the map. This appears to have been an important oversight, as targets given by the speech and language therapist would have been useful for the teaching assistant when planning the sessions each week.

One of the things that stood out immediately when observing this activity was the obvious relationship that the teaching assistant had developed with all pupils in the group. The children were supported throughout and a mutually respectful and trusting relationship was evident through the comments made by pupils. This has huge implications for the communication between teachers, teaching assistants and SENCOs – a much wider role was evident which encompassed teaching and learning but also the support of emotional, social and behavioural aspects of learning. However, for this to be effective, clear communication channels need to be open between all parties for successful collaboration to develop.

The activity was aimed at emotional and social development through a discussion on what is meant by the word 'happiness' which included some excellent examples of multi-sensory approaches to help engage the diverse range of learning needs which included both verbal and physical cues. The teaching assistant used resources from a published training pack which she had adapted to meet the unique needs of her group. The teaching assistant had used the pupils' strengths and interests to model what they thought happiness was and what it felt like. The use of a mirror to show facial changes when feeling happy was an excellent way to model this for the pupil with ASD, and to demonstrate that verbal communication is not the only way to recognize happiness in other people. This matched some of the expected outcomes on the provision maps, for example: 'to develop knowledge that his feelings have an impact on others' and 'to develop his basic social skills, including recognition of his own behaviour and the impact of others . . . identifying anxiety triggers'.

A range of behavioural management skills was also evident throughout the activity with the teaching assistant very skilfully drawing attention back from silly or inappropriate comments through targeted questioning and use of reinforcing language. The use of humour also helped defuse a number of potential problems – a strategy that would also be useful if used by the class teacher back in the classroom. Thinking about the impact of this group from the three perspectives – teacher, teaching assistant and SENCO – raises some interesting points.

The class teacher of the pupil with ASD was interviewed prior to the activity and seemed very unsure as to what the planning and intended impact was in regard to the nurture group. Although the 'existence' of a child with ASD was evident in the classroom, through the use of a workstation, visual timetable, etc, the responsibility of the continuity from nurture group to classroom seemed to fall on the shoulders of the teaching assistant. This matches the findings made by MacBeath (2009) where 'teachers often referred us to the LSA, as teachers themselves had very little contact with, or knowledge of, the children in question'.

In this case, the class teacher was happy for the teaching assistant to plan and deliver the activity independently with feedback coming from the provision mapping reviews carried out termly. This specialized awareness of individual needs was particularly evident through the feedback between the teaching assistant and the SENCO.

Feedback between the teaching assistant and the SENCO at the end of the activity was very productive. The teaching assistant obviously valued the chance to be observed by the SENCO and to receive feedback on their teaching and the impact on the children's learning. This was the first time this had happened in the school and it helped identify an area of continued professional development needed for teaching assistants, which the SENCO was keen to develop. To do this, there needs to be school culture with a collaborative ethos, where teaching assistants are given the opportunity to 'reflect on their practice, self-appraise and share ideas, expertise and knowledge with others' (Groom and Rose, 2005: 201).

What stood out from this feedback session was the level of expertise the teaching assistant had – she was clearly the 'expert' in outlining the learning needs of the pupils, particularly the boy with ASD whom she supports part-time in the classroom. The SENCO was very much in a collaborative relationship, actively taking on advice and suggestions from the teaching assistant. This was a rewarding example of the 'mutual respect and confidence and a shared purpose' described by Rose (2000: 194) and noted earlier in this chapter.

Comments made by the teaching assistant highlighted the need for this continuity and collaboration. These included:

Linking [this nurture group] to the classroom is a crucial part of what I do.

I am always thinking, how will this intervention benefit the class teacher?

I will take photos of [the pupil] in class when he is happy or when class mates are happy to show what it looks like. This can then be sent home to parents.

I will only feedback to the class teacher something that I feel is significant to the pupil's development. Otherwise informal verbal feedback is given although time constraints are an issue.

I feel that it is beneficial if teaching assistants linked to individual pupils are present in the nurture group. This saves having to find time to feed back after each session.

This contextualized learning event raised some interesting reflections regarding feedback. For the class teacher, this seemed to be almost a secondary role; there was an awareness of learning happening outside the classroom but the continuity in planning the learning that came after it was seen as the responsibility of the teaching assistant. In this context this worked, as the teaching assistant was confident and had a range of specialized knowledge regarding the needs of the pupils. However, the question would be who has overall responsibility for the progression of learning and who is monitoring the impact of intervention in the classroom? How is effective communication being utilized to ensure the 'seamless provision' (DfES, 2001, 5:27) for both parents and children with special educational needs in the classroom?

The feedback between the teaching assistant and SENCO was a powerful example of collaborative working where the SENCO gained from the experience as well as the teaching assistant. What was good to see here was that the SENCO acknowledged this and took recommendations on board. This meant that in this situation the teaching assistant felt valued and an integral part of the teaching and learning process.

With the SENCO taking up her new management role, this collaborative approach can only improve in this school, and may be evidence of the likely consequence of giving SENCOs a place in senior leadership teams. The role of teaching assistants in supporting the learning of children with SEN and/or disabilities is seen as crucial and the SENCO is already preparing to complete appraisals with the teaching assistants to identify training needs and also to deploy staff based on their strengths. This can only have a positive impact on collaborative working in this setting, which will help ensure quality teaching and learning for all pupils, enabling them to become independent learners and ultimately raise standards of achievement. (DfEE, 2000: 9).

References

Blatchford, P., Kutnick, P., Baines, E. and Galton, M. (2003) Towards a social pedagogy of classroom group work, *International Journal of Educational Research*, 39(1/2): 153.

DCSF (2007) *The Children's Plan: Building Brighter Futures*. London: HMSO.

DCSF (2008a) *21st Century Schools: A World Class Education for Every Child*. London: HMSO.

DCSF (2008b) *Personalised Learning: A Practical Guide*. London: HMSO.

DfEE (2000) *Working with Teaching Assistants: A Good Practical Guide*. London: DfEE.

DfES (2001) *Special Educational Needs: Code of Practice*. London: HMSO.

DfES (2003) *Developing the Role of Support Staff: What the National Agreement Means for You*. London: DfES.

Dyer, H. (1996) Where do we go from here? Issues in the Professional Development of Teaching Assistants, *Research in Post-Compulsory Education*, 1.

Gerber, S., Finn, J., Achilles, C. and Boyd-Zaharias, J. (2001) *The Enduring Effects of Small Classes*. New York: Teachers College Record, No. 103.

Gerschel, L. (2005) The SENCO's role in managing teaching assistants: the Greenwich perspective, *Support for Learning*, 20(2): 69–77.

Groom, B. and Rose, R. (2005) Supporting the inclusion of pupils with social, emotional and behavioural difficulties in the primary school: the role of teaching assistants, *Journal of Research in Special Educational Needs*, 5(1): 20–31.

MacBeath, J. (2009) *Border Crossing: Improving Schools*, vol. 12, no. 1. London: Sage. Available at: http://imp.sagepub.com.

Ofsted (2002) *Teaching Assistants in Primary Schools: An Evaluation of the Quality and Impact of their Work*. London: HMSO.

Ofsted (2006) *Inclusion: Does it Matter Where Children are Taught?* London: HMSO.

Ofsted (2009) *Inspection Report*. Available at: http://www.ofsted.gov.uk/oxedu_reports/download/(id)/105244/(as)/135052_319604.pdf.

Rose, R. (2000) Using classroom support in a primary school, *British Journal of Special Education*, 27(4).

TDA (2009) *The National Award for SEN Coordination*. London: TDA Publications.

17

BUILDING CONSENSUS: NEGOTIATING, LISTENING, INFLUENCING AND SUSTAINING COMMUNICATION
LEARNING FROM DANNY

Niki Elliot

Introduction

In schools much emphasis is placed on the analysis of 'hard' numerical data in trying to understand pupils' progress, but such data has its limitations. It tells you about outcomes and helps you pose questions, but it does not tell you about the processes and experiences that led to those outcomes. This kind of information emerges from the more eclectic data gathering that results in people's accounts of 'what happened' and 'why it happened', and our identification of particular events or observations that have challenged or informed our thinking. One way of describing these is as critical incidents (Tripp, 1993; Angelides, 2001).

This chapter makes use of a series of critical incidents to analyse practice in a school as it seeks to understand and respond to a new student, Danny, who is showing signs of distress. In particular, we are interested in role of the SENCO in building a partnership with the student and his mother and enabling collaboration and communication across the school.

For our purposes the critical incident analysis has three distinct phases:

1 The telling of the incident.
2 Analysing the responses to that incident.
3 Identifying what can be learned from it.

If the analysis is to be robust we need to ask well-focused questions:

1 What characteristics of this school enable it to identify and overcome barriers to Danny achieving, participating and belonging?
2 What role does the SENCO play in promoting effective communication and collaboration?

Critical Incident 1: Noticing Danny

'Hello, Mrs Jones – good to meet you. I'm Danny's form teacher Mr O'Riorden, and this is my colleague Ms Michaels. Danny says you are new to the area so we haven't really had a chance to meet before.'

Mrs Jones looked hesitantly from one to the other trying to read their faces. She decided on Mr O'Riorden because he was smiling, 'Danny doesn't want to come to school.'

Mr O'Riorden stopped smiling and looked at Ms Michaels, who seemed unsurprised, 'Well, he does seem pretty anxious to us and he hasn't managed to find any friends yet.'

'He's made a friend with the lad down the road but he doesn't come to this school . . . He didn't really get on that well at his last school. He's been worrying himself sick – I mean, *sick* all summer. He was such a bright happy little boy – interested in everything but when he got to Year 3 . . .'

'We think all children deserve a fresh start.' Mr O'Riorden tried smiling again, but Mrs Jones had stopped looking at faces.

Mr O'Riorden was very concerned. Danny barely spoke to anyone. In science lessons he looked interested but didn't seem to be able to get himself organized or follow instructions and his written work – well . . . The thing was Mr O'Riorden had very little information about Danny apart from his SATs results, which were worryingly low. When he phoned Danny's previous school his teacher described him as being a kinaesthetic learner, as having 'enthusiasms' but giving up very quickly. He particularly enjoyed PE and showed some talent. She had noted that his SATs results reflected his lack of persistence rather than his ability and commented that he consistently chose chatting to his friends over real work and could be uncooperative and argumentative when asked to 'knuckle down'.

There was no sign of that sort behaviour here, just sheer terror.

Ms Michaels, the SENCO, had spotted Danny early. She made a point of being around at breaks and lunchtimes when Y7 were new to the school. She had also picked up on Danny's SATs results and that he hadn't attended any induction. The teaching assistants had noticed Danny's isolation and his struggles to complete any work across different subjects and were also asking teachers for their observations.

The pastoral team have worked with the SENCO to identify how they can best share their expertise and knowledge of pupils. Together they have highlighted key events in the calendar for the different year groups to make sure that they focus their attention on good information-sharing and joint working at these times. The beginning of Year 7 is one such time. The form tutors work with the SENCO to identify students who are encountering barriers in school and conduct joint meetings with parents where there are concerns.

This school has a well-orchestrated induction and review process for its Year 7 students. Nonetheless, Danny and his mother have missed induction and that puts him at a disadvantage. Danny's form tutor makes good use of the transition information available to him and is proactive in contacting Danny's previous school.

The SENCO works closely with her teaching assistant team. They have half-termly meetings at which they discuss students who are of concern. This allows the SENCO to model practice in what to look for when observing students and how to make use of observations to help gain a holistic view of a student and avoid jumping to conclusions. The teaching assistants understand their role in observing students. They have a short team meeting every morning that ensures that information gets shared in a timely way.

Critical Incident 2: Finding out about Danny

'Mrs Jones, I can see that this is really worrying for you. We don't know much about Danny yet so I wonder if we could take some time to talk to you and Danny and try to understand what has happened?' Ms Michaels waited for a response.

'I can't . . .' There was a long pause, Mrs Jones wasn't used to being *asked*, mostly, in the past, she had been *told* about Danny. How he wasn't meeting his potential, how he wasted time, how he stopped other children from learning. She was hoping this school would be different. Perhaps . . .

'Would it be easier if I came to see you? School isn't always the best place to talk things through.'

Mrs Jones could feel Ms Michaels watching her carefully. She shifted in her seat and gathered herself together.

'I can't talk about it now but that might help. I could think . . . Danny could think . . . We . . .'

Ms Michaels was relieved. She could only guess at what had happened in the past but it seemed that Mrs Jones was struggling with schools too. There were some delicate discussions to be had.

This school values the views of parents and children, but does not assume that it is easy for them to express those views (Armstrong, 1995). Ms Michaels recognizes that school is an intimidating place for Danny and also for his mother so she is willing to meet them on their own territory.

She doesn't leap in with tests and diagnoses and 'what the staff at school think' but acknowledges that Danny and his mother already know a lot. In short, she is trying to establish a partnership between them rather than presenting herself as the expert with the solutions. She is asking not telling.

Happily for Ms Michaels, on their own patch both Danny and his mother are willing to think and talk, although Danny has his suspicions about her motives in visiting them.

Ms Michaels settled down in Danny's front room. Danny looked apprehensive, 'Hello . . .' Danny hesitated. 'Are you here because I'm stupid?' His eyes filled with tears.

'No, Danny. Mostly I'm here because I want to get to know you and find out what you are interested in. But I'd also like to find out what you think of school and how we could do things better.'

What emerged as they talked over tea was that Danny was actually very interested in lots of things. He told her a lot about his science lessons and what Mr O'Riorden had been teaching them. She asked Danny to take her through a science lesson and tell her about the good bits and the bad bits. The good bits were the ideas. The bad bits were all about reading, especially from the board, and writing. Danny also said he got annoyed with himself because he got muddled and forgot what he was supposed to do next.

Mrs Jones started talking about Danny's move from the infant school, where he was happy, to primary school, where he was seen as chatty and not trying hard. She was torn between thinking the teacher was right, and putting more pressure on Danny, and worrying that there might be an underlying reason for his lack of progress.

Danny looked cross. Sometimes he *had* just been chatting, but most of the time his friends had been helping him with reading and he had been helping them with ideas. He couldn't see what was wrong with that. He knew he wouldn't have anyone to ask at his new school and he had been worried about how he was going to manage and what people would think of him and whether all the different teachers would get cross with him like his last teacher had. He was also terrified of being late for a lesson and was confused by the timetable and the constant moving around in secondary school.

The discussions with Danny and his mother, together with the observations of the teaching assistants and teachers, had started to paint a pretty clear picture. Danny knew a lot about what was going on in his lessons, but he struggled with reading and writing and was a bit disorganized. In his new school he had no friends to help him out – the other Year 7s had noticed, with suspicion, his interest in their work and his tendency to hang around them to find out what to do next. They were not welcoming Danny into their groups of friends. Because Danny was frightened that the teachers would get cross with him he couldn't ask for help and tended to try to hide the work he was doing. That left Danny with no strategies to cope.

Soon after Ms Michaels' arrival in this school she started to work closely with senior leaders to discuss what they meant when they described the school as 'inclusive'. Over time the school has developed a very clear philosophy based on the social model of disability (Mittler, 2000). The social model starts from a position of thinking critically about the impact of the organization on the individual, considering any issues from his or her perspective. Ms Michaels and her colleagues set out with the intention of identifying the barriers experienced by Danny and other students.

Barriers can arise from attitudes, practices and systems. In Danny's case the attitude of a former teacher and the suspicions of his fellow students are stopping him from getting help, making it difficult for him to participate. The practice of focusing on written work as a means of assessing and recording achievement has stopped Danny from demonstrating what he is capable of, so his achievements are not properly recognized. Finally, the timing of induction activities in the school and his late arrival into the area meant that he had not been introduced to his new classmates and teachers. Consequently they know very little about each other, making it hard for Danny to feel welcome or to begin to belong.

The SENCO's role here is to understand the culture, attitudes and practices in her school and to work with colleagues to understand the impact that these have on different students (Booth and Ainscow, 2002). Essentially, Ms Michaels has to evaluate everyone's starting points and identify where the mismatches are.

Critical incident 3: Observing Danny

A teaching assistant watched Danny as the class wrestled with averages in maths. Danny was attentive. He sorted out some examples of when you would use the different sorts of average and even put his hand up to answer a question.

The words Mode, Mean and Median were written on the board. Danny wrote 'meed' in his book and seemed happy with this, then he wrote 'modan' and looked puzzled. The maths teacher was heading his way so Danny turned over the page. 'Come on Danny just three words to get down!' The teacher meant to be encouraging but Danny froze. He fought desperately not to cry, failed and ran out of the room. What would the other students think of him now? How could he ever go back into a lesson?

The observations from staff and teaching assistants were consistent. Danny was anxious and isolated, very easily put off his stride. He listened well and occasionally would volunteer an answer, but the minute he was asked to write or copy anything, he struggled and panicked. He was embarrassed by any attempts to support him and rejected help. Now he was refusing to go into any lessons.

Ms Michaels talked things through with Mr O'Riorden. There were three priorities: to address Danny's isolation and anxiety so that he could get back into his lessons, to get a better picture of Danny's ability than was offered by his SATs results, and to find out the exact nature of his problems with reading and writing.

The school ran a buddying scheme where Y8 students ran a breaktime club, so Ms Michaels asked one of the buddies to befriend Danny and invite him along. Mr O'Riorden asked two other boys from Danny's form to go along too and to try to get to know Danny.

Meanwhile, Danny worked with Ms Michaels and with teaching assistants in the Learning Centre. Danny was talking about science again to the science teaching assistant, Miss Sharma.

'Danny, that was really interesting; would you mind if I wrote it down for you so we could show Mr O'Riorden?' Danny and Miss Sharma showed his work to Mr O'Riorden, who was impressed.

Together the three of them worked out a plan to get him back into his science lessons. They talked about how Danny had worked with his friends in primary school and agreed that it would be a good way to work in science with his new 'buddies'. Miss Sharma would take some notes for him in the lesson, but *not* so it looked as though she was doing his work. Then they would finish any writing together back in the Learning Centre. Danny's mother was relieved when Mr O'Riorden phoned up to explain what they were doing. It was agreed that Miss Sharma would talk to Danny every day and let his mother know how he was getting on.

Danny started going back to his lessons. A note went round to Danny's teachers thanking them for their observations and saying that based on these the initial strategy would be to focus on his verbal contributions to lessons, taking the emphasis off written work. The teaching assistants supported this strategy by working with teachers to design alternative activities so that Danny could discuss and record his learning. These, in turn, helped the teachers to gauge more accurately the level at which Danny was working.

In addition to having a specialist teaching assistant, each subject area identifies a link teacher to coordinate work with students with additional needs. Teaching assistants understand the expectations and teaching approaches in their subject and are seen as part of the teaching team. Some teaching assistants also offer expertise in an aspect of SEN. As a result they are in a good position to work in partnership with teachers. Teachers and teaching assistants have made an early, thoughtful contribution to finding out about Danny. This, together with the partnership between Danny and the science staff, has informed the strategy which is put in place as Danny returns to his lessons.

Placing a teaching assistant in a 'key worker' role means that information can be gathered and shared systematically with Danny and his mother and, via the teaching assistants' briefing meetings, with Danny's teachers. Everyone is up-to-date and everyone is in a position to pass on any new information.

The SENCO's skill in this process is one of gaining and sharing information in a way which ensures that the people involved feel that their perspective is respected and influential in determining any changes to be made. She has thought about who the key players are and has created systems that make it easy for them to provide information. The SENCO has successfully built a consultative structure through which information is gathered, shared and acted upon.

Critical Incident 4: Learning from Danny

The teachers were pleased, and surprised, by Danny's levels of attainment. This was a good starting point for talking to him.

'How can I be good when I'm so rubbish at reading and writing?'

'What it means, Danny, is that you are good at thinking and understanding things, but we need to find out more about your reading and why that is so difficult for you. Can you tell me anything about that? What happens when you look at some writing?'

Danny pulled a face. 'This will sound stupid, Miss – the letters won't stay still.'

Danny told Ms Michaels that he did read stuff at home, but it took him a long time. He had some strategies for taming the moving letters but it was hard to use them in school and reading from the whiteboard was nearly impossible. Writing was a waste of time because it took him ages; he couldn't write what he wanted to say and what he did write was usually wrong.

In the past Ms Michaels had arranged to support students with difficulties similar to Danny's by taking them out of a couple of lessons a week, putting them on a special programme and providing some in-class support. But she felt that wouldn't be enough for Danny – he had said some things that troubled her. The barriers to Danny showing his real abilities and participating fully also came from how he was expected to learn and show his learning. She could help Danny to improve his reading skills but he would remain at a disadvantage. How could this school repair the damage of Danny's earlier experiences?

Ms Michaels invited a specialist teacher into the school to assess Danny's reading and writing difficulties. Together with the teaching assistants and link teachers they reviewed the issues that Danny faced, discussing his reading and organizational problems and what this meant for him in his different lessons. The link teachers and teaching assistants were able to identify examples of successful practice and resources they felt they could share. The teachers also acknowledged that they felt a bit uncertain about why Danny and other students experienced such difficulties. It was hard, with all the other pressures on their time, to 'get into Danny's shoes' and see a lesson from his perspective. As students' reading and writing skills often presented problems in lessons, it seemed sensible to build on this meeting. A 'getting into Danny's shoes' workshop would enable staff to work together to recognize the barriers students such as Danny faced, and draw on everyone's expertise in overcoming them. Danny liked the idea.

Ms Michaels wrote a report for the senior leaders and SEN governor on the school's experiences with Danny so far, and with students with similar difficulties. The report evaluated the provision the school had already put in place and pointed out the barriers that these students continued to experience. Among her recommendations Ms Michaels suggested the workshop as part of the school's raising achievement strategy.

Two important issues are raised by this critical incident. First, making specific provision for Danny is not enough for him to achieve, so change needs to take place throughout the school. Second, just issuing guidance on Danny's needs is unlikely to result in sustained changes in practice. Colleagues had commented that they need time to 'get into Danny's shoes'. Creating a workshop, based on the challenges that Danny faces, offers this time and an opportunity to build competence and generate solutions. From Danny's perspective, this is a school that wants to understand him, wants him to belong.

The SENCO has made good use of the systems that she has put in place to gather information but if she is to bring about changes in practice, she also has to gather support. Creating different forums that value the knowledge of a wide range of people enables the school to learn about itself and its practices. In a coordinating role it is difficult to *make* people do things so it is necessary to create opportunities that demonstrate, persuasively, the need for change and the wider benefits of any change. The SENCO engages with the issues faced by Danny in the different subjects and by doing so can make a strong case for action through formal reporting and decision-making processes. Her case addresses not only Danny's needs but also the wider priorities of the school.

Coda

The workshop did not solve all the problems for Danny. However, it did bring about changes in practice and created a platform for greater understanding. This helped Danny to settle into and benefit from his new school and helped his school to continue to learn from him.

This case study is a fictionalized version of real events. It draws on the practical experiences of the author in collaboration with the head of a learning support service. Our thanks to all the Dannys and their parents and schools that have contributed to our learning and to this chapter – who ask difficult questions of our education system and help us to improve it.

References

Angelides, P. (2001) Using critical incidents to understand school cultures, *Improving Schools*, 4(1): 24–33.

Armstrong, D. (1995) *Power and Partnership in Education*. London: Routledge.

Booth, T. and Ainscow, M. (2002) *The Index for Inclusion: Developing Learning and Participation in Schools*. Bristol: CSIE.

Mittler, P. (2000) *Working Towards Inclusive Education: Social Context*. London: David Fulton Publishers.

Tripp, D. (1993) *Critical Incidents in Teaching: Developing Professional Judgement*. London: Routledge.

18

THE GOVERNING BODY: AN (UNTAPPED) RESOURCE

Sue Pearson

Introduction

The title of this chapter reflects evidence that Governors have a valuable role to play in relation to special educational needs but that the extent to which this is developed varies across schools. SENCos have a role to play in ensuring that a positive, constructive relationship is built with the governing body and the SEN Governor(s).

The first part of this chapter sets out the current policy position before considering recent developments and evidence about practice, based on data from a national sample of SENCos. The final section suggests ways in which the potential of this group of stakeholders can be strengthened.

Policy context

Governors have an overall responsibility in relation to the school including issues such as the curriculum, policies and practices, budget, premises and extra-curricular activities. Each of these facets impinges on the inclusion of pupils with SEN, including the outcomes they achieve. Therefore the governing body of each school should proactively consider the implications of any decision on the whole school population.

Section 317 of the Education Act 1996 states the statutory responsibilities of Governors in relation to SEN. Their general duties were reiterated in the Code of Practice which linked these to the 'general policy and approach to meeting pupils' special educational needs for those with and without statements (DfES, 2001, Section 1.17). The Code of Practice states that the governing body must

- do its best to ensure that the necessary provision is made for any pupil who has special educational needs;
- ensure that, where the 'responsible person' – the Headteacher or the appropriate governor – has been informed by the LEA that a pupil has special educational needs, those needs are made known to all who are likely to teach them;

- ensure that teachers in the school are aware of the importance of identifying, and providing for, those pupils who have special educational needs;

- consult the LEA and the governing bodies of other schools, when it seems to be necessary or desirable in the interests of co-ordinated special educational provision in the area as a whole;

- ensure that a pupil with special educational needs joins in the activities of the school together with pupils who do not have special educational needs, so far as is reasonably practical and compatible with the child receiving the special educational provision their learning needs call for and the efficient education of the pupils with whom they are educated and the efficient use of resources;

- report to parents on the implementation of the school's policy for pupils with special educational needs (see Section 317, Education Act 1996).

- have regard to this Code of Practice when carrying out its duties toward all pupils with special educational needs (see Section 313, Education Act 1996).

Each of the phase-based sections of the Code of Practice provides further elaboration of the roles and responsibilities. Other recent pieces of legislation have extended these responsibilities into areas such as disability, including producing an access plan.

The governing body has specific responsibilities in relation to SENCos (DCSF, 2008). The content of this amendment was informed by the Select Committee report on SEN (House of Commons Education Select Committee, 2006). It requires that governing bodies should ensure that the SENCo is a trained teacher and that newly appointed SENCos gain the National Award in SEN Coordination.

In discharging their duties in relation to special educational needs, there has been a trend for schools to identify an individual Governor or a group of Governors to take a specific responsibility for this aspect of the school (Gordon and Williams, 2002). In the light of this, the term 'SEN Governor' has entered the lexicon with, for example, the DfES producing a video entitled 'Making a Difference: A Guide to Special Educational Needs (SEN) Governors' (DfES, 2003). This portrayed the role as a link between the school and the governing body, and emphasized that 'taking the time and effort to find out about SEN pays dividends in terms of [SEN Governor's] usefulness to the school' (DfES, 2003: 5). This is consistent with the generic guidance offered on Governornet with reference to link governors (e.g. those linked to literacy, numeracy, ICT, SEN) which foregrounds their responsibilities in relation to training, in terms of identifying training needs for new and existing governors, awareness of the LA training programmes, and attending LA training linked to their area of responsibility.

In the case of the SEN Governor(s), the role has been described as being a 'champion', a critical friend or a source of support. However, the responsibilities of the SEN Governor(s) are limited; the policies and practices remain the corporate responsibility of the governing body.

Evidence about the current situation

Research in relation to governing bodies and special educational needs is sparse, often reliant on a relatively small sample, and mostly somewhat dated (Scott, 1993; Baskind and Thompson, 1994; Wilson, 2001). Therefore, this section draws on two key sources; the evidence from the recent Lamb Report (DCSF, 2009) and from research commissioned by nasen (Pearson, 2008a, 2008b). Both these sources consider the role of the governing body although from slightly different perspectives.

The Lamb Report (DCSF, 2009), which was primarily concerned with parental confidence in SEN systems, referred to Governors, especially Chapter 4. It under-scored the importance of the role of the governing body and emphasized the need for training to support these committed volunteers to fulfil their role. The Report recommended the commencement in September 2011 of a training programme for Chairs of governing bodies and new Governors, and also recommended the development of an on-line resource about legal matters (available from September 2010). All Governors have access to advice and guidance through 'Governornet' (www.governornet.co.uk). The Lamb Report also recommended that the School Improvements Partner should include comments in their reports to governing bodies 'on the extent to which the school has promoted good outcomes and good progress for disabled pupils and pupils with SEN' (Recommendation 33). Thus the Lamb Report offered advice on training and support, and the sharing of information about provision. These feature in the linked Implementation Plan.

In 2007, nasen commissioned research into the 'Working Lives of SENCos', involving a postal questionnaire to 500 SENCos based in England. One section in this related to contact with the SEN Governor. Some 10.8 per cent of the respondents said the school did not have a SEN Governor. An additional question related to contact between the SENCo and the SEN Governor with 22 per cent either having no SEN Governor or no contact. Others were in a more fortunate position with frequent contact, and were very positive about the benefits.

These findings prompted further research to explore the issues in more detail, and to identify promising practices. An initial stage involved reviewing the resources available on Local Authority websites, the extent and nature of which are varied but mostly useful.

Reflection

What do current resources, and literature, suggest about relationships between schools or settings, and their governing bodies?

The findings from this phase informed the questions asked in a postal survey sent to a sample of SENCos; 191 responses were analysed. These were from mainstream schools for all age groups, but since the responsibilities are broadly similar, phase-based analysis was not undertaken. The survey considered both the role of the governing body as a whole and the links between the governing body and the school via the SENCo or the Head.

Table 18.1 Arrangements within the governing body in relation to SEN

One SEN Governor	Two or more Governors to share the responsibility	The Head acts as the named person	There is no SEN Governor	Not sure	Other
153	9	4	5	8	4

It was noted earlier that most governing bodies delegate the responsibilities to one or more Governors (Gordon and Williams, 2002). The data from the nasen research supported this view (Table 18.1).

'Other' was used by respondents where, for example, there was a sub-committee with this responsibility. In the cases where there were no SEN Governors, this may have been linked to changes in the governing body or be an apparent oversight.

> 'As far as I know there is no SEN governor. Any "post" addressed to the SEN Governor is put into my pigeon hole'.
>
> (Secondary SENCo)

Reflection

Does a conflict of interest occur in a school or setting if the Headteacher is also the SEN Governor? How might this affect the role of the SENCo?

Contact between the SENCo and/or the Headteacher, and the governing body including the SEN Governor was very variable. The data gathered considered both scheduled meetings and ad hoc ones. Perhaps the key question here should be about the SENCos' level of satisfaction with the arrangements, rather than their regularity. As an example of this, evidence about the adequacy of contact between the SENCo and the SEN Governor appears in Table 18.2.

Clearly, there are grounds for concern in this data but also evidence that some SENCos view the links more positively.

Reflection

Who should set the agenda for meetings between the SENCo and SEN Governor? How often should such meetings take place?

Developing a constructive relationship with the SEN Governor/ governing body

There are twin motives for developing a constructive relationship between the SENCo and the SEN Governor/governing body. First, to enable both to fulfil

Table 18.2 SENCos' view about the adequacy of the contact with the SEN Governor

	Not frequent enough	About right
Scheduled (n = 170)	76	94
Ad hoc (n = 145)	63	82

their duties as outlined above and, second, so that potential benefits are fully realized. Having completed the questionnaire for the nasen research, some respondents reassessed their relationship with the governing body, and the unexploited potential.

> Just goes to show how much support the department is potentially missing out on.
>
> (Primary SENCo)

> It has made me realize how isolated I actually feel without any real support from the governing body who don't seem to ask questions or ask how it is going unless there is an Ofsted inspection due then it's PRESSURE, PRESSURE, PRESSURE.
>
> (Middle school SENCo)

Several themes relevant to a constructive relationship emerged from the review of LA websites and the response from SENCos.

Clarity of roles

There is a need for all parties to be clear about their roles and responsibilities. Some LAs provide model descriptions of the role of the SEN Governor and some schools, through a process of negotiation, have developed such a document, suited to the circumstances of the school.

Appropriate sharing of information

Given that the SENCo is seen as 'pivotal' to SEN provision (DfES, 2004), sharing information with the governing body and the SEN Governor is vital and should be part of the role of every SENCo. However, in the nasen survey, only 65 per cent of the SENCos provided information to the Governors or the SEN Governor. Examples of materials shared included information about forms of provision, the staff available, the range of needs and needs of pupils.

Clearly the provision of information, with opportunities for discussion and clarification, is particularly valuable for newly appointed SEN Governors. Termly updates were used by many of the respondents to ensure that the data is current, and indeed the very discipline of regular sharing contributes to strengthening the links between the stakeholders.

Reviewing the special educational needs policy

Section 1.22 of the Code of Practice refers to the role of the Governors in school self-review and being fully informed about the school. The special educational needs policy document is significant for both the governing body, which is responsible for the school's strategic direction as outlined above, and for the staff of the school, since it underpins the provision for learners in the school. It provides a shared agenda that can cement the relationship.

Beyond reviewing the policy, the governing body is well placed to consider how it articulates with other school wide policies (e.g. behaviour policy, inclusion policy) and influences departmental policies.

Anonymized case studies

An approach used by a small number of schools involves providing (a group of) Governors with a case study about an individual child. The purpose of this is to contextualize the discussions about issues such as identification, provision and outcomes. These are complex, potentially contentious issues and exploring them in a non-threatening framework can be helpful. Some respondents regarded the Governors as 'passive' and this approach may engage them in a meaningful activity.

> 'We have used this way of explaining the needs of individuals at school and the processes that take place to support them in the mainstream setting'.
>
> (Primary SENCo)

However, difficulties exist with case studies in small schools where individual children are easily identified.

Flexible communication routes

There is no simple answer as to who should initiate the contact, the SENCo or the SEN Governor. The form and style of communication needed for both parties may vary at different points in the year or as relationships mature. Respondents provided some examples of reciprocal contacts with the emphasis on these being purposeful with a mixture of scheduled and ad hoc meetings:

> We meet as necessary but contact one another whenever appropriate and arrange meetings if needed.
>
> (Primary SENCo)

> Though it is not a fixed date – we meet regularly and email/phone each other often. She attends 2–3 of our Faculty meetings per annum.
>
> (Secondary SENCo)

Exploring the expertise of the Governors

As volunteers, Governors are frequently able to bring to their role expertise that they have gained elsewhere. Some of the respondents to the survey were very positive about how they capitalized on this, thereby enriching the provision in the school. For example, one SEN Governor was an occupational therapist who could share her professional knowledge. In other circumstances, the SEN Governor brings to the situation a fresh perspective which can produce some 'naïve' questions, the innocent enquiries that mean the status quo is critically re-considered. The SENCo needs to adapt to the strengths of the SEN Governor and take this into account when jointly planning the arrangements.

Sensitivity to potential difficulties

Given the confidential nature of some of the information about special educational needs, the SENCos were asked about issues such as confidentiality, conflicts of interest and ethical concerns. For the majority, these were either insignificant or manageable, although situations where the SEN Governor held other roles (e.g. Headteacher, TA or parent of a pupil with special educational needs) were more prone to being problematic.

Reflection

With reference to the themes outlined in this section, reflect on the constraints and opportunities for building constructive relationships between the SEN Governor, the school, and the wider school community.

There is a statutory requirement for the governing body of a school to be involved in issues relating to SEN provision; and evidence that this can be beneficial to the staff and pupils of the setting. In many schools, there is scope for improved practice, by approaches that establish collaborative relationships based on the desire to increase the benefits which accrue to the school, the SENCo, the pupils and their families.

References

Baskind, S. and Thompson, D. (1994) What role do governors play as representatives of special needs issues in their own schools? *British Educational Research Journal*, 20(3): 293.

DCSF (2008) *The Education (Special Educational Needs Co-ordinators) (England) Regulations 2008*. Available at: http://www.opsi.gov.uk/si/si2008/uksi_20082945_en_1.

DCSF (2009) *Lamb Inquiry: Special Educational Needs and Parental Confidence*. Nottingham: DCSF.

DfES (2001) *Special Educational Needs Code of Practice*. Nottingham: DfES.

DfES (2003) *Making a Difference: A Guide to Special Educational Needs (SEN) Governors*. Nottingham: DfES Publications.

DfES (2004) *Removing Barriers to Achievement: The Government's Strategy for Inclusion*. London: DfES.

Gordon, M. and Williams, A. (2002) *Special Educational Needs and Disability: A Governors' Guide*. Tamworth: NASEN.

House of Commons Education Select Committee (2006) *Special Educational Needs: Third Report of Session 2005–06*. London: The Stationery Office.

Pearson, S. (2008a) Deafened by silence or by the sound of footsteps? An investigation of the recruitment, induction and retention of SENCos in England, *Journal of Research in Special Educational Needs*, 8(2): 96–108.

Pearson, S. (2008b) *The Working Lives of SENCos*. Tamworth: nasen.

Scott, L. (1993) Confused and ill equipped? *British Journal of Special Education*, 20(4): 120–2.

Wilson, M. (2001) Comprehensive school governance and special educational needs provision: policy, practice and future priorities, *Educational Management and Administration*, 29(1): 49–62.

PART VI

Working in partnership

Introduction to Part VI

The final section contained within the Learning Outcomes framework is 'Working in partnership with pupils, families and other professionals'. The three chapters in Part VI are designed to show this aspect of the work of the SENCo. In Chapter 19, Christopher Robertson considers the Lamb Inquiry Report. A detailed account is given of the context of the Inquiry, focusing on the origins of the current SEN identification and assessment system in England, and the growth of parent partnerships. The need for the Inquiry is explained, in terms of systemic failures, but concentrating on improving the quality of such partnerships. The main recommendations that relate to parental voice are considered, in relation to the role of the SENCo. The chapter concludes by giving an overview of future trends in parent partnership. The Learning Outcomes contained in the theme 'Drawing on external sources of support and expertise' are evidenced here, particularly enabling SENCos to do the following:

- know the role and value of families and carers of pupils with SEN and/or disabilities;
- know the range of organizations and individuals working with pupils with SEN and/or disabilities and their role in providing information, advice and support.

Chapter 19 gives a reflective account of two important and developing themes. In the first, Christopher considers the way in which a changed perspective is evident around SEN, with the emergence of ways of thinking that challenge the power of the professionals involved, in making decisions on SEN provision, and place that power much more firmly in the hands of parents. The second theme looks at the way that the current system of identification and assessment, while under considerable strain, is capable of working better, if the full recommendations of the Lamb Inquiry are implemented.

Chapter 20 is by Lynne Cook who has written about multi-agency collaboration. The chapter is constructed as a narrative case study that details the events surrounding a pupil, whose special educational needs will be familiar to many. In introducing us to the pupil in this way, Lynne does not offer a view of how multi-agency collaboration should work; rather she opens a window into the often muddled way that practice develops, in a story that combines missed opportunities, difficult relationships, and competing perspectives, with the desire to reach out and help a young person to deal with the chaos in her life. In doing this, Lynne offers pointers to improved practice, and invites reflection, through a series of questions, on the fallibility of systems, when they rely on collaboration, communication and teamwork. This material addresses the Learning Outcomes from the theme 'Drawing on external sources of support and expertise', namely:

- know the principles of multi-agency working, building a 'team around a child', and the Common Assessment Framework and how to use it, where appropriate, for pupils with SEN and/or disabilities;
- develop effective working partnerships with professionals in other services and agencies, including voluntary organizations, to support a coherent, coordinated and effective approach to supporting pupils with SEN and/or disabilities;
- know how to interpret specialist information from other professionals and agencies to support appropriate teaching and learning for pupils with SEN and/or disabilities and support colleagues in making use of such information.

Lynne has highlighted here the constant need for the system that has been built up around meeting the needs of children and young people to be self-evaluative. A reflection on the seeming inability of that system to successfully protect all of the young people it is designed to look after, despite a succession of initiatives, policies, and legislative frameworks to ensure that it does, might highlight the changing role of the SENCo, in moving from process management to strategic leadership.

In Chapter 21, Barbara Bradbury, Alison Feeney and Anne Gager contribute a powerful chapter on Hearing the Voice of the Child. The chapter begins with a consideration of how the need to hear pupil voice has become a central part of current practice in schools, and suggests that this is fraught with inherent complications in the case of pupils with additional needs. Three case studies of pupils, each of whose voice is likely to go unheeded, are offered. There is an acknowledgement of the variability with which pupil voice is heard; the SENCo is seen as the facilitator of change in this area, capable of overcoming the inertia that prevents the adoption of uniformly good practice. The need for systemic flexibility, embodying genuine consultation, is seen as an antidote to tokenistic practice; this is exemplified in a discussion focusing on difficulties with the structure of meetings. The chapter addresses Learning Outcomes within the theme 'Consulting, engaging and communicating with colleagues, parents and carers and pupils', by enabling SENCos to do the following:

- ensure that pupils with SEN and/or disabilities are involved, whenever appropriate, in planning, agreeing, reviewing and evaluating the provision made for them;

- communicate effectively with parents and carers of pupils with SEN and/or disabilities, taking account of their views.

Three important themes for reflection can be drawn from this chapter. The first considers the rights of the child which, although clearly and aspirationally defined, can be difficult to enact. This leads to the second, that of the disenfranchisement of pupils where the voice of the child is ignored, either because it cannot be elicited or because it is misunderstood or where a surrogate voice, for example, that of the parents, is heard in preference. Finally, the chapter challenges us to consider the weight that should be given to any of the voices that surround the pupil, in a system that thinks it always acts in the best interests of those pupils.

Although written to address one of the themes contained within this section of the Learning Outcomes framework, each of the chapters in Part VI could as easily address the remaining themes. Chapter 19, on the Lamb Inquiry, has important messages for pupil voice as well as for parent partnership, and the work of Lynne Cook has at its heart the need for all involved in provision for pupils with SEN and/or disabilities to be aware of the need for good communication.

Similarly, the themes that can be developed from each chapter, by a reflective analysis, can be used to evidence learning outcomes from other areas of the framework. Chapter 20, on multi-agency collaboration, could as easily have been written to exemplify those Learning Outcomes that address internal collaborative practice, within Leading, Developing and Supporting Colleagues, or flexible and innovative use of the existing workforce, from Coordinating Provision. Chapter 21, on valuing pupil voice, resonates with Learning Outcomes in Professional Contexts, such as how a child's development can be affected by their SEN and/or disability; with Coordinating Provision, for example, planning approaches that minimize barriers; or from Strategic Development, to understand the potential of new technologies to support communication. Finally, Chapter 19 has a strong foundation in Professional Contexts, in looking at statutory and regulatory frameworks, and in Strategic Development, by influencing the alignment of policy to school evaluation processes.

19

WORKING IN PARTNERSHIP WITH PARENTS
Christopher Robertson

Introduction

> Good, honest and open communication is key to the development of positive
> working relationships and requires practitioners who listen to parents and
> are trusted by them. Parents' confidence in the SEN system and in schools
> and local authorities in particular, is significantly coloured by the quality
> of communication with them. Personal contact is a key factor for parents of
> children with SEN and no information system will be valued that does not
> make provision for face-to-face communication.
>
> (Lamb, 2009, p. 40, para. 3.1)

This chapter will focus on a key aspect of the role of the SENCO, that of working in
partnership with parents, to secure the best possible outcomes for children with special educational needs (SEN).[1] The importance of this dimension of the role is clearly
reflected in the learning outcomes for the National Award for SEN Coordination,
although these almost certainly underestimate the amount of time that needs to be
invested in collaborative partnership activities.

The chapter will look closely at some of the findings and recommendations
outlined in the final report of the Lamb Inquiry, focusing particularly on recommendations concerned with giving parents a stronger voice in their child's education
and associated provision. Before doing this, it is worth reflecting on the development
of SEN-related parent partnership practice that has evolved over many years, and
commenting on the strengths and weaknesses of this.

Developments in parent partnership

It is too easy to think of the Warnock Report (Warnock, 1978) as belonging to another
era, and as mistaken in many of the ideas it outlined as important for the shaping of
what came to be the 'modern era' of special education policy in the UK (particularly
England). Indeed, Baroness Warnock herself has been fiercely critical of the report
that her Committee of Enquiry produced (Warnock, 2005, 2007, Warnock and

Norwich, 2010). Notwithstanding some of conceptual problems that she and other commentators have identified in the report and some of the implementation difficulties that distorted or failed to follow through with recommendations, it did place a high value on parent partnership. It did this – in a chapter specifically concerned with parents as partners – by emphasizing the value of providing parents with clear practical advice and information, and by arguing that the right for parents to be involved in decision making in the education of their child with SEN should be strengthened. Some of the recommendations in Chapter 9 of the report could have been written in the very recent past. For example, the importance of key workers (a single point of contact) is stressed, and so too, is the entitlement to short breaks for children and their families. Both of these have been the subject of policy campaigns and initiatives during the past five years.

During the 1980s, and following the implementation of the 1981 Education Act (concerned directly with SEN), it became apparent that commitments made to work closely with parents, by local authorities and schools, did not always result in better practice. Although many education professionals thought that they were working in partnership with parents and communicating effectively, the experience of many parents showed that this was not the case (Goacher et al., 1988). In particular, many problems seemed to arise in relation to meeting the requirements of the statutory framework for special education, and aspects of formal assessment in particular. Too often, it seemed that professionals were behaving like 'street level bureaucrats' (Weatherley, 1978), in making it difficult for parents of children with SEN to ensure that their needs were met in accordance with legal requirements. Practice in schools was not so heavily criticized, but variability in the quality of partnership working with parents was a characteristic of the time.

Formalizing parent partnership

In an effort to address some of these difficulties, the first *Code of Practice on the Identification and Assessment of Special Educational Needs* was introduced (DfE, 1994). The Code placed a strong emphasis on the role of parents as partners with their child's school, and formalized the role of parent partnership schemes. It also highlighted the role of SENCOs as key to developing effective partnership practice, although this proved difficult as they found themselves struggling to meet the demands of the role (Ofsted, 1997). With regard to working with parents, some of the intrinsic problems linked to an imbalance of power began to be recognized (Armstrong, 1995). New models of parent partnership began to emerge, that challenged the linear way in which partnership had been conceptualized, and recognized the complexities and tensions involved (Dale, 1995), pointing to the need to acknowledge that parents, schools and local authorities should try to resolve differences of opinion through negotiation.

Systematic reviews of the implementation of the Code pointed to the need for updating and refinement (Lewis et al., 1996), leading to the introduction of the revised *SEN Code of Practice* (DfES, 2001) that still serves as a key framework for practice, providing practical advice and statutory guidance. The importance of parent partnership – for both local authorities and schools – is identified as a fundamental principle in the Code (para. 1.5) and a critical success factor (para. 1.6). More important still, is the inclusion of a chapter at the beginning of the Code that focuses explicitly on working with parents. This chapter states that:

> Parents hold key information and have a critical role to play in their child's education. They have unique strengths, knowledge and experience to contribute to the shared view of a child's needs and the best ways of supporting them. It is therefore essential that all professionals (school, LEAs and other agencies) actively seek to work with parents and value the contribution they make.
>
> (para. 2.2)

This central tenet is developed in three sections; the first outlines ways in which parents should be supported and empowered (para. 2.2); the second sets out clear principles for all education and other professionals to incorporate into their practice and professional cultures (para. 2.7), and finally, the third gives guidance on the ways in which the roles and responsibilities detailed will be discharged; these are summarized in a table at the end of the relevant chapter (p. 26). This guidance is important for SENCOs, in providing clear statutory information, and in setting out principles for good practice, which will help SENCOs to work effectively with parents.

The need for improvement

Despite the good intentions of the Code of Practice, it became apparent in the middle of the first decade of the twenty-first century, that a significant number of parents did not feel that they were being treated as equal partners in the education of their children. These concerns mirrored wider professional concerns about whether or not the SEN system was fit for purpose. The Audit Commission (2002a, 2002b), and the House of Commons Education and Skills Select Committee (2006, 2007) were highly critical of the system, referring to evidence about what was not working received from aggrieved parents. Mary Warnock's (2005, 2007) influential views heightened concerns which were added to by the SEN commission established by the Conservative Party (Balchin, 2006, 2007). In response, the government followed the advice of the Select Committee's report *Special Educational Needs: Assessment and Funding* (House of Commons, 2007), to look anew at causes of parental dissatisfaction, acknowledging that these were inextricably linked to SEN assessment issues.

A formal Inquiry, chaired by Brian Lamb, was set up to advise on the most effective ways of increasing parental confidence in the SEN assessment process. The Inquiry commenced work in March 2008 and, in December 2009, published a final report which addresses issues that extend well beyond those pertaining to assessment issues (Lamb, 2009). The report includes 51 recommendations that, in combination, are intended to ensure that the system will be improved to the extent that parents will be confident that it works for them.[2]

At first glance, SENCOs may feel that the Inquiry Report includes too many recommendations. However, another way of thinking about its content is to view it from a parent's perspective. If all of the recommended actions are addressed, and the SEN system does increase parental confidence, then the benefits for SENCOs are likely to be manifold. It is worth noting too, that although the Inquiry does make a lot of recommendations, it also (p. 12) points out that most parents (85 per cent) of children with SEN are happy with their child's current school placement (Lewis et al., 2007; DCSF, 2010).

The box below illustrates the eight recommendations that focus on giving parents a stronger voice.

A stronger voice for parents

The core offer developed through Aiming High for Disabled Children is extended to provide a set of principles for engagement by schools and children's services with parents of children with SEN. (Recommendation 13)
This offer will outline a set of expectations for how children with SEN and/or disabilities and their families will be informed and involved as their needs are assessed. It covers: information and transparency; assessment; and participation and feedback. Guidance (a 'toolkit') should help schools and SENCOs to understand their role in contributing to the core offer, making communication with parents clear and more effective.

Current improvements in parent engagement should take full account of disabled children and children with SEN. (Recommendation 14)
This recommendation should ensure that schools and SENCOs pay particular attention to ensuring that parents of children with SEN are fully included in initiatives to improve parent engagement. The Achievement for All project provides a more focused way of engaging with parents of children with additional needs, including those with SEN.

The mandatory content of schools' SEN policies is simplified and schools should consult with parents on the content of the policy. (Recommendation 15)
Schools and SENCOs have struggled to ensure that school SEN policies are compliant, fit for purpose and used to inform practice. Simpler policies acknowledge that some information can readily be included in other policies (e.g. teaching and learning). This inclusive approach means that the SEN policy will simply 'signpost' the relevant policy. Government publications can be 'signposted' in the same way to show key information for parents, avoiding unnecessary duplication.

Importantly, this recommendation also suggests involving parents in the planning and review of policy content.

The requirement to produce and publish an SEN policy is extended to pupil referral units. (Recommendation 16)
Although this recommendation is not directly related to the work of SENCOs, it highlights the need for mainstream SENCOs to liaise with units/short stay schools to aid pupil transfer. This liaison will also be vital for parents.

Annual review meetings for children with a statement include a consideration of information needs of parents and children and young people. (Recommendation 17)
Many schools have developed effective and innovative ways of involving children and parents in reviews but further guidance and the sharing of good practice will be

appreciated by schools and SENCOs. A revised SEN Code of Practice is likely to include more detailed guidance on these information requirements.

The DCSF re-launches parent partnership services to provide parents with expert, high-quality advice. They should be trained in the statutory framework and their role in advising parents of their rights should be reinforced. (Recommendation 18)
The Inquiry report notes that many parent partnership services are 'dogged by the notion of neutrality' (para. 3.49) and it calls for a shake-up. This will require a sharpening of focus and tightening of remit, which will be difficult for some local authorities to accept. However, schools and SENCOs may also benefit, particularly if they are given clearer advice about how parent partnership services work with parents and schools.

The DCSF commissions the National Strategies to work with local authorities to ensure that parent partnership services are appropriately deployed. (Recommendation 19)
This seeks to clarify what a parent partnership should do, and what other local authority staff should do to support partnership working with parents. This will be important for parents, but for schools and SENCOs too.
    The biggest challenge linked to this recommendation concerns the number of families who do not access parent partnership services. This means, at the national level, that many families who are most in need do not receive support or guidance. Ideally, schools and SENCOs should be in a position to take a proactive role in recommending parent partnership service referrals, and working with these services to support families.

The DCSF commissions and promotes a dedicated independent advice line for parents of disabled children and children with special educational needs. (Recommendation 20)
The development of an easily accessible helpline, could, if it is appropriately resourced and staffed, be helpful to schools and SENCOs. They should certainly be aware of its existence so that they can tell parents about it. At the same time, schools are likely to be regarded by parents as key contact points and sources of advice, so SENCOs need to be supported in developing 'in-house' advice provision that is available when needed. Face-to-face communication with someone that parents know and trust is crucial (Penfold et al., 2009).

Of course, many other recommendations in the Lamb Inquiry final report will be of interest to SENCOs, some of which will have direct and immediate relevance. For example, Recommendation 5 calls for the Training and Development Agency for Schools (TDA) to develop guidance on the effective deployment of teaching assistants. Others, such as Recommendation 50, concerning the evaluation of different types of educational psychology service model, will be important but the impact is likely to be more indirect, and to occur in the mid to long term.

A final reason for wanting to emphasize the importance of the Lamb Inquiry, for both SENCOs and parents, is their joint experience of the SEN system. In a recent study of the perspectives of SENCOs and parents on multi-agency working to support children with SEN (Barnes, 2008) it was noted that both groups experienced similar difficulties in accessing timely and well-coordinated support. The Inquiry's findings and recommendations should therefore be regarded as being about improving the SEN system for parents and professionals.

The longer term

Given the number of recommendations made in the Lamb Inquiry's final report, it may be seen as surprising that it took the view that the SEN system could be made to work well, if it was re-balanced to take note of parental and other concerns. It is surprising too that it did not recommend revising the current SEN Code of Practice but plans to do this are noted in the government's detailed response to the Inquiry (Department for Children, Schools and Families, 2010).

By way of conclusion, it is worth noting that debates about changing the fundamental architecture of the SEN system have been taking place for a number of years. For example, Wilkins (2008) has argued that the system could be radically improved if parents are given greater freedom to choose a school for their child with SEN, one that is not necessarily under the control of a local authority. This idea is similar to that alluded to in the second report of the Commission on Special Needs in Education (Balchin, 2007):

> [We] want to help parents to be able to make their own decision instead of being forced to be powerless onlookers; we want them to be involved, instead of being, too often, bystanders of a state-controlled process.

A further report, by Gillinson and Green (2007), advocates the need to move from an SEN system that involves partnership working with parents, to one that is co-produced with them. The report includes interesting case study examples that show how schools have made positive changes to the way that they work, that foster close collaboration with parents. SENCOs will be able to identify ideas in the report that could be implemented in their own contexts, so that all interactions with parents are as positive as they can be.

Finally, with talk of radical changes to schooling, and greater choice and empowerment for all parents, including those of children with SEN, it is worth remembering that such freedoms are rarely brought to fruition (Clarke et al., 2007). So, although the texture of partnership work between schools, SENCOs and parents may be affected by structural changes to the education system in the future, there will still be a need for the best kind of collaborative practice that takes place in many schools already. This brings me back to the extract from the Lamb Inquiry at the very beginning of this chapter. It captures, very succinctly, what parents of children with SEN both want and need from an SEN system; this involves good communication and opportunities for face-to-face discussion rather than anything more complex.

Notes

1   Throughout this chapter 'parents' includes all those with parental responsibility, including corporate parents and carers. The term 'child' or 'children' is also used, rather than the longer 'child and young person'.

2   These recommendations were accepted in full by the Secretary of State for Children, Schools and Families.

References

Armstrong, D. (1995) *Power and Partnership in Education*. London: Routledge.

Audit Commission (2002a) *Statutory Assessment and Statements of Special Educational Needs: In Need of Review?* Wetherby: Audit Commission Publications.

Audit Commission (2002b) *Special Educational Needs: A Mainstream Issue*. Wetherby: Audit Commission Publications.

Balchin, R. (2006) *Conservative Commission on Special Needs in Education: Interim Recommendations for Consultation*. London: The Conservative Party.

Balchin, R. (2007) *Conservative Commission on Special Needs in Education: The Second Report*. London: The Conservative Party.

Barnes, P. (2008) Multi-agency working: what are the perspectives of SENCOs and parents regarding its development and implementation?, *British Journal of Special Educational Needs*, 35(4): 230–40.

Clarke, J., Newman, J., Smith, N., Vidler, E. and Westmarland, L. (2007) *Creating Citizen-Consumers: Changing Public and Changing Public Services*. London: Sage.

Dale, N. (1995) *Working with Families of Children with Special Needs: Partnership and Practice*. London: Routledge.

DCSF (2010) *Improving Parental Confidence in the Special Educational Needs System: An Implementation Plan*. London: DCSF.

DfE (1994) *Code of Practice on the Identification and Assessment of Special Educational Needs*. London: HMSO.

DfES (2001) *Special Educational Needs Code of Practice*. Nottingham: DfES Publications.

Gillinson, S. and Green, H. (2007) *Beyond Bricks and Mortar: An Alternative Approach to the SEN Debate*. London: RNID.

Goacher, B., Evans, J., Welton, J. and Weddell, K. (1988) *Policy and Provision for Special Educational Needs: Implementing the 1981 Education Act*. London: Cassell.

House of Commons Education and Skills Committee (2006) *Special Educational Needs. Third Report of Session 2005–06, Volume 1 [HC 478–1]*. London: The Stationery Office.

House of Commons Education and Skills Committee (2007) *Special Educational Needs: Assessment and Funding. Tenth Report of Session 2006–07 [HC 1077]*. London: The Stationery Office.

Lamb, B. (2009) *The Lamb Inquiry: Special Educational Needs and Parental Confidence*. Nottingham: DCSF Publications.

Lewis, A., Neil, A. and Campbell, J. (1996) *The Implementation of the Code of Practice in Primary and Secondary Schools: A National Survey of the Perceptions of Special Educational Needs Coordinators*. London: NUT.

Lewis, A., Parsons, S. and Robertson, C. (2007) *My School, My Family, My Life: Telling It Like It Is*. Birmingham: Disability Rights Commission/University of Birmingham.

Ofsted (1997) *The SEN Code of Practice: Two Years On: The Implementation of the Code of Practice for Pupils with SEN*. HMI 23. London: Ofsted.

Penfold, C., Cleghorn, N., Tennant, R., Palmer, I. and Read, J. (2009) *Parental Confidence in the Special Educational Needs Assessment, Statementing and Tribunal System: A Qualitative Study*, RR117, National Centre for Social Research for DCSF. Available at: www.dcsf.gov.uk/research.

Warnock, M. (1978) *Special Educational Needs: Report of the Committee of Enquiry into the Education of Handicapped Children and Young People*. London: HMSO.

Warnock, M. (2005) *Special Educational Needs: A New Look*, Impact (pamphlet 11). London: Philosophy of Education Society of Great Britain.

Warnock, M. (2007) Foreword, in R. Cigman (ed.) *Included or Excluded? The Challenge of Mainstream for Some SEN Children*. London: Routledge.

Warnock, M. and Norwich, B. (2010) in Terzi, L. (Ed.) *Special Educational Needs: A New Look*. 2nd Edition. London: Continuum.

Weatherley, R. (1978) *Reforming Special Education: Policy Implementation from State Level to Street Level*, Cambridge, MA: MIT Press.

Wilkins, L. (2008) *Learning the Hard Way: A Strategy for Special Educational Needs*. London: CentreForum and Policy Exchange.

20

MULTI-AGENCY COLLABORATION

Lynne Cook

Introduction

This chapter describes and analyses a year in the life of a pupil with behavioural, emotional and social difficulties (BESD) in receipt of support from a number of agencies. Suggestions will be made about the purpose of each support intervention, and who benefits from each experience.

Case study: Emma

Background to case study

Emma is a Year 11 student at a large 11–18 mainstream comprehensive school (1,800 on roll). She is the eldest of two girls and lives with her mum and stepfather who are both currently unemployed. Mum was addicted to heroin but now only uses 'soft drugs' occasionally; she likes to get drunk every weekend.

In the primary phase Emma changed school three times because mum either had arguments with the Headteacher and withdrew her, or Emma was being bullied. A friend of the family sexually abused Emma at the age of 8. He was sent to prison and committed suicide there. Emma and mum accessed support from The Ark, a voluntary organization that provides help for children who have been sexually abused and their families. Her younger sister, then aged 6, did not attend at mother's request and neither did stepfather. When the perpetrator committed suicide, they stopped attending because mum told Emma he could never do it again. Despite encouragement to continue, mum disagreed because as Emma was so young she wanted her to forget about it rather than keep talking about it. A social worker was allocated to the family but they refused to engage with her and eventually visits to the house ceased. There are no records of Emma being put on the child protection register.

Secondary school

Emma had a poor start at secondary school. She was a victim of bullying and changed schools at the end of Year 7. She made a reasonable start to Year 8 at her new school but had trouble with friendships and her peer group and was referred to the School Counsellor by the Head of Year, who introduced Emma to a Circle of Friends (Newton et al., 1996) and a sixth form student was allocated as a mentor. For the remainder of Year 8 and at the start of Year 9 Emma enjoyed a settled period at school, made friends, enjoyed learning and made good progress.

However, she started to present with increasingly bizarre and disruptive behaviour in the last term of Year 9 and this continued into the beginning of Year 10. She became a frequent truant. Her behaviour was highly disruptive and as she was a bright girl and in top sets for some subjects, this was having a very bad effect on her classes and on Emma herself. Breaks and lunchtimes were supervised to prevent her truanting, smoking and harassing others to leave school with her. The Head of Year informed her parents about the truanting by letter but there was no response from them. The form tutor made a referral to the Special Educational Needs Coordinator (SENCo) expressing his concerns and, following discussion with the Head of Year, the advice to Emma's teachers was to follow the school behaviour policy guidance, use appropriate rewards/sanctions and monitor behaviour patterns. Emma was encouraged by her form tutor to talk with the School Counsellor but Emma refused.

At the start of the Spring term of Year 10, with increasing concerns for Emma's own safety and that of other students and teachers, the SENCo called a school case conference. Parents were invited to the meeting to discuss the concerns but they refused to attend with mum giving the reason that Emma's behaviour was also making home life unbearable and she would like her put into care.

The school case conference was attended by some of Emma's subject teachers, the School Counsellor, KS4 Alternative Programme Manager, form tutor, Head of Year and Emma. During the meeting Emma's behaviour was disturbing, bizarre and alternated between crying and screaming. Emma still refused to engage with the School Counsellor. The outcome of the meeting was that Emma was put onto School Action of the SEN Code of Practice because her behaviour was affecting her learning and a referral was made to the school's Education Social Worker (ESW) to prioritize an immediate home visit because of the concern about deteriorating behaviour and truanting. A referral was also made to be put on the waiting list to see the school's educational psychologist.

Following the ESW home visit, Emma returned to school and was put on a flexible part-time timetable which the SENCo had arranged through the KS4 Alternative Programme Manager. This included a reduced number of GCSEs, study support and part-time working in the school crèche as it was agreed by all that returning to a full timetable was unlikely to be successful. This would allow Emma to catch up on work missed and hopefully give her an opportunity to experience success in a placement, as she had expressed a desire to train as a nursery nurse. She continued to truant from lessons but she received an excellent report from the crèche placement.

However, after four weeks Emma received a five-day fixed term suspension for violence against another pupil and was requested to stay at home pending a meeting with parents. The parents refused to come to school and Emma remained at home for three more weeks with the ESW making home visits to try to get the parents to attend a meeting.

Emma's infrequent attendance over Year 10 now meant she was behind with her studies and this caused additional difficulties if and when she did attend lessons. The SENCo called a second case conference inviting subject teachers, form tutor, Head of Year, ESW, School Counsellor, KS4 Alternative Programme Manager, parents and Emma. A decision was made to offer a period of home tuition in the summer term of Year 10 to do some intensive catch-up work on a limited range of GCSE subjects in preparation for returning to school. She was allocated six hours per week and the expectation was that Emma would also do a work experience placement for one/two days per week. The school KS4 Alternative Programme Manager was assigned as the home tutor. Mum was requested to seek medical advice and take Emma to see her GP regarding her behaviour.

Emma was extremely excited about doing school work at home and engaged with the home tutor straightaway. Together the tutor and Emma made a plan of subjects to cover, coursework to catch up on and set targets to achieve. The tutor noted that there was an immediate rapport and sensed from the outset the Emma felt she could trust her.

On her second visit the home tutor asked Emma how she felt about school. Emma shared her thoughts readily and said 'It seems hard to believe that in Years 7, 8, and 9 I was a real boffin. I was really good and did all the work and I behaved well.' Emma explained to the tutor that recently she had been very naughty. She described how she had thrown a chair at a teacher in English and she had skived 80–90 per cent of the week and sometimes skived the whole week. She got caught smoking on the field all the time. Sometimes she and her friend would get out of lessons and run down the corridor shouting and laughing really loud. 'Teachers would try to catch you – it was funny. I would get internally suspended and run away from that. In lessons that were really boring I would make loud weird noises so that the teacher sent me out. They thought I was going mad but it was funny. I really liked English but I had loads of teachers because they kept swapping my group if the teacher couldn't control me. I like writing and using my brain to write poems and stories about feelings. I know why I went off it and started acting crazy; it was because of what happened with my stepdad.'

The home tutor encouraged Emma to say what happened and suggested that she may be able to help or get someone else who can help sort things out. The tutor recorded the conversation that then ensued. Emma and stepfather were watching a film about prostitutes in China and 'he asked me to touch him in a private place. I wouldn't and he went really mad with me and started hitting me. I managed to get away and went upstairs and packed a bag and ran to his real daughter's house. The next day I phoned my mum and told her what had happened, she said I was lying just like I was when I was younger. His daughter said I should call the police but I wouldn't. I went home and no-one would speak to me, not my mum, sister or him.' The tutor reassured Emma that she had done the right thing in sharing this because she could now get Emma some help. Surprisingly Emma agreed and they both went to the school together without offering an explanation to mum.

Following the disclosure the tutor followed child protection guidance and informed the School Counsellor who was also the designated teacher. She informed social services. Two social workers took Emma home and talked to mum and step-father. He said Emma was lying and that she had made it all up just like she did with his friend when she was in primary school. Mum was asked to decide who she believed and she chose to believe her partner and she said Emma was always telling lies. Emma and her sister were considered to be at risk and were immediately taken into emergency foster care.

They went to live in a small village with emergency foster carers but after making a fire on the rug in the lounge and stealing personal possessions, they were then taken to another foster home but this didn't work out either. There was a succession of short-term placements and during this time neither of the girls was enrolled at another school because they kept running away from their foster carers. The girls would often make their way back to their Nan's house and eventually Nan agreed to take care of both of them. It turned out that Nan had adopted Emma's mum after she had fostered her as a young girl.

On their return to their home town a case conference was called and the school accepted both girls back. Emma's sister attended school. Emma's home tutoring was resumed (at Nan's home) as she had now been out of mainstream lessons for several months and it was agreed by everyone that a sudden return to school was unlikely to be successful. Interestingly Emma asked if she could have the same tutor as she said they had got on well together. However, the relationship between Emma and Nan proved extremely difficult and was breaking down after only a few weeks. Social services convened a meeting with parents and Nan with the outcome that if mum and stepfather wanted they could try having the girls back to see how it worked out.

Emma told her home tutor, 'It's alright being back at home most of the time. My mum says I lied about my stepdad to get him into trouble but I didn't. Sometimes when they are arguing and bringing it all up again I feel like the end of the world has begun. My stepdad is very, very strict with me even if I am just five minutes late in or something but it's not too bad. They are strict and I have to do jobs and they make me do my sister's turn and my dad's turn at the washing up and I do it but it's not fair.'

Emma requested to be allowed to return to school for the final term of Year 11 before study leave started as she 'wanted to finish school properly like everyone else'. Her timetable included English, Mathematics, Art, and work experience in the school library. She described this period as boring because all her friends were doing GCSEs but she was not entered for any. She described how she would go to lessons and help friends with their work and how she did a past paper in maths and got a higher mark than her friend but the teacher said she didn't want to put pressure on her and it was too late to enter.

Talking to her tutor she said, 'I'm not thick but I sometimes feel I am when I am in class. I sometimes feel I'm not the same as everybody else. I think I feel differently inside to other people my own age. My mum says I shouldn't compare myself with anyone else and then no-one will know if I am different or not.'

What can we learn about supporting children with BESD in mainstream school from this case study?

From a young age Emma was potentially 'at risk' from mother's substance/alcohol abuse but when stepfather came into their life there appeared to be a period of stability. Little is known or recorded about the support the family received when Emma was in primary school. This may be because she attended three schools in a short space of time. The first records of Emma accessing support from professionals is following the first occurrence of sexual abuse when the family attended, spasmodically it seems, a counselling service for children who have suffered sexual abuse. When this support ended there is no record of any further individual support for Emma or family despite the fact that the perpetrator committed suicide when in prison for his conviction. This was accepted by the family as 'the best thing that could have happened to him' with no apparent support offered to Emma.

It was at secondary school when Emma first accepted help from the School Counsellor to help with friendship problems and some months later disclosed to her home tutor that her stepfather was sexually abusing her. In this case, support was accessed promptly and Emma and her sister were both removed from the home and put on the child protection register.

As is so often the case with children, the emotional and social difficulties of the child impact on behaviour, and escalation of situations can happen quickly so that a prompt response is required to the situation rather than pre-planned action based on initial concern.

It could be suggested that the signs were there from a relatively early age that Emma required multi-professional support but that although support was accessed over time there was perhaps insufficient continuity of monitoring and support for this family.

Reflective questions

- What were your first impressions of Emma?
- What do you think of the steps the school made?
- Was home tuition a good decision?
- Do you think education was a priority for her?
- Was education a main priority for her by the school?
- Do you think she should have been on the special educational needs register?
- Are there other routes you would have taken to support Emma?

Reference

Newton, C., Taylor, G. and Wilson, D. (1996) Circles of friends: an inclusive approach to meeting emotional and behavioural difficulties, *Educational Psychology in Practice*, 11(4): 41–8.

21

HEARING THE VOICE OF THE CHILD: ENSURING AUTHENTICITY

Barbara Bradbury, Alison Feeney and Anne Gager

Introduction

> I believe that giving children and young people a say in decisions that affect
> them will impact positively on . . . inclusion.
>
> (DfES, 2004)

The importance of children's voice has been a regular and recurrent theme in education in general and in SEN specifically. The SEN Code of Practice gave pupil voice a high priority, emphasizing that children 'should feel confident that they will be listened to' (DfES, 2001: 27). However, despite such legislation and frameworks of guidance, there remains a noted frustration among young people with SEN/ disabilities, which is that teachers do not listen to or understand their needs (Turner, 2003). More recently the Lamb Inquiry recognized that, 'The voice of children needs to be strengthened within the system' (DCSF, 2009).

It has been found that where schools do involve pupils with SEN/disabilities in shaping and making decisions, pupils are able to provide insights into what makes school life difficult for them and offer solutions. Pupils' solutions are often practical and simple and the impact of them would appear to enable pupils to have greater access to learning (DCSF, 2009: 42). However, there is considerable variation in whether teachers listen to disabled pupils. 'Best teachers are considered to be those who listened and remembered specific issues and needs of pupils, however a common theme was that many teachers did not listen to disabled children and young people' (Turner, 2003: 40).

If pupil voice is to be heard and taken seriously, cooperation and development are needed on many levels and it is likely that this facilitation becomes the responsibility of the SENCo.

This chapter seeks to look at ways in which schools seek to 'hear' the voice of the child. Three scenarios will be presented. Through the consideration and analysis of these situations, there will be the opportunity to assess the processes which can facilitate hearing the child's voice and those which may impede it. The effectiveness of these will be questioned and some key considerations offered.

Scenario 1: Amid
Context
Y11 Mainstream school MLD (moderate learning difficulty)
Learning style/current strategies
Amid learns best when there is repetition and over-learning of tasks. He retains understanding of tasks when they can be practically executed.
Issues
Amid lacks confidence and does not easily express opinions. He does not join in extra-curricular activities. Parents want him to live at home and attend part-time provision for adults with significant learning needs. Amid has confided once with a teaching assistant that he wants to live with other students in supported living.
Amid: Transition Review (from high school to further education) The SENCo chaired a 'person-centred' transition review for Amid, based upon a conviction that this would enable his views to be taken into account and highlight his strengths and skills, openly and informally. Adults continually asked Amid for his views. When his form tutor asked what Amid hoped to do when he left school, he surprised all by stating his desire to be a pilot. The Social Care transition worker briefly mentioned supported living options and residential college. Parents gave a clear indication about Amid continuing to live at home. Amid made no comment.

Considerations for the SENCo:

- Appraisal of Amid's cognitive capacity to evaluate the options available.
- Amid's likelihood of complying with a dominant view or that of key stakeholders, such as his parents.
- The validity and stability of Amid's views and his feelings of freedom to express these.
- The extent to which school is expected to act as advocate for known but unexpressed wishes (such as Amid's expressed desire to live in a supported living scheme).
- A potential conflict of interest between working in partnership with his parents and Amid's desires.
- Encouragement for Amid to have aspirations, and the responsibility to challenge and 'adjust' dreams until they are attainable.

- The effectiveness of the approach in fulfilling the SENCo's aims.
- Scaffolding and development of necessary and unusual skills needed by a young person to participate meaningfully.

To hear a young person's voice, we must understand their means of communication and offer participation in decision making which is meaningful. Difficult to express ideas cannot be rushed and sensitive advocacy may be needed to help difficult to raise issues to be raised. However strong the conviction of adults involved that they know what would be best for the young person, personal agendas need to be bracketed and sufficient space and time and a suitable forum provided for the young person's authentic voice to emerge. How do we walk the tightrope between crushing someone's dreams (which would be demoralizing), and introducing realism to those dreams?

Scenario 2: Becky
Context
Y4 Mainstream school SCLN (Speech Communication and Language Needs)
Learning style/current strategies
Becky learns best in an auditory environment. She needs staff to sign in order to facilitate two-way conversation. In addition, she is encouraged to use her communication aid to answer simple questions.
Issues
Becky is increasingly self-conscious and is reluctant to use methods of communication which make her feel different.
Becky: Resource provision Following an external assessment of Becky's communication needs, a high tech. communication aid was identified by the specialist Speech and Language Therapist. After a lengthy assessment period, funding was sought and granted (£8,000) and parents and school staff were trained on programming the aid. The communication aid has a range of uses and has been set up for home and school use. When Becky uses it to answer a question it takes her a long time to get to the correct overlay and subsequent answer. Increasingly she is deliberately 'forgetting' her communication aid and shows clear annoyance at using it. She prefers to answer questions by a combination of pointing, signing and making sounds. Usually adults and pupils manage to understand what she means; however, there are occasions that they do not manage to decipher her meaning.

Considerations for the SENCo:

- What is Becky communicating by persistently forgetting her aid?
- How confident can we be that the aid was desired by Becky from the outset?
- Should Becky continue to struggle with a method of communication with which she feels uncomfortable?
- Is it likely that with more practice Becky will become more positive about her aid?
- Are professionals more likely to continue with a communication method because considerable money and time has been already been spent on it?

To some extent, the value of any aid is limited by the confidence of those involved in its use, its utility in overcoming the barrier it seeks to alleviate, the patience of those involved to gain proficiency or to listen for the expressed voice and the potential loss, in skill terms, of substituting other means of communication.

Scenario 3: Lee
Context
Y9 mainstream EBSD (Emotional Behavioural and Social Difficulties)
Learning style/current strategies
Lee has a TA for 15 hours a week. These hours are shared with one other pupil.
Issues
Lee finds it difficult to conform to social expectations of school and is prone to verbal outbursts with both pupils and staff. Lee has a good relationship with the SENCo and has mentioned to her that he hates being 'minded'.
Lee: Incident After a difficult lunchtime when Lee was sent in from the yard to his Head of Year, his TA was asked to collect him and accompany him to afternoon registration. Out of concern for Lee, she asked him about what had happened, triggering a significant verbal outburst during which he rejected her concern, in no uncertain terms, called her names, swore and walked off, smashing his fist into the wall. The Head of Year, witnessing this, called Lee back into her room.

Considerations for the SENCo:

- What is Lee communicating by his behaviour?
- Is the TA's concern for Lee's well-being sufficient justification for what may be an ill-judged intervention?
- Would the subsequent interpretation of Lee's behaviour as either a 'disciplinary issue' or the result of a 'special educational need' influence the likely outcomes for Lee?
- Will the fact that Lee has broken so many rules mean that he is more or less likely to have his authentic voice heard?
- Should the TA take the initiative to ensure that the relationship is repaired, and when?
- Could restorative justice offer more positive approaches than a purely disciplinary response?

If the manner of expression is socially unacceptable and strident, this may challenge the system to breaking point, risking exclusion for the child with SEN. Children who have social, emotional and/or behavioural difficulties are at higher risk of exclusion and, indeed, their behaviour may seem focused upon achieving this. Arguably, these are the young people who can least afford the experience of rejection. How can we assure children whose behaviour may even endanger others or themselves, that they are valued, supported and worthy of 'unconditional positive regard' (Rogers, 1961)? Indeed, we might wonder if the child with severe behavioural issues might be just as unlikely to have their true voice heard as a child with significant communication barriers.

Reflection

It seems that some of the enabling and disabling factors which impinge upon the process of listening to children's voices are legislative, procedural or directed beyond the school, others are institutional and the SENCo can lead or participate in the change process and others, importantly, fall within the sphere of influence of the SENCo.

The rights of children in this country are fraught with contradiction. It could be argued that children's rights are few and this contrasts with the imperative in the *SEN Code of Practice* (DfES, 2001) to work with pupil participation in decision making. Furthermore, the *United Nations Convention on the Rights of the Child* (UNCRC) (1989, Article 12) endorses the child's 'right to express . . . views freely in all matters affecting the child, the views of the child being given due weight', and the *Every Child Matters Green Paper* (HMSO, 2003) upholds these principles. Indeed, it is evident that the *UN Convention* (UNCRC, 1989) refers to all children without exception although the guarantees offered by Article 23 might be argued to be compromised by reference to the 'eligible' child and a caveat about 'available resources'. However, the imperative that the child attains 'the fullest possible social integration and individual development' is clear. We might consider the extent to which, in denying the voice of the child, we are limiting our understanding and empathy for the desires of the child and therefore misunderstanding their needs. Ultimately, those without conventional means of communication might be argued to belong to a 'linguistic minority' (Article 30) and their rights are upheld in the Convention. It is questionable, however, to what extent the child's rights are upheld within the educational system.

It may be of relevance to ask to what extent it is the norm for those in education to consult children in matters relating to their current and future lives. Do the systems which have been generated conspire to deny them a voice? When, for example, they are invited to take options in secondary school, to what extent are these decisions a reflection of their own desires and preferences? Equally, it is important to ascertain whether the system can respond with flexibility and humility to the agendas which may be set by children. We need to secure that children are not only consulted, but that they feel that the consultation is genuine and has some prospect of initiating change. The National Youth Agency (available at: www.nya.org.uk/hearbyright, accessed on 19 November 2009) argues that progress towards this will be impaired unless there is an acceptance that the prevailing attitudes within organizations involved with children need fundamental change. They argue further that unless we are prepared to engage with the challenges of enabling pupil voice, we risk not only disenfranchising the children and young people, but also retrenching outdated policies and structures, missing out on the valuable contribution which might be made to communities and society by hearing those voices and returning the 'often excluded' to the main body of society.

Institutional change may be impaired due to inertia. Additionally, thoughtless implementation has the potential to call initiatives into disrepute and may lead to tokenism (Hart, 1992, 1997). 'Territorial' and power-guarding behaviours may threaten communication while organizational and personal resistance to what may be perceived as criticism, may impair the listening process. There is a danger that, in its endeavour to listen to the voices of their children, schools may find themselves staging 'events' rather than adopting changed ways of 'being'. The SENCo may be instrumental in identifying and eliminating those retrograde forces while working in a system which is, perhaps, compromised by pragmatism and appearances.

There may be a danger that those with a professional involvement with children and, indeed, their parents, think that their experiences and expertise equip them to have a superior grasp of what children really need or what is 'best' for them and we may need to 'bracket' our assumptions, our personal and culturally determined constructions of reality, what we perceive as our wisdom, and be prepared to enter into the child's own reality, appreciate their aspirations and the pressures they experience. If some children do not have the capacity to express a view or to make a genuine choice, the challenge may be not only to address this issue, but also to avoid this being extrapolated to children for whom teacher expectations are low.

Some of the problems with meetings may be *that* the meetings exist, *how* they are instigated, facilitated and conducted, *who* is present, the extent to which the voices are heard, the belief of all present in the efficacy of the process used and the potential influence which may be had over the outcomes. The settings within which involvement of children is commonplace, such as Individual Education Plan review meetings or Annual Reviews (DfES, 2001) can be thought of as providing an environment which is not conducive to a genuine dialogue and may contain subtle and more overt pressures to offer conventional or socially acceptable responses. It might be argued that professionals may collude with the notion of deception or secrecy in order to shield children from unpalatable truths. Positive strategies which may be considered by the SENCo might change the format and focus of the meetings involved. For example, person-centred planning approaches such as PATH, MAP (http://www.circlesnetwork.org.uk/what_is_person_centred_planning.htm, accessed on 22 March 2010), or perhaps the implementation of suggestions such as Martin et al.'s (2006) IEP meetings led by children might suffice, although these need careful planning and evaluation to secure that they meet their aims and they reveal the genuine views of the children involved. It might be suggested that a method is only as potentially effective as it is suitable, and is limited by the quality of its implementation and the extent to which subsequent evaluation is viewed formatively.

If advocacy is used to access the pupil's voice, the effectiveness of an advocate may be limited by their own beliefs and assumptions, sculpted by their prior experience, shaped by their cultural expectations and held in check by their capacity for empathy and skill in eliciting the child's genuine views. We might wonder if we enable a child's voice as a pure 'emitted' reflection of their true feelings and desires, or whether there is a tendency to 'focus' or 'groom' the voice we hear.

If the child is able to offer their view, there needs to be a careful consideration of the weight this view should be given. Children's views may not be stable over time and their priorities may not always be in their best interests. Issues such as the influence of hormones and the stability of moods may affect the outcomes when a child's views are sought. As Bragg (2007: 515) cautions, 'We should not underestimate the complexities of pupil voice.'

Beyond this, we might speculate that this is about far more than listening, involving and acting. There is a climatic and attitudinal issue which may act to suppress children and young people's voices before we even seek their view. This may originate in the language used with and about them by adults, messages conveyed to them about values, experiences of power differentials and exclusion. Do we allow voices to remain unheard because it may be easier not to hear or, alternatively, do things ourselves, because pace is not sufficiently flexible or because it may take so long to *really* hear the voices? We might argue that this may indeed be a reflection of a wider disenfranchisement of young people by society. It might also be argued that some young people are far easier to disenfranchise than others. Those without a physical voice, those whose capacity to make informed choices need skilful and careful development and those with a strident, aggressive voice (perhaps accompanied by what manifest as socially inappropriate or antisocial behaviours) may all be at risk of being misunderstood.

According to Smith (2002, p. 73), Prout and James (1990) state that 'Psychological concepts which inform Western orthodoxies about childhood view development as an inexorable universal path from immaturity and incompetence towards rationality, competence and autonomy.' We must consider how we may promote a sense of personal agency among children and young people and ask ourselves to what extent the problem of accessing and enabling children's voices is a reflection of a system which still does not see them, and allow them to be seen, as individuals. The challenge for the SENCo is to ensure that frameworks are flexible and responsive and place a premium upon hearing the voice of the child while recognizing that undue weight cannot be given to whimsical or transitory ideas.

While reflecting upon the task of writing this chapter, the team wrestled with the possibility and dangers of suggesting that some voices may, as yet, be beyond our skill to enable. Perhaps more hazardous yet, though, is the mistaken delusion that we are enabling children's voices when, at best, what we are hearing may be constrained and compromised by external forces acting institutionally, within the children themselves and within ourselves. We need not only to hear the *obvious* voice and facilitate the less forthright, but to become ever more skilled in understanding and interpreting the *behaviours* children use to communicate their authentic desires and the quality of their experiences. We need to exercise caution in our interpretations while questioning our own motives and the powers which stabilize the status quo.

The SENCo is uniquely placed to interface with numerous external agencies, with their colleagues, the parents, their children and institutions and systems within which those children are educated. The role offers the opportunity to influence and model practice from individual interactions, through leadership, setting the tone for interactions with children by other adults, by shaping procedures and policies, challenging assumptions and prejudices and by sharing in setting priorities and assuring accountability.

References

Bragg, S. (2007) 'But I listen to children anyway!' – teacher perspectives on pupil voice, *Educational Action Research*, 15(4): 505–15. Available at: http://ebscohost.com.

Circles Network [online], *What is Person Centred Planning?* Available at: http://www.circlesnetwork.org.uk/what_is_person_centred_planning.htm (accessed 22 March 2010).

DCSF (2009) *Lamb Inquiry: Special Educational Needs and Parental Confidence.* Available at: http://www.dcsf.gov.uk/lambinquiry/downloads/8553-lamb-inquiry.pdf (accessed 23 March 2010).

DfES (2001) *Special Educational Needs Code of Practice.* Nottingham: DfES Publications.

DfES (2004) *Working Together: Giving Children and Young People a Say.* Available at: http://publications.teachernet.gov.uk/eOrderingDownload/DfES%200134%20200 MIG1963.doc (accessed 23 March 2010).

Hart, R. (1992) *Children's Participation from Tokenism to Citizenship.* Florence: UNICEF Innocenti Research Centre.

Hart, R. (1997) *Children's Participation: The Theory and Practice of Involving Young Citizens in Community Development and Environmental Care.* Florence: UNICEF.

HMSO (2003) *Every Child Matters.* Norwich: The Stationery Office (Cm. 5860).

Martin, J., Van Dycke, J., Christensen, R., Greene, B., Gardner, E. and Lovett, D. (2006) 'Increasing student participation in IEP meetings: establishing the self-directed IEP as an evidence-based practice', *Exceptional Children*, 72(3): 299–316.

National Youth Agency: Hear by Right (2009) *Involving Children and Young People: An Introduction.* Available at: www.nya.org.ul/hearbyright (accessed 19 November 2009).

Rogers, C. R. (1961) *On Becoming a Person.* London: Constable & Robinson.

Smith, A. B. (2002) 'Interpreting and supporting participation rights: contributions from sociocultural theory', *The International Journal of Children's Rights*, 10: 73–88.

Turner, C. (2003) *What Disabled Children and Young People in Wales Think about the Services They Use.* Available at: http://www.barnardos.org.uk/engfinal_1.pdf (accessed 23 March 2010).

United Nations (1989) *United Nations Convention on the Rights of the Child.* Available at: http://www.dcsf.gov.uk/everychildmatters/strategy/strategyandgovernance/uncrc/united nationsarticles/uncrcarticles/ (accessed on 19 November 2009).

Index

The *McGraw·Hill* Companies

What's new from Open University Press?

Education... Media, Film & Cultural Studies

Health, Nursing & Social Welfare... Higher Education

Psychology, Counselling & Psychotherapy... Study Skills

Keep up with what's buzzing
at Open University Press
by signing up to receive
regular title information at
www.openup.co.uk/elert

Sociology

 OPEN UNIVERSITY PRESS

M c G r a w - H i l l   E d u c a t i o n

21223244R00134

Printed in Great Britain
by Amazon